Karin Dahlberg
Nancy Drew
Maria Nyström

Reflective lifeworld research

Studentlitteratur

Art. No 7606
ISBN 91-44-01695-6
© The authors and Studentlitteratur 2001

Printed in Sweden
Studentlitteratur, Lund
Web-address: www.studentlitteratur.se

Printing/year 1 2 3 4 5 6 7 8 9 10 | 05 04 03 02 2001

Contents

Preface   7

Preface   13
   by Nancy Diekelmann and Helen Denne Schulte
         References   15

Introduction   17
      Patients' and students' lifeworlds   20
         A model for caring and teaching   21
         A human science research model   23
      The book structure   24

1   Paradigms and their influence   25
      The idea of paradigms   26
         World view   28
         Scientific view   30
         Paradigm competence   31
         Researcher interest and research direction   33
      Knowledge development in paradigms   34
         The scientific status of caring   36
         The scientific status of education   37
         Can paradigms be mixed?   38
         Can paradigms change?   40

2   The philosophy of lifeworld research   42
      Phenomenology   42
         "Zu den Sachen selbst"   44
         The natural attitude and the lifeworld   45
            The subjective body   49
            The body in health and illness   53
            Embodied knowing and knowing bodies   54

Intentionality 55
    Temporal appresentations 58
Transcendentality 59
Intersubjectivity 63
    Understanding others through indirect
    appresentation 65
    Lived relations with others 68
Hermeneutics 70
    Hermeneutics as theory of interpretation 71
    A premature idea of lived experience 74
    The phenomenological turning point in hermeneutics 77
    The idea of an open hermeneutic 80
        The history of effect – Wirkungsgeschichte 81
    The dialectic of explanation and understanding 85
    Language 88
Phenomenology and hermeneutics – no separate
magnitudes 90
    The lifeworld perspective 91
    The issue of pure description 92

3 **An open lifeworld approach** 95
Openness 96
    An open stance 97
Openness as an open and immediate mind 99
    Examples of openness in the conduct of research 104
    Openness as an antithesis to "method" 110
Intersubjective openness 112
Meaning 113
Uniqueness 116
Pre-understanding 117
    The idea of pre-understanding 119
    The need to influence pre-understanding 122
        Questioning the pre-understanding 126
        The cognitive aspect of pre-understanding 129
        The social aspect of pre-understanding 130
        The emotional aspect of pre-understanding 132
    The historical nature of understanding and pre-
understanding 134

Self-awareness, self-reflection and reflection   138
    Self-reflection   139
    Professional and scientific reflection   142

4   Methods for lifeworld research – data gathering   146
    Narratives   149
    Interviews   154
        The reflective dialogue   156
        Limitations of an interview as dialogue   157
        Sequence of the interview   158
        Immediacy in interviews   160
        Dramatized interviews   161
        Other supportive sources   164
        Preparations for an interview and its after-work   164
        Transcribing recorded interviews   166
        Ethical reflections on interviewing   167
    Fieldwork and observation   169
        Anthropology and ethnography   169
        Fieldwork   172
        Participant observation   174
        Preparing for observation   176
        Realization of fieldwork and observation   178
        Ethical reflections on observing   180

5   Analyzing data and presenting results   182
    Phenomenological analysis – description   183
        Whole – parts – whole   185
            Phenomenological parts   188
            A new whole   192
        Dialogal research   194
        An embodied moment of encountering violence and
        aggression in mental health nursing – an empirical example
        of phenomenology   196
            Findings   196
    Hermeneutic analysis – interpretation   201
        A scientific interpretational attitude   203
        Whole – parts – whole   205
            Hermeneutical parts   206
            A new whole   208

Trying out the interpretations   209
The enigma of severe mental illness – an empirical example
of hermeneutic analysis   211
    Findings   213
    Comparative analysis of the existential
    interpretations   220
    The main interpretation – an interpreted whole   221
Phenomenography   222
    Categories of understanding   225

6   Generalization and validity in lifeworld research   227
Application of the results to new contexts   228
Validity and objectivity   230
    The researching subject   232
Validity of the data analysis   236

Concluding reflections   240

Bibliography   243

Index   257

Preface

Rollo May once stated that people of like mind find each other. Across an ocean two scholars discovered that their world views were remarkably alike and decided to collaborate. The collaboration between Nancy Drew and myself began with the discovery of our mutual dismay about our health care and education, the enchantment with technology to the exclusion of subjective experience, and perhaps more importantly, the subjective body. The discovery that we held similar views on the nature of human science, and in particular, philosophy, generated a desire to submit our views for others to consider. Shortly, two articles were co-authored and published in 1995 and 1997. The next logical step was elaboration of our beliefs in a larger format. During the late 80:s and early 90:s I had been working on the explication of phenomenographic and phenomenological methodology, and as a result of that work a Swedish book on qualitative methods for health care research was published (Dahlberg, 1993, 1997). We decided to let that manuscript be a starting point for our international book. We thank Bob Kaill who took his time and translated the Swedish book into English.

I am deeply grateful to Nancy Drew, who without any hesitations joined me in this undertaking. Even if we are twin souls in many respects it is not easy to collaborate with an ocean in between, despite all the help of modern technology the real intersubjective event is still something that happens between people that meet, to paraphrase Nancy Drew herself. And that has not been possible to such an extent, as we had wished. However, a number of visits have been possible and I thank the University College of Borås, School of Health Sciences and the county council of Södra Älvsborg, as well as Saint Joseph College, Hartford, CT, who have supported our collaboration. I also want to thank the two husbands involved, Bengt Dahlberg and John Nolte, for their thought-ful support throughout this project.

We decided early that this book should draw upon philosophical and epistemological knowledge as well as concrete lived research experiences. Nancy Drew and I have most of all practiced pheno-menological research and therefore Maria Nyström was also invi-ted. Maria has to be described as being born to be a "hermeneuti-sist". She is constantly, and very rapidly, interpreting the world around her, trying to openly understand it in different ways, and from different perspectives, at the same time. She was my first stu-dent to achieve a doctoral degree, and to be her advisor meant at the same time to be her hermeneutical partner, interpreting her research data as well as the whole world around us. Together we investigated the hermeneutical realm of the world, theoretically and practically. I am very grateful that she wanted to participate in this book project, and I am especially grateful that I am still invited to be a discussion partner even after the degree was conquered.

Merleau-Ponty (1968) says that genuine conversation gives us access to thoughts that we did not know ourselves capable of, that we were not capable of before our words were responded to by another. Hours of such conversations have been a source of much growth and mutual respect in the relationship between the authors of this book. However, also others have been involved in the con-versations during the writing of this book. First I am especially gra-teful for the opportunity to get to know Steen Halling who, so free from superiority, takes time to collaborate with a horse-loving Swede. Steen has contributed with many important thoughts on openness in chapter 3 and has also commented upon chapter 2 and chapter 5. I also want to thank Jerry McClelland, who has challenged my thoughts from a critical interpretive perspective and has hosted me, and cared for me, while I have been teaching at the University of Minnesota. Jerry has contributed with educatio-nal ideas in chapter 1 and commented on several of my texts that this book is based on.

Gunilla Carlsson is one of my doctoral students and the most pure of phenomenologists, she does not even like to talk about interpretation. She is always anxious to encounter the world in such a way that lets the world speak. For her it has therefore never been the case that she takes a method and stays there. In order to really meet a complex world, she saw it necessary to try new ways of doing research, which has enriched this book in a concrete way. I am grateful to that methodological contribution and to her comments on the text as a whole, and for the opportunity to participate in her lifeworld research.

Another of my doctoral students that I have learned much from is Margaretha Ekebergh. Even if her work is not a concrete part of this book, her ideas are. I am grateful for the benefit of being the advisor of her fascinating research on reflection, and especially her interest in the enigma of the human mind.

Besides those students named I wish also to thank all other students which I continue to learn from. I am especially grateful to the group of doctoral students that regularly meet at Pajebo Gård, my private oasis in the south-west of Sweden. Some special thanks also go to the University of Minnesota, whose students have taught me how I must argue in order to make the theory of phenomenological research graspable and trustworthy. One student in particular has to be thanked, Patricia Schaber. She has read and commented on most of the chapters, and given good advises both linguistically and epistemologically. I wish all the students good luck in their phenomenological research. I also thank Jane Plihal who thought phenomenology enough interesting to invite me there in the first place.

There is a special room in my phenomenological heart for Jan Bengtsson and Amedeo Giorgi, both have been my teachers and friends for years. Jan gave me the map and Amedeo gave me the compass, without which I had never managed to orient myself in the philosophical jungle. I am especially grateful to both of them for enduring my endless questions and epistemological whims, and for their permission to go my own way. I will also always be grateful to Bengt-Erik Benktsson, an amazing man who took me by his hand and guided me through Martin Heidegger's philosophy.

To let one's professional lifeworld be influenced by phenomenology was not always a wonderful choice. Mainstream science is still – let's say – different. Even a strong-willed and stubborn mind as mine needs a friendly and encouraging atmosphere once in a while. This purpose has been served by the International Human Science Research Conferences whose participants I have had the favor of meeting with from 1988 onwards. I am grateful for all conversations that have been offered me by these likeable people of whom I already have mentioned Amedeo Giorgi and Steen Halling. I also want to thank Chris Aanstoos, Steinar Kvale, Johan Lindström, Max van Manen, Ference Marton, and Donald Polkinghorne for many and wonderful discussions and debates.

However, it is not only the big clubs that is important for independent thinkers. Therefore I want to thank the people at the Borås university college that have supported me and my ideas. I especially want to thank Kerstin Segesten, who tries to teach me not to make all the mistakes myself, but listen to those who are more experienced. I want to thank Birgitta Davidsson and Maj Klasson, who both have contributed to the methodological discussions in a creative way. Also connected to the college is Carl-Magnus Stolt, who I owe many thanks for challinging as well as confirming discussions.

Another group I want to thank is the hermeneutic circle around Staffan Selander and Per-Johan Ödman in Stockholm. They have firmly objected to the Husserlian approach Maria and I presented there; at the same time they proof that real scholars debate vividly but are always close to a smile!

Groups that encourage an academic debate are indeed important. Such a group is the Studentlitteratur "caring science expert group" that regularly meet in Lund. I want to thank Ann Langius and Eva Matell for being such good discussion partners and especially Liselotte Rooke who also thoroughly read and commented on the manuscript.

Last but not least, my thoughts and thanks go to my former advisor, Claes-Göran Wenestam, who taught me what it means to be a researcher in the first place.

The result of all these conversations named above, and all these conversations that are not named but are no less important, is this book, which we offer as a bridge between philosophy and method for reflective lifeworld research within all kinds of human sciences. The human sciences know their philosophers well – Husserl, Heidegger, Merleau-Ponty, and Gadamer, to name four of the most often cited thinkers. In this book we have attempted to make explicit the connections between the philosophy of these thinkers and the actual practice of human science lifeworld research.

The authors of this book are basically nurses. All three of us are also teachers by education and are still employed as university teachers, and we are at present time teaching within the health care research area. Karin Dahlberg is a professor in health care sciences at Borås University College, School of Health Sciences in Sweden, Nancy Drew is a professor in nursing at Saint Joseph College, School of Nursing, West Hartford, CT, US, and Maria Nyström is assistant professor at Borås University College, School of Health Sciences. All three are trained in the psychiatric area of health care, all have some education in psychotherapy, one (MN) is a psychologist, and one (ND) is a psychodrama therapist. Two of us (KD, ND) have doctoral degrees in general pedagogy, and one (MN) has her degree in health care pedagogy.

When we, in this book, talk about the human science disciplines that, conscious of it or not, acknowledge and build upon the primacy of human intentional experience, we mean disciplines such as health care, including nursing, medicine, physiotherapy, occupational therapy, and education, counseling, psychotherapy, social work. Most of the examples in the book are from the health care area. Examples too often become "models" of thought and even if we prefer this to not happen, we mean that if our examples are being used they should at least be carefully thought through in the first place! Thus we prefer lived through examples.

Also, some practical remarks. All italics etc. in quotes are original. English translations of quotes that come from Swedish texts are undertaken by the authors.

I dedicate this book to my grown up children, Helena, who is a philosopher by education, and Christian, who is a philosopher by life. I thank both for the fights and the love they are giving me with their endless challenges of my thoughts.

Sjömarken, Sweden, in the bright beginning of 2001

Karin Dahlberg

Preface

by Nancy Diekelmann and Helen Denne Schulte

Lifeworld arrives as a surplus of meaning.
Significance is given to all.

Phenomenology challenges and extends scientific scholarship by prying open the otherwise unquestioned underlying presuppositions that form the basis of the claim to universality in science. The play of confluences in human science theories and practices is enriched by explorations into the philosophical situatedness of contemporary scholarship. En-abling human sciences research to uncover the philosophical situatedness of *all* studies, including scientific studies requires a literature that supports these endeavors. This is just such a book for phenomenology.

Reflective Lifeworld Research contributes to an exegesis of phenomenology in the context of human sciences scholarship and reveals the similarities and differences between the transcendental phenomenology of Edmund Husserl and the hermeneutic (interpretive) phenomenology of Martin Heidegger. As more than an explication of commonalties, this book *revisions* the very demarcations that make philosophical phenomenological labeling possible. Of significant import is the discourse on how researchers, as residents of the lifeworld, influence or constitute their research results. Attention to the epistemological assumptions and openness to the richness of the lifeworld reveal neoteric paths for reflective thinking.

Confronting the predominance of theory and science, phenomenology offers otherwise forgotten or overlooked possibilities for increasing understandings in contemporary human sciences. Phenomenology as a questioning, gathers scholars, practitioners, students, teachers, and citizens into persistent thinking and converging conversations around complex contemporary issues, including those of method. These converging conversations are phenomenological and work to reveal what has been dismissed, ignored, or simply forgotten in contemporary human sciences research. It is through these converging conversations that we hear ourselves and create a silence sufficient to hear and respond to others.

> In the midst of the constant noise of our modern world,
> we need to create sufficient silence to hear ourselves and others.
> (Fletcher, Sorrell, & Silva, 2001, p. 23)

Moving beyond methodological nationalism in scholarship, this book reflects how explicating interpretive methodologies, specifically phenomenology, can raise complex, multifaceted questions to elicit and encourage continuing inquiry. In poetic ways, the assumptions of scientific research are explicated and challenged. The all too common practice of destroying the worthfulness of the predominate paradigm to create a place for new approaches is assiduously avoided. The narratives in this book are compelling. Phenomenological studies are a beginning; a questioning that gathers continued conversations around complex issues. They call out to human science researchers to respond in new ways by examining their day-to-day practices in a new light.

Contemporary research demands attention to the philosophical perspectives of knowledge generation and approaches to knowing that situate research. For example, as health professions research becomes its history, the nuances of thinking and the philosophical backgrounds that shape thinking come to the forefront in the research literature generated. Terms like "quantitative" and "qualitative", while still present in the human sciences research, receive much needed explication in order to reveal problematic presuppositions. The authors caution against the "increasingly glamorous research designs presented as qualitative research." (Chapter Six, p. 7) Just as it is no longer acceptable to present a study as scientific as if the kinds of approaches to science do not matter, so to for phenomenology. Knowing a scientific study embraces a post-positivist approach is important to every aspect from reading the research report to interpreting the results. Likewise a phenomenological study must reveal what specific approaches to phenomenology are being embraced in a study.

14

Perhaps for too long, graduate students in the human sciences have been introduced to phenomenology only tangentially in required methods and research courses. Allotted little emphasis in predominantly scientific methods required coursework, phenomenology remains relegated to an obscure or highly specialized approach to research. Critical social theorists, feminists and post-modernists, share with phenomenologists a concern for how particular methods are selected to teach research to graduate students. However, until this book, there has not been a resource for students to understand in breadth and depth phenomenological methods in the context of lifeworld research. Openness and pre-understanding as well as concerns for objectivity and validity are explored with rigor in this book. A view of epistemology as a lifeworld approach to human sciences research opens up a way to exploring phenomena that draws on the work of Husserl, Heidegger, Merleau-Ponty and Gadamer.

This book is vanguard. For example, revisionist thinking shows up in the claim that in *Being and Time,* Heidegger did not reverse or abandon the philosophy of Husserl, rather he explored in particular significance the ontological dimension of intentionality. This book offers both experienced interpretive researchers and students a view of phenomenology that is thoughtful and thought-provoking.

Nancy Diekelmann, PhD, RN, FAAN
Helen Denne Schulte, Professor
University of Wisconsin-Madison School of Nursing

References

Fletcher, J., Sorrell, J., & Silva, M. (2001). Harming patients in the name of quality of life. In N. Diekelmann (Ed.), *Interpretive studies in healthcare and the human sciences: Vol. 1. Power, oppression, and violence in healthcare and the human sciences.* Madison, WI: University of Wisconsin Press.

Introduction

In order to outline a methodology and researching principles that aim at explicating the world of humans, our starting point must be to consider the relationship between humans and our world. There remains a central question: what is the human world? Despite the fact that knowledge of the human world has been the subject of research in many disciplines for several decades, there exists no unequivocal answer to this question. Why is this?

The answer to this question may lie within Capra's (1991) ideas about western ontology in relation to eastern philosophies, which value the wholeness of experience and a holistic perspective of humans as a part of nature. What it means to be human cannot be totally captured in language, and by no means by numbers, but is understood in its fullness only through experience of it. We share the conviction of Capra and other contemporary scientists that human understanding of nature is undergoing a tremendous change. We believe that the human sciences[1], those disciplines that acknowledge and build upon the primacy of human intentional experience, have a crucial role in the evolving post post modern[2] approach, that is beginning to be characteristic of the way that the natural sciences as well as the human sciences are understood, researched and taught. In fact, we might very well be standing at the threshold of a revolutionary change in the way that

1   The concept human sciences is not uncomplicated. We have chosen that to make clear the purpose of the book that is mentioned here. A concept close to human sciences in, for example, the US is social sciences.
2   I thank Donald Polkinghorne for this term for the contemporary movement within humans sciences, which meaning in short is, that we have left the positivistic idea of absolute scientific rigidity and objectivism, we have also left the postmodern idea of nihilism and relativism, and arrived at an idea of science that offers an open but at the same time rigorous methodological approach.

humans relate to the world as our home and to our fellow world dwellers. It is to this end that we have undertaken this book. It is our attempt to contribute to the humanizing of the professions that in one way or another provide nurturing, growth and support to the human family.

The very nature of human being in human science research is characterized by complexity. When someone is, for example, caring for or teaching another person there is at least both intersubjectivity and intentionality involved. This is true whether the caring or teaching activity in question takes the form of caring or educational practice, or research in those areas. Also, both caring and teaching have to deal with the uniqueness as well as the generalities of human beings.

Recognizing the complexities of human life is nothing that is characteristic of traditional and contemporary science. "Science manipulates things and gives up living in them"... "it comes face to face with the real world only at rare intervals", says Merleau-Ponty (1989/1964, p. 159). He thereby takes up a thread from Bergson (1992)[3] who is critical to the philosophical, and scientific, movement, and especial to its influence on people's understanding of the world, meaning that everything in the world is being reduced into something measurable. Bergson takes emotion and pain as example. He is critical to how these characteristics of life are limited to a spatial understanding. We talk about an emotion as if it is something concrete and permanent in time and space, thereby comparing emotions and measuring them as more or less intensive. This cannot be done, says Bergson. Emotions, as well as pain, do not exist concretely, and cannot thus be fixated and measured. Instead what we have to do is to understand how these characteristics of life are lived. We need a scientific approach that does not give up living in the things that we explore.

When arguing for hermeneutics, Palmer (1969) puts forward the idea that human science must try to formulate an epistemology and a methodology reflective of and tailored to the act of understanding, which transcends established science's reductionistic objectivism. For human science researchers, phenomenology and hermeneutics is the equipment with which to return to the whole-

---

3   Originally published 1889 as *Essai sur les donées immédiates de la conscience.*

ness of life. For human sciences the return to the fundament of the lifeworld requires finding a perspective other than either of the extremes of psychologism, subjectivism and relativism on the one side, and scientism and objectivism on the other. From the phenomenological point of view what is desired is neither the specific, personal perspective nor the depersonalized, "objective" perspective, rather, the perspective of subject experience as such (Kohák, 1977). Hermeneutics contributes to the perspective of the human subject as such by showing us how knowledge can increase through describing, interpreting and understanding such experience.

Capturing the full complexity of human being is not however easily done, in part, because of its tacit nature, its embodied silence. When, for example, caring or teaching is undertaken, regardless of the particular discipline or specific area of practice, much of what is done is accomplished without the guide of a formal structure for the actions and decisions involved. Human caring or teaching behaviors, those responses that are in answer to another's being in need of care or knowledge, are often carried out with an unspoken understanding, that silent knowing which we have just begun to acknowledge and explore.

Caring and teaching practices are not new. They have a long history of traditions which, however, have not been articulated adequately for a science of caring or a science of teaching. The most that can be said with any consensus is that the so far formalized knowledge in these areas speaks about our concern for others and thereby it also speaks about our relationship with the world of others and the world of things. However, in this book we are not content to leave caring and teaching in such a vague state. Having recognized the difficulties of articulating caring and teaching we propose to plunge ahead and express our understanding of this most basic aspect of human existence.

The tacit knowledge that operates in encounters between caregivers and patients[4] or teachers and students[5] is an area in caring

---

4   In this book we use the term patient for the person who in one form or another receives care, it be general health care, hospital care, social care, psychotherapeutic care, etc. Using the term "patient" we draw upon the old understanding of the word, which means "a person who suffers" (Eriksson, 1993).

and teaching which is not fully understood. Tacit knowledge is an important part of praxis, as several scholars have revealed (Polanyi, 1966; Polanyi, 1978; Schön, 1983; Benner, 1984). A great deal of caring and teaching praxis is intuitive. If one observes, for example, an experienced nurse, it seems that s/he instinctively knows what to do, appearing wholly immersed in the activity of caring, drawing on, and taking for granted, the knowledge and understanding needed at the moment. From a phenomenological perspective, this caring knowledge can be understood as embodied and implicit (Merleau-Ponty, 1968; Merleau-Ponty, 1995). Tacit knowledge can be further understood as a process, a perfect understanding between individual and culture (Polanyi, 1978). According to Polanyi, when knowledge is formed it is a result of one's belief in, and reliance on the knowledge derived from personal experience. Knowledge thus obtained enables the practitioner to make decisions and to act effectively in acute situations without awareness of acting. It is possible to describe tacit practical knowledge (Polanyi, 1966; Polanyi, 1978; Schön, 1983; Rolf, 1991). We believe that it should be described. Understanding tacit knowledge and how it functions in caring and teaching will help illuminate praxis beyond the usual reporting of objective caregiver and teacher actions and behaviors.

Patients' and students' lifeworlds

The patient is the most important and the central person in caring; the student is the most important and the central person in teaching. The patient is "the suffering person" (Eriksson, 1994), the person cared for, the one that the care is aimed for. The student is the learning person, the person that is taught. The central position of the patient and the student must be clearly pointed out here, because when it comes to the reality where political and practical decisions are being made, this is not obvious. Neither is this clear when traditional science in these areas is being scrutinized. This

---

5   We use the term student for the person who is the object of teaching and who is supposed to learn from teaching activities.

does not mean that caregivers' or teachers' perspective could not or should not be focused in research. It means, that if we are to understand caring and teaching we first of all have to understand the lifeworlds of patients and students. We have to make explicit how patients experience and relate to their health processes and to the care being given. We have to make explicit how students experience and relate to their learning processes and the teaching they are offered. With this central aim in mind we can begin exploring the lifeworlds of caregivers and teachers as well.

A model for caring and teaching

What is said above means that here exists a need to express the lifeworlds of the patients and students, and a need to express the lifeworlds of caregivers and teachers, not least the tacit part of caring and teaching knowledge. At the same time we are aware of the fact that we cannot describe this fully, but we want to describe it as near as possible, explicate it as much as possible. In order to do this, and in order to outline a methodology, we started out with some ideas about caring, a guiding caring model (Drew & Dahlberg, 1995). What we now want to do is to extend that guiding model to encompass even some basic ideas of teaching and learning, which then will serve as an ontological and epistemological starting point for this book.

In the caring – teaching model there are some central ontological components that are described as *encounter*, *openness*, *uniqueness*, *immediacy*, and *meaning*. These concepts, which emerged from our (KD, ND) research, suggest a philosophy for a holistic caring perspective, as well as a holistic teaching perspective, that is characterized by intersubjectivity and interpersonal confirmation, a perspective that, emphasizing upon the cared for or learning person, fosters growth and well-being for both individuals in the professional relationship.

Encounter, the core concept, is understood as an intersubjective and meaningful, I-Thou meeting (Buber, 1970) between a professional and patient or student in which the growth of the latter is of primary importance. No specific tasks or goals have greater importance than the degree to which humanly meaningful relating occurs between the two individuals in the caring situation.

Openness can be understood as a state of mind in which one, in a self-aware way, is sensitive to the other's experience, a willingness to increase one's capacity for empathic response to others. Openness is the capacity to be surprised and sensitive to the unpredictable. Swanson's (1993) concept of "being with" conveys some of the quality of openness. It means seeking to discover and understand the other person rather than seeing the other through a lens of assumptions.

Uniqueness denotes the belief that caring or teaching cannot be explained by their designations. Neither can the complexity of the individuals in a caring or teaching situation be grasped through analytic maneuvers or explanatory theories. Uniqueness reminds us to accept the complexity and ambiguity that are inherent in human caring or teaching situations.

Immediacy has many meanings in philosophy. In a general sense we want to refer to the meaning that Merleau-Ponty's (1995) gives the term, as a direct and primitive contact with the world through one's body. Closely related is an unself-conscious immersion in one's experience of the moment, which confirming regard from, and engagement with, a caring or teaching professional can bring about.

Every caring or teaching encounter is, or should be, directed towards *meaning*. The meaning in a caring relationship is related to suffering and health, while the meaning in a teaching relationship is related to learning. In both a caring and teaching encounter there must be an amount of shared meaning. A true caring or teaching encounter offers the opportunity for contributing to the meaning, and perhaps meaningfulness, for both, of their mutual situation. Meaning is never static, but always expandable. The caring or teaching professional's obligation is to discover and understand meaning as the other experiences it.

These described five concepts are also the foundation for the model for human science research which follows. However, whereas the core concept for practice is encounter, in the research model the primary concept is openness.

A human science research model

The five concepts of encounter, openness, meaning, immediacy, and uniqueness were also described as significant for human science research (Dahlberg & Drew, 1997). The purpose of this book is to further explicate this idea and outline a model for reflective lifeworld research based on the mentioned caring – teaching concepts. However, the goal of research is different than the goal of caring and teaching practice. Whereas the goal in practice is the individual patient's health and student's growth, the goal in research is the scientific development of knowledge. The proposed research model reflects a structural shift from the ontological focus of the practice model, with encounter as the core concept, to an epistemological focus with a core concept of openness. For caring and teaching, epistemology is the search for answers to the question, How can research provide knowledge for caring and teaching and such human science areas? Both practice, with its emphasis on health and growth, and research, which aims toward knowledge and understanding, are understood from the perspective of the lifeworld. A lifeworld perspective, with its return to everyday phenomena, demands a research methodology in which openness is the central concept. In the proposed research model, the researcher's capacity for openness assumes priority over the other four concepts of meaning, immediacy, uniqueness, and intersubjectivity (Dahlberg & Drew, 1997).

There is however a small difference between the earlier published research model (Dahlberg & Drew, 1997) and the one presented in this book. In the third chapter, where the empirical epistemology is presented, we emphasize more on the awareness of pre-under-

OPENNESS	NARRATIVES	
IMMEDIACY	INTERVIEWS	
INTERSUBJECTIVITY	?	OBSERVATION	MEANING
MEANING	context	DRAWINGS	ANALYSIS
UNIQUENESS	OTHER SOURCES	

LIFEWORLD PERSPECTIVE
INTENTIONALITY
PHENOMENOLOGY   HERMENEUTICS

Figure showing an epistemological model for reflective lifeworld research.

standing and reflection, than was done earlier. The word encounter is changed in favor of intersubjectivity.

Many central and important phenomena in the world of human being are immeasurable. In human science research we have to deal with a complexity and an ambiguity that does not allow for reductionism or atomism without loosing this world's vital meaning. In the world of human being we have to manage intentionality, reflectivity, intersubjectivity, and tacit knowledge – all of which a part cannot, probably, be verbalized at all. At least not yet. We thus need, we desire, a certain kind of research approach to meet these demands without reductionism. We mean that reflective lifeworld research, the methodology for human science research as it is outlined in the model above, offers such an approach.

The book structure

The research model, described at page 19, serves as a structure for this book. We begin the book in a general epistemological discussion tied to paradigm theory, which says that a paradigm cannot be judged from an outside position, because all scientific work is always carried out from within a paradigm. In chapter two we give the philosophical epistemological basis for human science research, as the main philosophers in the traditions of phenomenology and hermeneutics, Husserl, Heidegger, Merleau-Ponty and Gadamer developed it. The emphasis is on human intentionality and reflection. In chapter three we transform the philosophical epistemological ideas to an empirical epistemology. Mainly we do that by using the concepts openness, immediacy, intersubjectivity, meaning and uniqueness, but we also deal with the empirical consequences of the philosophical phenomenological reduction. Then, when the epistemology is settled, we outline some methodological principals for data gathering and data analysis that serve the purpose of a reflective lifeworld research. In the last chapter we offer some brief discussions of generalization and validity.

1 Paradigms and their influence

The individual is always encased by a tradition; and we do not choose that tradition, rather, if we look and understand, we find that we are living within a particular tradition (Heidegger, 1962). Gadamer (1994) clearly asserts that we exist through tradition. These statements imply that we always carry within us our historical and traditional point of view. Even when we do not consciously choose to work within a particular tradition we are active within a tradition. Our thinking is always influenced in some way by the tradition of our culture or our time. Just as we are never context-less, we are never traditionless.

The health care that we give today and the teaching that we do are part of a tradition. To understand the present, and in particular the development of caring and teaching knowledge, we need to look back and see how the past has influenced the present. Philosophers Heidegger and Gadamer stress the importance of tradition.

Traditions condition our existence and confer upon us the beliefs and values that we later learn to recognize as assumptions. In the case of science, its traditions contain assumptions which guide research, often in ways of which we are not aware. In Gadamer's (1994) words, these scientific assumptions can be as invisible for us as water is for fish. But though assumptions may be silent and hidden, they nevertheless contribute to the framework within which a discipline and its researchers function.

The notion of a paradigm conveys the idea that the tradition and the basic assumptions that steer the activities of science can be recognized and described. Paradigm comes from Greek, meaning example, in the sense of model or pattern. A paradigm functions as a mold, it shapes our perceptions of the world around us. A paradigm can also be thought of as a lens. Just as we learn not to see our glasses when we look through them, neither do we see the accepted paradigm of our discipline. Instead, we understand *with* it, just as we use our glasses in order to see. Depending upon the angle, strength or color of the lens, we see the world with varied sharpness, or in different colors, or in other qualitatively different ways. Rolf[1] (1991) writes about paradigms as patterns:

> Normally scientific endeavors are carried out according to particular patterns when we formulate the problems, solve them, and evaluate the solutions. These paradigmatic patterns ("disciplinary matrix") tell us how the world in general is, which methods are legitimate, which laws and symbols can be used in explanations, and finally a number of concrete successes which function as learning examples. (p. 87)

As researchers we see the world from within certain paradigms. Even though a paradigm may be invisible to us its effects continue to operate, making it all the more important to discover and consider the paradigm that is guiding our activities, and particularly, how the paradigm influences epistemological and methodological decisions for research.

The idea of paradigms

Kuhn (1970) is held as the founder of paradigm theory, a foundational epistemological idea that a certain theory or a set of beliefs rules the scientific work. In *The Structure of Scientific Revolutions* he rejected the accepted view of empirical science as an ideal, a view that had been unquestioned since the burgeoning of the natural sciences in the 18th century. With his ideas about paradigms Kuhn created "one of our decades most encompassing scientific theoretical debates"[2] (Lindholm[3], 1981, p. 22). Kuhn's challenge to the sci-

---

1   B. Rolf is a Swedish philosopher.
2   The judgment of T. Kuhn (b. 1922) is hold in the same way by the Oxford Companion to Philosophy (Honderich, (ed.), 1995). They name *The Structure of Scientific Revolutions* "the most influential book in modern philosophy of science" (p. 451).
3   Without being a philosopher S. Lindholm has written some important contributions to the Nordic philosophy of science.

entific community was meant to answer basic questions such as: What constitutes a legitimate scientific problem and how does science decide its legitimacy? How do the methods used to address such problems develop? What is considered an acceptable answer to a scientific question? Neither the natural nor social sciences had considered these questions prior to Kuhn.

Kuhn's claim was that a paradigm enjoys no strictly logical reason for its existence, but that it arises from the prevailing perspective of the scientists who govern the discipline. A discipline's scientific problems and methods arise from within its paradigm, that set of models, theories, beliefs that ultimately determine the problems that are seen, the questions that are raised and the methods selected to answer them. Eventually the models/theories and beliefs become research traditions. Researchers are therefore not "free" to practice science, but are steered by the dominant paradigm in many, often subtle, ways. The paradigm provides researchers with a pattern of scientific assumptions and foundational questions, which bring about a variety of positions taken by individual scientists as they think about their problems. These scientific assumptions, questions, and positions steer the discipline's work. The paradigm becomes be the scientific prototype for the formation of knowledge. The paradigmatic position that researchers take when making basic choices influences the direction of subsequent thinking and choices. The paradigm directs what the discipline's scientists and researchers are prepared to believe in. Similarly, the paradigm's epistemology influences scientists' and researchers' belief about what is possible to discover, what they hold to be true and scientific.

Even though Kuhn is credited with raising the paradigm issue, it has been argued that he was not the first to use the term, but rather, borrowed it from Wittgenstein[4], who in turn, found the term in Lichtenberg's 18th century philosophy (Rolf, 1991). Similar ideas were also held by Ludwik Fleck who published *Entstehung und Entwicklung einer wissenschaflichen Tatsache – Einfurung in die Lehre von Denkstil und Denkkollektiv*, a work that has become more prominent today than when it was written in 1935. By asserting that

---

4   L. Wittgenstein (1889–1951) is often described as the most important analytical philosopher of the twentieth century.

knowledge is contextual dependent, Fleck reveals the conditions and determinations of knowledge and knowledge development. Through examples from medicine Fleck shows that scientific knowledge by no means exists in an objectivistic vacuum. Instead, he says, scientific facts are products of history and society, and thus these facts change when history and society change. Fleck's classical work is now considered a forerunner to Kuhn[5].

Paradigm is a complex concept. Kuhn (1970) himself uses the term with a number of different meanings. However the core meaning of Kuhn's notion of paradigm is that, in part, it depicts the development of knowledge and in part it is a description and an explanation of how the models which create the premises of scientific research are formed. It is important to note that Kuhn had no normative intentions.

If we are to increase the possibilities of understanding science and its rules, we have to understand its paradigms, which each researcher carries, and which effect the researchers' understanding of the world and the science they conduct. Every paradigm has its own criteria, which define what is good science and good methods. A useful to describe paradigms is to identify their components or directing factors. Well-known concepts in paradigm theory are: world view, view of science, competence, and interest (Lindholm, 1981; Törnebohm, 1982; Eriksson, 1986; Lindström, 1990).

World view

A paradigm is known by its world view. A world view is made up of a collection of general assumptions about the part of the world in which a discipline's scientists are engaged in researching, Törnebohm (1985) says. A world view is the answer to the ontological question: What *is* the world? A world view describes basic assumptions about the way the world is comprised.

There are two basic, classical world-views. The first is that everything in the world, including people, are best understood by being

---

5   Also M. Polanyi held a paradigm idea similar to Kuhn's. Even though Polanyi did not use the term paradigm, he maintains that a tradition can be fully judged only from within the tradition itself (Rolf, 1991).

divided into isolated parts or variables (atomism), and/or reduced to the smallest, often physical, common denominator (reductionism). The second classical view is that the world is structured in patterns of internal interacting parts, where the whole influences the parts and the parts the whole (holism)[6]. In a holistic world view, humans and their being in the world cannot be understood by procedures that reduce them to autonomous parts, but can be fully understood only within a context where relating and meaning are primary.

The crucial aspect of the world view of human science research is its ontological understanding of the human being in the world with others. As it is to all human science disciplines, this view of humans is central to all caring and teaching. In order to understand how care is best given it is necessary to reflect upon what it means to each individual to be in need of care, to learn the meaning of the individual's situation. Other ontological questions that must be asked are: What does it (ontologically) mean to be a caregiver? What is the difference between a caregiver and a caretaker? What is care? What is the difference between care in general and professional care? What is holistic care? For example, holistic care is often talked about, especially in health care theory. It is generally agreed that patients should be understood and cared for from a holistic perspective. The results of a phenomenographic interview study (Dahlberg, 1992) however, indicated that a holistic perspective is a many-faceted phenomenon. A holistic caring perspective can be thought of as the combining of the different disciplines of medicine, psychology, sociology, and the spiritual into a whole. Another perspective concentrates on the unique individual behind the role of patient. Finally, holistic care is thought to exist if there is an egalitarian and collaborative relationship between the caregiver and the person receiving care. These different ways of understanding a holistic perspective in health care mirrors different views of humanity and are also expressions of a world view.

Likewise, we can see how different world views govern various approaches to teaching. Here certain ontological questions have to be asked such as: What does it mean to learn? What does it mean

6   This holistic view is also described in, for example, systems theory.

to teach? What is the difference between being a teacher and being a student? Cherished ideals in education, such as the influencing students, and grading, must be analyzed with reference to ontological meaning.

Scientific view

All scientists and researchers have a view of science, which is the way that they understand their field of scientific work. One's scientific view is related to one's world view; it is also built upon epistemological assumptions that guide questions about the world and the subsequent methods chosen to answer those questions. In addition, a paradigmatic view of science includes assumptions about how the discipline evolved, how it relates to other disciplines, and how it should be developed in the future, all of which promulgate the discipline's arena of research and beliefs about how the research should be conducted (Törnebohm, 1985).

Lindholm (1981) describes a paradigmatic view of science as a group of norms or ideas that delineate *what* should be researched and *how* it should be done. He identifies three aspects to the question, What should be researched? The first concerns seeing something *as* a problem in the first place. The second aspect is deciding whether the problem can be answered with scientific research. The third aspect is deciding what problems belong to the discipline and what should remain outside of it. For example, the subjective experience of health care has frequently been defined as an unscientific topic and therefore has not been considered as appropriate for study within health care research.

Lindholm further describes a continuum along which science raises the question, How should a problem be researched?[7] The continuum begins with general questions shared by all disciplines and proceeds to more encompassing, epistemological questions. Examples of such questions are: What is knowledge? How is it possible to obtain knowledge about a particular phenomenon? What is appropriate and scientific? How authentic/applicable is this

---

7   Also other questions could be raised her, such as, is knowledge by generated? Created? Discovered? Investigated? Explored?

knowledge? These epistemological standpoints lead one along the continuum to a point where more concrete questions are being raised and where the concrete choice of a particular method, which is suitable to both the problem and the paradigm, is made. The view of science may be very different between different paradigms, not least according to the how-questions. A basic assumption in mainstream science is that there is one and only method that serves the purpose of scientific truth and thus suffices for all types of research problems. We put forward the basic assumption that one general method is unacceptable. Instead, diversity of methods is sought and is dependant on the nature of investigation, the questions raised, and the purpose to be open to the phenomenon[8].

Paradigm competence

Törnebohm (1982) cites the researcher's competence as a crucial component of paradigm theory. The competencies which researchers bring to their area of interest help to create the culture of the paradigm; the culture, in turn, exerts great influence over researchers and the work that they engage in. Historically, the cultural paradigm created within the natural sciences has been given priority beyond the natural science domain, for example, in health care, while the cultural paradigm values of the human sciences have been considered of less consequence. The task of human science research is to describe the important phenomena of the human being in the world and the values that are central to the human culture. In order to foster a human science research culture its own perspective and paradigm must be allowed to develop and to have an influence on the world of science. As Polkinghorne (1986), Kvale (1989), and Giorgi (1988) and others many times have pointed out, human science researchers have to build their own scientific culture. It is only within this context that we can adequately answer challenges from positivistic sciences regarding scientific truth, objectivity and rigorous methods.

8   This idea is symbolized by the ? in the research model on page 19.

Researchers' competence forms the paradigm, which, in turn, influences how the researchers communicate scientific knowledge both within and outside of the paradigm. Being able to speak to each other within a cultural community is necessary in order to facilitate discussion about issues of praxis and dissemination of research. For a paradigm to flourish as a scientific culture researchers must first have the ability to converse with others within the same paradigm, and second, the ability to communicate with people from other paradigms. We must be able to listen, understand and learn from each other. As a meta-paradigm, the common culture that belongs to human science researchers promotes intra-paradigmatic (within human science research[9]) as well as inter-paradigmatic communication (e.g. between researchers in human science and researchers in natural science, or between researchers in different paradigmatic areas within human sciences). Communicative competence increases the likelihood of interdisciplinary cooperation, which is rapidly becoming the standard in the global scientific community.[10]

In addition to linguistic and communicative competence (Törnebohm, 1982), every paradigm depends on the social competence that contributes to understanding the researcher role, and the creation and establishment of the research area. Being socially competent as a researcher means comprehending the ramifications of overt as well as potential ethical issues. It means having respect for others, including all those who participate in research, as well as a keen sense of the professional roles that arise within the research process. These social considerations pose for scientists the problems that, when ethically and adequately addressed, can establish the paradigm as a useful one for society and its members.

In addition to the paradigmatic influence associated with a particular research area, one's formal education is the most important source of paradigm influence. Doctoral students are paradigmatically vulnerable and tend to accept the paradigm of their profes-

---

9   We mean that it is of crucial importance for the development of human sciences that all researchers within that field have a foundational knowledge about phenomenology, and for example about intentionality and reflection.

10 For example, Capra (1991) shows how a fruitful inter-disciplinary conversation can be carried out.

sors. It is of concern that students, who conduct research as part of their formal learning, and teachers, who engage in their discipline's research, takes seriously paradigmatic issues and open up these issues for discussions and debate.

Researcher interest and research direction

Just as paradigms direct what gets researched, paradigms themselves are influenced by the research direction and researchers' interest and investment in their research. As researchers, we always have a personal history with whatever we choose to study (Heidegger, 1967; Gendlin, 1967). The choice of a phenomenon for study stems from one's own pre-dispositions, values, and the researchers' personal investment in solving a problem that often fires the inception of a study. Research is planned and conducted because the phenomenon in question matters in some way to the researcher; no one plans and executes a study that is meaningless to her/him. It is the cumulative, committed interest of researchers that guides the direction in which research develops in their field. Also, and maybe more important, the choice of research plan is not only the researcher's since it is also influenced by the scientific context of the researcher. That is, a paradigm is often mirroring in the common research interest within the paradigm. It is likely that a researcher does not choose to work with a research problem that is not opportune in the ruling paradigm. In order for a paradigm to develop it is important that the unwritten rules about what is 'come il faut' are discussed and exposed to change.

A paradigm has been compared to a lens, but it is also analogous to an iceberg: only the top is seen; the largest portion is hidden and difficult to discern. Ordinarily it is difficult to see the paradigm or the traditions that we carry within us. Gadamer (1994) asserts that we see and understand only a part of it, that is, that which is above the surface, but that we are unaware of the rest, and as a result the paradigm is not verbalized very often. Instead a paradigm shows itself indirectly in the research problems that are chosen, the methods that are used and the criteria against which resultant knowledge is judged.

Knowledge development in paradigms

Science does not, of course, develop apart from the society of which it is a component. The results of scientific endeavors reflect the perspective and thought which guided their discovery. We may conclude therefore, that scientific facts are integrated parts of theoretical structure and "there are no absolute criteria for what is true" (Brante, 1981, p. 45). Similar to Kuhn (1970), Brante[11] (1981), urges us to question the generally accepted view of science as a solely rational and independent activity. Indeed, as scientists we are urged to maintain a healthy skepticism for any accepted body of knowledge.

What is considered a truth and what serves as a scientific method is partly due to the current paradigmatic period. During the paradigmatic period that is referred to as normal science, which is characterized by a stabile paradigm that does not allow any discussions or objections against it. During this period the scientific work is analogous to puzzle-solving, and clean-up work, which, as Brante (1981) expresses it, is "slow, laborious and, for the outsider, rather boring work" (p. 48). During a period of normal science, the goal is to strengthen the prevailing theoretical structure, which may result in a developing rigidity within the science when reality is forced into an established, relatively fixed form that the paradigm demands.

Science is not only a theoretical but a social phenomenon as well. The scientists who develop the theories also control the paradigm. Included in the paradigm is an array of social norms, which regulate the scientists' actions. Every scientist becomes part of the collective consciousness as a result of the socialization process of the scientific discipline, which may or may not depict a valid picture of that science. For example, scientists may be socialized as researchers who see their work as a strictly rational process, which is steered by objective criteria. Historically, the positivistic view of science has contributed to just such a picture of the nature of science by avoiding the paradigmatic notions and by insisting on one

---

11 T. Brante is a Swedish sociologist who has contributed to the philosophy of science in the Nordic countries.

kind of method, based in mathematics, as a guarantee for scientifically valid research.

Science is a theoretical and sociological activity, and it is a human one (Brante, 1981). However, the researcher as subject often disappears from the debate as a result of the objectivistic demands of science. Bärmark[12] (1984) says that many scientific models deny this important aspect of scientific work. Instead, science is often understood as a "research machine in which one puts empirical information and from which scientific knowledge then comes out" (p. 64). The important point that Bärmark is making is that it is impossible to omit the human subject in science. He describes a research project that studied researchers within either natural or social sciences and revealed them as deeply engaged in their research and "everything but neutral in relationship to their theories" (p. 65). In this respect he thus found no difference between the researchers. We cannot say with impunity that some scientists are more scientific than others, depending upon what type of research they are doing. All researchers invest themselves, more or less, in their research (Anderson, 1981).

The main stream view of scientific knowledge portrays researchers and their observations as neutral, ahistorical and contextless. Paradigm theory disputes this idea. It is of crucial importance that we consider the human subject's role in science, and maintain that in order to understand science and its research we must also understand the researcher as subject. Scientists observe the world, of which they are part, always from their own historical and cultural positions (Gadamer, 1994). Also quantum physics teaches us this foremost principle: there are no neutral methods; every tool is loaded with a paradigmatic value.

---

12 J. Bärmark is associate professor at Göteborg university, the department of philosophy of science, and has thoroughly been analyzing metascientific problems.

The scientific status of caring

What is the paradigmatic status of health science[13]? And what is the paradigmatic character of the western health care system? For more than a century the natural science paradigm has directed the development of healthcare. The result is a highly technologically-oriented system of care. This is especially true in the United States, where, in addition to a preoccupation with technology, healthcare is characterized by a market orientation. Sweden, which has been more open to holistic and humanistic practice has fostered a less objectivistic approach to its healthcare, but is nevertheless influenced by the United States, as is much of the world. Since the middle of the 1980's, the development of health care science in Scandinavia has increasingly taken a human, holistic and health centered perspective (Eriksson, 1986, 1999).

According to paradigm theory, caring science is an immature science because it does not have a unique and autonomous theoretical basis for scientific practice. As part of the healthcare system, caring science is influenced by the same political and social factors that constrict and shape all of the related health care disciplines. Research is in an even more vulnerable position with respect to the influence of the dominant paradigm. A result of the current paradigmatic situation in healthcare is that caring science researchers run the risk of following the line of least resistance and uncritically appropriating the biomedical and technologically oriented paradigm, thus accepting its norms and methods, and too often, a positivistic conception of science.

It is difficult to put forward changes that accentuate the importance of focusing on the unique and individual in the treatment of disease and health promotion when the ruling paradigm emphasizes the opposite. The lack of flexibility and along with the possessiveness that has been characteristic of the biomedical culture, inhibits new ideas from gaining ground (Stolt & Dahlberg, 1998). But then, that is precisely the nature of the early stages of an

---

13 This is not an unproblematic term and much debated. In this book health science equals caring science and means an approach to health care that is not limited by certain professionals.

approaching paradigm shift. We can watch with interest as the struggle for dominance ensues.

That a new health care paradigm is developing can be evidenced by the emergence of a new caring science language. New concepts suggest that traditional science is indicating a wish to discover, describe, and discuss ideas which have not previously been of scientific interest. However, linguistic changes do not always keep pace with paradigms shifts. Because a new paradigm is born out of the old one, it is expected that concepts from a formerly prevailing paradigm remain for a while in the new paradigm. The problem is that often the old concepts are used in new ways, and become a source of misunderstanding. An example of this is the frequent appearance of medical terms in nursing literature. The term nursing diagnosis indicates an incomplete transition from the biomedical paradigm to a holistic, caring paradigm.

The scientific status of education

What is then the paradigmatic status of education? While education research also continues to be dominated by the positivistic model, there has been a fractious debate during the last 30 years regarding the legitimacy of varying approaches to conducting research (Bredo & Feinberg, 1982). Interpretive researchers first challenged the adequacy of the positivistic model to research educational questions, and the critical science and post-modern researchers have more recently challenged the adequacy of both positivistic and interpretive research models.

The competition among views has been oversimplified and cast as quantitative versus qualitative research paradigms. The debate about quantitative and qualitative research has been explicit in a deluge of publications (e.g., Eisner, 1992; Keeves & Lakomski, 1999; Popkewitz, 1992; Schrag, 1992). It is less visible but equally present when editorial decisions are made about which articles and books are published, funding decisions are made about grant proposals, and hiring decisions are made to fill research positions, as Diesing (1991) notes.

One result of many researchers' objection to positivism and the wish to expand the understanding of scientific methods and the ensuing competition among other models has been the increasingly exotic research designs coming under the umbrella of qualitative research. Too little attention is now paid to the coherence among the epistemological assumptions, research question asked, and results of investigations. Another result of the competing views and increasing variability of research methodologies and designs is a quandary over what criteria should be used for judging the quality of research (Lagemann & Shulman, 1999).

Researchers are selecting different kinds of problems and topics to research today compared to the middle part of the last century when the physical science model was used exclusively. Earlier, research problems were more general and "were defined by the fundamental psychological processes of learning, such as memory, transfer, and problem solving" (Lagemann & Shulman, 1999). The application to practice was indirect; research findings slowly made their way into teacher education literature and textbooks. Today, many education research projects are small in scale, idiosyncratic to the context in which they are studied, and more holistic; Harry Wolcott's (1983) study, "Adequate Schools and Inadequate Education: The life history of a sneaky kid" illustrates this. School improvement is an example of a current research topic that has been pursued in larger scale studies and reflects increased concern about linking research and practice closely (Slavin & Madden, 1987; Comer, 1995; Levin, 1988).

The positivistic model continues to dominate educational practice as well as research. Technical subjects, such as math, are valued more highly than literature, drama, or art. Curriculum in general is strongly oriented toward technical knowledge about the world; even teacher education is technical in nature, focusing on techniques of teaching. Meaning of phenomena, for example, is seldom made explicit in learning and teaching; in teacher education the meaning of teaching is infrequently included in syllabi or textbooks.

Can paradigms be mixed?

Sometimes the question is raised as to whether paradigms can be mixed. Usually the question arises because one has found it diffi-

© Studentlitteratur

cult to belong to or affirm a single paradigm. Especially students, when touching upon the scientific questions for maybe the first time, find this very problematic. Health care and education, respectively, can be understood from both a natural science and a human science perspective. For students it is often appealing to encompass both perspectives. To get a better grasp of this problem we turn to Eriksson (1986) who proposes a picture of science at four different levels[14]:

Practical level:	*Here the skills are developed (the art of caring, the art of teaching*
Technological level:	*Here the "know-how" knowledge is developed (a kind of applied knowledge development)*
Theoretical level:	*Here "knowing-that" knowledge is developed (theories and models)*
Metatheoretical level:	*Here the disciplines are developed as science*

It is at the fundamental metatheoretical level that the paradigm is discussed and developed, and the paradigm and other theoretical and scientific questions are discussed. The other levels are never far outside our awareness, however. At the theoretical level of health care science for example nursing can be discussed from a variety of disciplines, such as psychology, medicine, or sociology. In a research project on the everyday care of Alzheimer patients, theories from psychology as well as from biomedicine could be used in order to better understand the needs of these patients. Further, at the technological level is the choice of methods, for example, interviews, observations or other sources of data. The most concrete instance, the practical level, gets its power from being

14 Eriksson's idea is originally valid for the understanding of health care and its science. Here we broaden the idea of Eriksson to encompass also education and its science.

anchored at the technological, theoretical, and the metatheoretical levels. The positions that one takes on metatheoretical and paradigmatic questions influences the theoretical and technological development of knowledge.

Accordingly, at the metatheoretical level it is **not** possible to mix paradigms. This means that when we grapple with fundamental questions such as one's world view, we must take a position. One cannot see a human both as a complex, indivisible whole as well as the sum of parts, which can be reduced to a common denominator that can be measured. The necessity of taking one position or the other becomes apparent when one engages in scientific work. However, when the basic paradigmatic and metatheoretical questions are decided upon, it is then possible to mix theoretical perspectives – it must however match the foundational choice. Let us give an example:

After the basic worldview is established it can be interesting to view humans and human problems from different theoretical perspectives. It can also be fruitful to use different methods to illuminate particular aspects of human existence. From the same thought process a unique caring action or a unique research activity can seem very different from another one, even if both come from the same ontological assumptions of mankind and the world.

The same is true for teaching. A teacher who is based in a certain pedagogic paradigm, and has explicated the metatheoretical choice, benefits from different learning theories. The foundational assumptions of the paradigm guide the choices made on higher levels. It all depends on the purpose and goal for the actual action.

Can paradigms change?

A frequent question is, do paradigms change? And if so, how? Before change can happen, researchers must be clear about the paradigm in which they function. In large part, discovery of the prevailing paradigm happens through the discussions in which researchers engage with each other in order to articulate, thematize and reflect on the scientific work that is being done within their area. Finding one's own position in and relation to the actual paradigm, and determining which paradigmatic rules will guide one's work, depends on developing awareness of the foundational assumptions, beliefs and values that guide the paradigmatic choices. It is more likely that a paradigm changes when it is made evident by clarifying and specifying the basic choices and positions which have resulted in a world view, with an accompanying epistemology and methodology. However, there are good reasons to believe that paradigms are continually emerging, being altered and being left behind as a matter of lifetime evolution.

2 The philosophy of lifeworld research

Phenomenological and hermeneutical philosophy are essential elements of the epistemology[1] that provids a foundation for human science research. While phenomenology and hermeneutics are broad and rich traditions, each with a distinct line of development, it is also obvious that they have a common ground. In this chapter we present and discuss the epistemological similarities and differences that characterize these two traditions, and that serve as a foundation for human science research.

Phenomenology

Phenomenology is not and has never been a single philosophy. Phenomenology appeared as a concept in philosophy during the 18th century and was understood during the 18th and 19th centuries in a variety of ways that nevertheless shared a common focus on "the apparent" as opposed to an "absolute truth" (Bengtsson[2], 1991). Phenomenology evolved into a broader understanding when Edmund Husserl (1859–1938) introduced the first part of *Logical investigations*[3] at the turn of the last century. In this book he challenges his own philosophical background, and he is especially critical to the psychologism that was influential by that time (Bengtsson, 1999). We see here an emerging pattern in Husserl's

---

1 Epistemology generally means the theory of knowledge.
2 J. Bengtsson is a Swedish philosopher. His main work is within the field of phenomenology.
3 Originally published as *Logische Untersuchungen,* 1900–1901.

philosophy, the serious and well-grounded critique of reductionism, which was and still is a dominant force in mainstream philosophy and scientific research. Husserl's philosophical texts began to be noted in the early 1900's and as a result there emerged a new way of understanding the world.

In addition to the critique of reductionism, another idea emerged early on in Husserl's philosophical work and was articulated in his analysis of the crisis of European sciences (1970b[4]). This idea, which also became influential among his colleagues and in understanding of modern science, meant an observation that natural science's tremendous progress, including a burgeoning technology, lead to a totalization of natural science as a governing ideal and the view that the natural sciences were a superior method to reach truth. As a result of this totalization, the social sciences were especially, and detrimentally, influenced by positivism. Husserl warned that cultivating the scientific ideal of positivism would sever science from the everyday world, ultimately resulting in the dehumanization of society rather than producing the anticipated benefits that scientific knowledge were expect to bring about. Husserl (1970b) writes that,

> [M]erely fact-minded sciences make merely fact-minded people. The change in public evaluation of science was unavoidable, especially after the war, and we know that gradually it has become regarded with hostility among the younger generation. In our vital need, so we are told, this science has nothing to say to us. It excludes in principle precisely the questions which man, given over in our unhappy times to the most portentous upheavals, find the most burning: questions of the meaning or meaninglessness of the whole of this human existence. (p. 6)

Referring to this concern of Husserl, Bengtsson (1987a) says that a science that is too far removed from the human world runs the risk of creating a crisis of confidence.

---

4   In the English translation by Carr (1970) it is said that *Die Krisis der europäischen Wissenschaften und die transzendentale Phänomenologie* was originally published in German 1954. However, since Edmund Husserl died 1938 it is interesting to note when he wrote this important piece of philosophy. According to Carr, he worked on it for some years and until 1937, but 1936 he published an essay that contains a great part of these ideas.

> A science that has lost its contact with the lifeworld will soon also lose its importance for everyday people, it will estrange rather than increase understanding or set free, and it will sooner or later be called in question by researchers who discover that it has changed to a pure instrument or an intellectual game. (p. 20)

Unfortunately, we recognize this all too much in contemporary science. Accordingly, Husserl's phenomenological alternative to an epistemological foundation for science is still valid and relevant.

Husserl's solution to the problem of a dehumanized science was to reinstate the everyday human world as the foundation of science. To this end, he saw phenomenology as the first philosophy, that is, the guiding foundation, or stance, for all scientific thinking because phenomenology takes into account the scientist's relationship with research projects, thereby assuring the objectivity[5] upon which that science is founded. The way to accomplish the new foundation was, in Husserl's (1970a) words, "to go to the things themselves".

"Zu den Sachen selbst"

An oft-repeated idea, and slogan, in phenomenological philosophy is "to go to the things themselves. The phenomenological idea of going to the things themselves means to do full justice to the everyday experience, to the lived experience (Husserl, 1970a). This idea also includes the aim to approach the world as it is experienced, in all its variety. The things of which Husserl spoke, and which are the objects of all research, are not to be understood as existing solely in themselves (the main idea of realism). Nor can they be reduced to mere aspects of the subject's conceptual world (the main idea of idealism). Things, rather, are things of experience. The term experience denotes the relationship we have with the world in which we are engaged. Phenomenology, which can be said here to function as a link between realism and idealism, turns to the world as it is experienced. Phenomenologically

---

5   It is important here to differ objectivity from objectivism, which means being caught in the belief that research does not involve the researcher as subject and that the researched world is "out there." See also chapter 6.

expressed, "going to the things" means that, as researchers, we stand in such a way that the things can show themselves to us, and thus "the thing" is understood as a phenomenon.

Phenomenon is a central concept within phenomenology. In order to express the meaning of phenomenology, Heidegger[6] (1889–1976), one of the most important and original among the students of Husserl's, says that it is the science of phenomena (1998, p. 50). The concept phenomenon, Heidegger explains, goes back to the Greek word *'phainomenon'*, which in turn is derived from *'phainesthai'*, which signifies "to show itself". Phenomenon thus means, Heidegger says, "that which shows itself in itself", or, that which becomes manifest for us. A phenomenon can then be understood as an object, a "thing" or a "part"[7] of the world, as it presents itself to, or, as it is experienced by, a subject. This is the core of the lifeworld perspective.

The natural attitude and the lifeworld

Rather than holding an obscure and elite place in the world, Husserl envisioned science as part of the world. Although he was critical of it, Husserl was also clear about the inherent power of what he called "the natural attitude", which he wanted to describe and understand through the intentional consciousness, an idea that understands consciousness as directed towards the world[8].

Human existence is characterized by the natural attitude, which is the primordial position for all researchers. The natural attitude as Husserl (1970a) conceived of it, is the everyday immersion in one's existence and experience in which we take for granted that the world is as we perceive it, and that others experience the world as

6 The philosophy of Martin Heidegger will be more thoroughly presented in the section on hermeneutics.
7 The words thing and part, are put in quote marks here because we do not refer to things and parts as the words are used in everyday language, something that is understood as something just concrete, in time and space only. With things and parts we mean anything within the human world of being that could be an object for consciousness, concrete "things" as well as abstract "things".
8 Intentionality is an important part of phenomenology which we will return to later in this chapter.

we do. In the natural attitude we do not critically reflect on our immediate action and response to the world, but we just do it, we just *are*. We live the natural attitude, so to speak. Thus, the natural attitude is the bottom-line for the everyday world where we live our lives and which we take for granted in all of our activities Bengtsson (1993a). For Husserl, this is a naïve approach to the world. As we shall see, in this attitude we do not stop to consider all possibilities for each situation in which we find ourselves. The natural attitude lacks the sophistication that would make it suitable as a framework for science.

The natural attitude characterizes activity in which humans are completely directed towards, immersed in, and absorbed by the activity, or the being, of the moment. To be in the natural attitude means that one does not consciously analyze what one is experiencing. When playing a piece of music a pianist is immersed, immediately, in the music, rather than thinking through every step involved in striking the right keys and keeping the tempo, etc. It is only when a mistake is heard that the pianist stops and thinks through the musical score and its rendering in an analytic way. In the natural attitude, one is immersed in, and thus in a sense lost in the actual activity. As a result, the things that we are closest to are the things that are most hidden from us (Heidegger, 1998). What we are immersed in we assume exists in the way we experience it. Daily activities appear obvious and are taken for granted in the same way we take for granted the air we breathe, or a fish does with the water it lives in. In the natural attitude we do not consider it necessary to analyze those things which are closest and which seem obvious, that is, our tacit or implicit experiencing of the world. However, in a scientific attitude[9], broadly understood, scrutiny of the tacit is necessary. A first step taken in that direction brings us to a deeper understanding of the notion of lifeworld as it is understood in phenomenology.

Husserl's idea of the lifeworld (*Lebenswelt*) emerged out of his notions of the natural attitude, where all science and research has

---

9   This book can be understood as a demonstration of what we mean by a scientific attitude. However, this far we want to explain, that by 'scientific' we refer to a methodical and systematic handling of research data (cf. Merleau-Ponty, 1964).

46

its origins. Husserl (1970b) was the first to describe the lifeworld as an epistemological idea and to outline a lifeworld theory. His intent was for lifeworld theory to become the new basis for all philosophy and human science research. Many interpreters of Husserl's philosophy, such as his French successor Maurice Merleau-Ponty (1908–1961), say that it was not until towards the end of his life that Husserl identified *Lebenswelt* as a central theme of phenomenology. Although this is right about the notion of the lifeworld being a central theme of phenomenology, Merleau-Ponty and others are not entirely correct in saying that this idea came late in Husserl's life. It is important to note that Husserl, according to Bengtsson (1998), introduced the notion of *Lebenswelt* in a research manuscript, dated as early as 1916[10].

For Husserl, phenomenology begins within the concrete and lived existence in the world. It was his intention to philosophically examine the lifeworld as a tacit ground for science. Phenomenology seeks to avoid reductionism and to grasp and describe the world in the way that it is experienced by humans. The concept of the lifeworld implies an epistemology for human science research in which the question of meaning is primary. Human science research seeks to understand meanings in our everyday experience, and in lifeworld, meanings that often are implicit or "tacit". Referring to Husserl, Gadamer[11] (1995) says that the lifeworld itself is tacit. It is "the world in which we are immersed in the natural attitude that never becomes an object as such for us, but that represents the pregiven basis of all experience" (pp. 246–247). This understanding of lifeworld is obvious in Gadamer's philosophy, since he also understands the lifeworld as "the whole in which we live as historical creatures" (p. 247).

The lifeworld theory was further explicated, and became a lifeworld phenomenology, by Merleau-Ponty (1995[12]). Merleau-Ponty expresses lifeworld as "*être-au-monde*". His understanding of "lifeworld" signifies how we are *to* the world, that is, how we relate to

---

10 Husserl's manuscript has the title: *Lebenswelt – Wissenschaft – Philosophie: Naives Hinleben in der Welt – Symbolisches Festlegen durch Urteile der Welt – Begründung.*
11 The philosophy of Hans-George Gadamer will be more thoroughly presented in the section on hermeneutics.
12 Originally published as *Phénoménologie de la perception*, 1945.

and interact with the world. Accordingly, the lifeworld for Merleau-Ponty is a phenomenal field. He describes the notion of lifeworld in a poetic way:

> To return to the things themselves is to return to *that* world which precedes knowledge, of which knowledge *always* speaks, and in relation to which every scientific schematization is an abstract and derivative sign-language, as is geography in relation to the countryside in which we have learnt beforehand what a forest, a prairie or a river is. (1995, ix)

Merleau-Ponty asserts that the lifeworld is a necessary condition for knowledge. Indeed, he says that the lifeworld precedes all knowledge. It is clear, that for Merleau-Ponty, Heidegger, Gadamer, as well as for Husserl[13], we can never escape the lifeworld, the complex, qualitative and lived reality that is there for us whatever we do. Husserl puts it in this way:

> The knowledge of the objective-scientific world is "grounded" in the self-evidence of the life-world. The latter is pregiven to the scientific worker, or the working community, as ground ... If we cease being immersed in our scientific thinking, we become aware that we scientists are, after all, human beings and as such are among the components of the life-world which always exists for us, ever pregiven; and thus all of science is pulled, along with us, into the – merely "subjective-relative" – life-world. ... The concrete life-world, then, is the grounding soil [*der gründende Boden*] of the "scientifically true" world and at the same time encompasses it in its own universal concreteness. (1970b, pp. 130–131)

The arena of phenomenology is characterized by Merleau-Ponty as a phenomenal field. The phrase "phenomenal field" suggests that the world we investigate has a duality. We cannot judge about the world other than in relation to our experience of it. On the other hand, the world or an object of the world is present, even if we are not aware of it at the moment. It is there whether or not we experience it. And it is present, as lifeworld, already when we start think-

---

13 This is not an uncomplicated understanding of Husserl's lifeworld theory. In several texts where he outlines the transcendental phenomenology his aim is to go beyond the natural attitude and the lifeworld. It is however our understanding, that he is clear about the lifeworld as the pre-given and pre-scientific world.

ing and doing our scientific work. The lifeworld is thus pre-scientific and pre-reflective. This is a notion that we must keep in mind when we later on turn to Husserl's idea about transcendentality.

Scientific work is a human activity and, as such, is part of the lifeworld. Although science has not always recognized that its theories originate in scientists' implicit experience of the lifeworld, it begins in the lifeworld. Knowledge of the lifeworld can be acquired through science, but knowledge is something other than the reality of what is known. Theorizing and reflecting on the concrete, lived world involves a loss of the concrete lived world as we know it, but at the same time expands the store of knowledge that is at a more abstract intellectual level (Bengtsson, 1993a). With Husserl's idea of phenomenology it becomes possible to confront the human everyday world in a scientific way that clarifies the lifeworld underpinnings of any explanations that science might propose. It was Husserl's contention that science begins with and extends from a lifeworld perspective. He saw phenomenology as the key to the grounding of science in the lifeworld, an approach that later was adopted by hermeneutics. The lifeworld theory is an epistemological and methodological tool with which the multifarious world of human being is revealed and understood. The overall aim of lifeworld research is the description and elucidation of the lived world in a way that expands our understanding of human experience.

The subjective body

The lifeworld is for Merleau-Ponty also the lived world (*monde vecu*), that is, the world we have access to through our bodies. Thus, in his understanding, all knowledge that we develop is embodied knowing. The notions of subjective body and embodied knowing are other aspects of the natural attitude and the lifeworld approach. As Merleau-Ponty expresses it, "I am to the world as body".

> [W]hen I reflect on the essence of subjectivity, I find it bound up with that of the body and that of the world, this is because my existence as subjectivity is merely one with my existence as a body and with the existence of the world, and because the subject that I am, when taken concretely, is inseparable from this body and this world. The ontological world and body which we find at the core of the sub-

> ject are not the world or body as idea, but on the one hand the world
> itself contracted into a comprehensive grasp, and on the other the
> body itself as a knowing-body. (p. 408)

It would be difficult to overstate the centrality of the subjective
body to Merleau-Ponty's (1995) understanding of the human
world. The human body can never be understood merely as a biological thing or as an object that can be moved around the room in
the same way as furniture and other things[14]. "If my arm is resting
on the table I should never think of saying that it is beside the ash-
tray in the way in which the ash-tray is beside the telephone" (p.
98). The body is distinguishable from the objects in that we can
turn away from the latter whereas we can never turn away from the
body. Instead, the body "is constantly perceived" (p. 90). It is
through the body and the bodily experience that the surrounding
world becomes meaningful for us. "My body is that meaningful
core which behaves like a general function", says Merleau-Ponty
(p. 147). And also, it is the body that gives us a world in the first
place, being "our means of communication with it" (p. 92). It is
the living body which offers a connection to the world and which
carries out all living actions. "The body is the vehicle of being in
the world" (p. 82) and it is "the horizon latent in all our experience
and itself ever-present and anterior to every determining thought"
(p. 92). We can never free ourselves from this embodiment, never
come away from or stand outside of ourselves as subjective bodies.
On the contrary, it is precisely through the body that we have
access to anything such as a world, it is the body that connects us
to that world and roots us in the world. In short, the "body is our

---

14 "To say that it [the body] is always near me, always there for me, is to say
    that it is never really in front of me, that I can not array it before my eyes,
    that it remains marginal to all my perceptions, that it is with me." (p. 90).
        Merleau-Ponty further shows the relationship between the body and
    the external world: "In so far as it sees or touches the world, my body can
    therefore be neither seen nor touched. What prevents its ever being an
    object, ever being 'completely constituted' is that it is that by which there
    are objects. It is neither tangible nor visible in so far as it is that which sees
    and touches. The body therefore is not one more among external objects,
    with the peculiarity of always being there. If it is permanent, the perma-
    nence is absolute and is the ground for the relative permanence of disap-
    pearing objects, real objects." (p.92)

anchorage" (p. 144) in the world. As long as we live we have a world, and the connection is the subjective body.

Accordingly, the human being does not "have" a body, but "is" the body. Consequently, the phenomenological understanding of the body as subjective consequently is complex. We cannot step outside the body, instead, we experience it from both inside and outside simultaneously. The subjective body replaces the old dichotomy and problem of body and/or soul, because the subjective body means "a fusion of soul and body" (p. 84)[15]. The relation to ones body is characterized by immediacy. One relates to one's body and to oneself in the natural attitude, which is characterized by an unreflective awareness. Most of what we do in our day-to-day lives we do without reflection, without being consciously aware of it. We walk, eat, read or type, without being aware of every single movement or action. But that does not mean that we live randomly. What we do is generally both meaningful and coherent. In Merleau-Ponty's words, our body is "a nexus of living meanings" (p. 151).

According to Merleau-Ponty, Heidegger and Husserl, all of whom have similar standpoints, human beings and their existence can never be understood without being considered as a living whole. Objective findings such as test results, x-ray pictures, grades and other so called objective signs are important tools in the health care and education, but are of limited value. Understanding other humans and their existence can never be complete without the perspective of their subjective experience, their lived viewpoint of body, health, knowledge and existence.

Similarly, Merleau-Ponty emphasizes the human in relationship with space and time, and says that we must "avoid saying that our body is in space, or in time. It inhabits space and time" (p. 139). He also states: "I am not in space and time, nor do I conceive space

---

15 Merleau-Ponty makes this understanding in another quote: "Man taken as a concrete being is not a psyche joined to an organism, but a movement to and fro of existence which at one time allow itself to take corporeal form and at others moves towards personal acts. Psychological motives and bodily occasions may overlap because there is not a single impulse in a living body which is entirely fortuitous in relation to psychic intentions, not a single mental act which has not found at least its germ or its general outline in psychological tendencies." (p. 88)

and time; I belong to them, my body combines with them an includes them" (p. 140). As humans we live both space and time. Consequently, a room is not a room in itself, as a physical fact. Neither is the room to be understood just as something cognitive or subjective. Instead the room is something that we are in relationship with. As subjective bodies we relate to the room. In front of, or behind, above, and below – can be only in relation to a subject, that is, the bodily subject. Thus we have a living horizon that is constantly shifting as it, so to speak, moves with us. As subjective bodies we are therefor always "here" and we are always also "now". We are used to talking about past time as time that is no longer, and future as time that is no yet. However, according to Merleau-Ponty,

> What is past or future for me is present in the world ... Past and future exist only too unmistakably in the world, they exist in the present, and what being itself lacks in order to be of the temporal order, is the not-being of elsewhere, formerly and tomorrow. (p. 412)

In the lifeworld "now" has no temporal character, Merleau-Ponty says. Instances of "now" could not accordingly occur in sequence. In regard to our temporal relationship with the world, Merleau-Ponty comes very close to Heidegger (1998), who is critical of the conventional notion of time as "a succession, as a 'flowing stream' of "nows", as the 'course of time'" (p. 474). "Now" is not something that we calculate or track. "Now" is something that we live in the moment. Just as we always stand in a living relationship with the world we always stay in a living relationship with time.

Memory is also to be understood as embodied. The body is the medium of our temporal and spatial communication and therefor significant in the function of memory (Merleau-Ponty, 1995). Memory is, "an effort to reopen time on the basis of the implications contained in the present" (p. 181). Implications of space and time are communicated to us bodily. For example, if we walk on a certain path where we walked as children, and this walk then is filled with memories of the earlier walk, we can "sense the mood of the earlier time manifested in the present" (Smith, 1992, p. 104). The bodily memory makes it "a reverie" of the past, "playing out here and now".

The body in health and illness

Health is silent, is an old saying. Gadamer (1996) confirms this when he says that it is not health but illness which "objectifies" itself. When healthy, we have a natural attitude to our subjective body and to the idea of health itself, which we take for granted. As Gadamer says, "[h]ealth does not actually present itself to us" (p. 107). One could say that there is a hidden character to health. When ill, however, we do not enjoy easy and natural access to the world. Our relationship with the world is disturbed when we are ill. Gadamer (1996) states that "illness as the loss of health, as the loss of one's undisturbed 'freedom', always involves a sort of exclusion from 'life'." (p. 55). In illness, we can no longer count on the freedom to participate in everyday activities as we once did. Illness is far more than symptoms, diagnoses, and treatment. It is also the loss of abilities that hinder easy and unmindful living. The lived body, and even more profoundly, lived illness, make clear what it means to have access to the world. When our bodies are healthy and strong we meet the world unafraid. But when we are in pain and weak, our bodies become obstacles that keep us from immediate engagement with the world. A break down of one's body means a break down of life (Toombs, 1993). Every illness has a particular meaning that alters one's attachment with the world. A headache may mean an inability to concentrate on one's writing; arthritis may mean an inability to go horse back-riding. Toombs (1993) points out that chronic or life threatening diseases not only effect one's immediate engagement in the world, but also "portends the 'inability to' carry out future projects or to complete anticipated goals" (p. 63). Furthermore, in illness certain activities "are no longer within my bodily scope", as Toombs (p. 63) puts it.

Consequently, illness could be understood as bodily dissonance. The possibility of productive access to the world and the opportunity to do what one anticipates is radically changed when something disturbs one's sense of the subjective body's well-being. Bodily dissonance is a conflict of wanting and not being able to, lacking bodily autonomy. Bodily dissonance means having a fragile body.

Embodied knowing and knowing bodies

As humans we live as subjects in and through our bodies. All understanding, our memory, perception, emotional and cognitive relations to the world, is embodied. Such embodiment is evident in health care practices as well as in teaching. For example, nurses practice embodied knowing when they intuitively care for patients. As Benner (1984) describes it, the experienced nurse spends little time in reflecting about what s/he is doing, but simply proceeds in a natural way in which knowledge is embodied. Benner exemplifies this embodied knowledge in those situations in which an experienced nurse knows immediately when something is wrong with a patient and takes action to correct the situation. Embodied knowing is fairly easy to recognize. For example, an experienced psychotherapist, despite years of formal education, does not act according to rule-bound techniques with pre-designed answers or actions. Nor does the therapist act like a reed shaken by the wind, randomly making her/his decisions as the result of powerful emotions. With embodied knowing, the therapist knows what to do and how to respond to the patient naturally, with knowledge and experience that are integrated bodily.

Another example: a teacher of children "reads" the classroom to determine if students are ready to move on to the next step of the lesson. At the same time s/he considers how s/he will make the transition to the next step and monitors which students are off-task. The teacher's knowledge of pacing the lesson and moving to a location in the room to silently beckon inattentive students back to the lesson is embodied. The whole subjective body is needed and deployed when the teacher teaches expertly.

The subjective body is also very prominent in the lifeworlds of students. A general review of pedagogic and educational research literature gives a clear picture of a one-sided, and thereby also biased, perspective of learning as something cognitive. Learning theories have been developed from psychological, sociological, biological and physiological disciplines, but there is no account of the lived body in learning. Even from recent research[16] about learning one gets the picture of brains or cognitions lined up above

16 See for example Marton, F. & Booth, S. 1997. *Learning and awareness.* New Jersey: Lawrence Erlbaum Assoc. Publ.

the school desks, and in front of them is one more cognitive object, the one teaching. In a study by Dahlberg, McClelland and Plihal (1999) [17] this understanding of learning is being challenged, and a conceptualization of embodied learning is emerging. The lived experiences of university students' learning reminds us we are in the world bodily, not just as cognitive beings. For example, a meaning of the subjective body in the learning situation is bodily excitement. That is, while the student is learning, her or his body is energetic, alert, and fuels the student's learning. Another constituent is the body sensing the emotional climate of the classroom. The body responds to discomfort that may in turn precipitate learning as it did for a student whose "stomach bothered" her. In her family therapy class, a churning in her stomach during a discussion of homosexual couples signaled to her she was biased. This realization was not cognitive so much as it was bodily.

Intentionality

In addition to the lifeworld perspective, Husserl's theory of intentionality is central to phenomenology. In Ideas I, Husserl (1998[18]) clearly states that intentionality is a main theme of phenomenology. Understanding intentionality is crucial in human science research that is based on phenomenological philosophy. Intentionality refers to our primordial approach to the world, in which we are spontaneously, rather than critically engaged. Intentionality characterized the most basic mode of being. When we are, we are intentional, so to speak.

Franz Brentano, one of Husserl's early teachers in Vienna, introduced the phenomenological theory of conscious intentionality. Husserl (1970a) exposited the theory of intentionality as an epistemological concept in order to clarify and elucidate the natural attitude. Intentionality refers to the relationship between a person and

---

17 This is from a paper with the title *University students' bodily learning experiences*, presented at the International Human Science Research Conference Sheffield, England July, 1999.

18 *Ideen zu einer reinen Phänomenologischen Philsophie, Erstes Buch* was first published 1913.

the object or events of her/his experience, or more simply, one's directed awareness of an object or event (Husserl, 1907, 1998). There is always an intentional relationship with the things that make up our everyday lives, that is, we understand the meaning of the things that we use and that we see around us as the things, activity and places that belong to and signify our world. Merleau-Ponty (1995) explains Husserl's theory of intentional structures with the statement, "consciousness is consciousness of something" (p.137). Consciousness is always directed toward some object, perception what is perceived, the wish what is wished for, the thought what is the idea. When we experience something, it is experienced as something which has meaning for us. A person doing phenomenological research is interested in the way that consciousness grasps an object or event as something, as it is meant. To say that something is understood as meant, indicates a contextual and historical relationship between ourselves and the essential structures of a phenomenon; because we live in the world of which this phenomenon is a part, it has meaning for us and we bring this meaning to subsequent encounters and perceptions of it.

In the moment of perceiving we experience the world in an all-at-once way, implicitly understanding what it means. We perceive an object or an event and we see the particular characteristics of the object or event. In the phenomenological frame of mind, we see the aspects, or patterns, that let us grasp the essence of the phenomenon, that is, that which makes the object or event into that particular phenomenon. This active relationship in which we experience the things and events of our world as endowed with meaning, as meant, is the intentionality of which Husserl spoke.

Thus, there is always an intentional relationship with the things that make up our everyday lives, that is, we understand the meaning of the things that we use and that we see around us as the things and places that belong to and signify our world. Intentionality also involves the completion of partially accessible qualities or characteristics of an object which are not directly presented but which nevertheless are present in our conscious experience of it. Husserl (1970b) says that every perception has a horizon belonging to it, a horizon that emerges with the act of perceiving.

> Even if I stop at perception, I still have the full consciousness of the thing, just as I already have it at the first glance when I see it as the thing. In seeing I always "mean" it with all sides which are in no way given to me, not even in the form of intuitive, anticipatory presentifications. (1970b, p. 158)

The object's horizons, the partially accessible characteristics that contribute to our experience of the thing as something, which are not immediately presented to consciousness, but nevertheless exist in our consciousness, is what Husserl also named "apperceptions" or "appresentations" (1992[19]). Bengtsson (1998) explains that in every particular experience there is such an appresentation, which transcends the immediate given, and makes possible an existence in space and time which our senses give to us as a whole. A specific concrete reality is presented in the experience. Along with that which is accessible to sight, or hearing, for example, the parts of the object which are not directly presented are nevertheless experienced, we fill them in, so to speak, so that the experience is of whole cloth. An example may help.

When Helen sits in her study she can lift her gaze from the keyboard and see the end of the neighbor's house and the lilac hedge, which is a continuation of the wall of the house. That house and its lilac hedge are at that time directly given to her, or in Husserl's words, they are presented to her experience. Even though the end of the house and the lilac hedge are all that she can see of her neighbor's place, the part of the house that is absent from her view is included in her experience of looking at the house. If she should go around the lilac hedge, she will find a terrace with sun chairs and inside the terrace door is a room, etc. These portions of her neighbor's place which are not immediately presented to consciousness, but nevertheless exist in her consciousness, are what Husserl named appresentations. Appresentations, which in this example include the house's terrace and interior, are the object's inner horizons, its interior. If we go further and discover that behind the neighbor's place is another house and beyond that house is a street, we have come into contact with the object's outer

---

19   See footnote 24, p. 65.

horizons. The object's outer horizons could thus be understood as its immediate context.

These intentional structures are important to understand if we want to understand an object's meaning. Intentionality means making experience into a full, concrete or abstract picture. For that purpose, consciousness completes the experience of seeing a situation or an object, integrating appresentations with actual presentations. This is what happens in the example of Helen, in which she makes into a whole the spatial presentations and appresentations of the experience. It is important to note that the appresentations, that make the experience into a whole, are not directly given in consciousness, but can be made accessible to consciousness in a direct experience (Bengtsson, 1993). In the example above, Helen can leave her computer, go out, and have a look at the neighbor residence, and thereby make the appresentations into direct presentations for consciousness.

Temporal appresentations

The presented meaning of intentionality is valid also in reference to temporal presentations. Consciousness, Husserl (1964[20]) asserts, is time-consciousness. He sees lived experience as a consciousness of perception that is, "nothing other than temporally constitutive consciousness with its phases of flowing retentions and protentions" (p. 176). Every mental process, Husserl says, has an infinitely fulfilled temporal horizon. It is like a stream of mental processes, a stream of experience, without beginning and end. When we are reflective and using our consciousness actively, we are constantly moving in this endless temporal space. Reflective activity relates the past, that is, the now-incidents that have been, and the future, that is, the now-incidents which are to come, to the present moment.

A certain function of memory, which Husserl calls a primary memory, comes into the picture. When we try to make sense of something we perceive, consciousness brings together past intendings of objects, especially of that actual kind, and objects in general (retention). That is, past experience of that (kind of) object affects

---

20   Husserl gave these lectures between 1905–1910, but the text was published (with a preface of Heidegger) 1928.

the present relationship with it. Furthermore, if one says, for example, that "Paris is the capital of ...", the listener will immediately understand that the statement is about France, even if that is not part of what is directly presented in the act. Thus consciousness includes "a horizon of original, even if entirely empty, expectation, an expectation at first purely passive (protention)" (Husserl, 1970b, p. 160). Husserl's theory of intentionality emphasizes that perception is related only to the present. "But this present", Husserl asserts, "is always meant as having an endless past behind it and an open future before it" (p. 160).

The connection between the present moment and past experience might also be thought of as a juncture or nexus in which new and expanded understanding is possible (Merleau-Ponty, 1991a). If we are aware of the historical connections to the present moment, the past events that we recall have an integrative function, in which the present situation and the past are transformed into a new whole. Meaning is never finally complete but is always expandable, limited only by our readiness to enlarge our understanding.

Natanson (1973) clarifies that this process of bringing together past and future is not a cumulative but regenerative intentive process. This means that we draw on all of our experience, both past and anticipated, and that such experience becomes a moment in the present as we consider meanings and import for decisions and understanding.

Transcendentality

Husserl's notion of transcendence and transcendental subjectivity has been and continues to be the source of much philosophical discussion and dispute among human science researchers. Typically, such discussions become debates between extreme and opposing positions. One viewpoint sees transcendence as standing aside from one's subjective experience in order to observe the world or a particular phenomenon from a pure epistemological and totally objective perspective. One might imagine a free-floating platform upon which the phenomenologist sits and which provides an unhindered view of the phenomenon in question. The other perspective holds that such a position of pure transcendence is impossible, and as such, transcendental subjectivity should be considered a hypothetical notion that ought to be discarded altogether. In what follows we will argue for a somewhat middle position.

Transcendentality is the notion with which Husserl (1998) aims to go beyond the natural attitude. He offers a radical alteration of the natural stance of position. According to this idea, we can step out of the natural attitude and "put out of action" or "exclude" or "parenthesize" parts of the world from our consciousness, a conscious act that frequently is referred to as "bracketing" (*Einklammerung*). Thus, a reduction has taken place. Giorgi[21] (1997) explains that the reason for this maneuver is that we must question what we experience, instead of assuming that it is something real (in the word's most primordial meaning). Phenomenology, he says, "wants to understand what motivates a conscious creature to say that something 'is'" (1997, p. 239). He continues, "even when one encounters in experience things and events that 'obviously' have existence, the reduction directs one to step back and describe and examine them as presence". This stance of scientific openness, which Husserl (1970b) calls the phenomenological-psychological reduction, is an important notion for researchers who want "to go to the things themselves". In this regard, a researcher must,

> neither concur nor refuse, nor remain in problematic suspense, as if he had some say in the validities of the persons who are his subjects. So long as he has not acquired this posture as a serious and consciously established one, he has arrived at this true subject matter; and as soon as he violates it, he has lost his subject matter. (p. 240)

Bracketing, however, does not mean that the event or object that has been set aside is lost. Husserl says (1998, p. 61) that even if we choose to parenthesize the world, it will always remain there for us, as an "actuality" to consciousness. Within the reduction, or this epochè, as Husserl (1970b) also calls it, "neither the sciences nor the scientists have disappeared for us who practice the epochè. They continue to be what they were before, in any case: facts in the unified context of the pregiven life-world" (p. 136).

---

21 A. Giorgi is an American psychologist who has developed a phenomenological psychology based in the philosophy of Husserl and Merleau-Ponty.

However, it is clear that Husserl's transcendental subjectivity has limits and is constrained by the very fact that it is part of the world. Given the understanding of consciousness that Husserl himself presents in the theory of intentionality we have to conclude that there is no pure consciousness per se, and therefore there is no possibility to achieve pure knowledge per se. It is impossible to bracket all pre-understanding that there is in the lifeworld. Being in the world, and therefore being human, is a limitation from which we can never be free. Phenomenology and the hermeneutics that was developed after Husserl adopted this approach to epistemology. The transcendental platform of understanding above and apart from the world, is an illusion. The discovery of a pure ego and objective consciousness, was Husserl's ultimate goal, and at the same time an unreachable, unrealistic goal. He never fully, satisfactorily solved the problem of how a pure transcendental position could be attained, and even more so, he never solved the problem of the transcendental subject in a lifeworld. Some questions remain to be answered by researchers; is it credible to keep the idea of transcendentality?; is it possible to withhold past knowledge?; and, can a researcher avoid making existential claims for the objects which obviously are already there, in the world?

Toward the end of his life's work, Husserl acknowledged the primacy of the lifeworld and began to develop his ideas about it more thoroughly than earlier (Husserl, 1970b). A plausible explanation for his concern about the lifeworld might be that he believed that the concept of the lifeworld ultimately would support his lifelong efforts to present transcendence as a useful and workable tool for explicating consciousness. We may, however, also speculate that, by this period in his life, Husserl might have surrendered his dream of developing a pure transcendental phenomenology, and instead, turned to the notion of the lifeworld as a median point between the difficulties with transcendence and the need for an approach with which to begin the work of phenomenology. It seems clear that Husserl had not entirely given up his struggle to make transcendence an acceptable premise for the mental labors of phenomenology. In Eugene Fink's (1995) explication of Husserl's unfinished sixth meditation, he asserts that the concept of transcendentality designates subjectivity and its constituting function in relationship to the natural attitude and, therefore, to the world.

Transcendentality places us "in antithesis to the world and to the natural attitude" (p. 143). Fink is clear that Husserl's transcendental subjectivity has obvious limits. Fink argues for the impossibility of bracketing all pre-understanding (p. 36). His premise is that being in the world and therefore, being human, is the pre-understanding from which we can never be totally removed; the transcendental platform of observation above the world is an illusion. A more creative way of approaching this particular epistemological dilemma might be to emphasize the continuum, or pathway, between the two positions of pure consciousness and lifeworld embeddedness. We can imagine that although the purity of the platform is impossible to reach, the path that lies between the natural attitude and the point of pure transcendence is accessible to us and provides an entry point from which to develop a perspective of critical scrutiny for research.

This is how we find the solution to the epistemological dilemma that Fink offers, and that other philosophers suggest as well[22]. Self-awareness can be understood as an aspect of the human capacity for transcendentality, an ability to reflect on our own consciousness and perception. Consequently, self-awareness is an important part of that continuum upon which the transcendental platform is the extreme end position.

Self-awareness belongs to phenomenological epistemology and methodology, the approach that has its origins in the lifeworld and an emphasis on openness. The gulf between those who dismiss transcendence as a goal that is impossible to achieve and those who insist that it can be accomplished is less problematic than it might appear. Certainly it is a philosophical issue that will not be resolved here. What is important for research, however, is understanding that the capacity for bracketing and self-awareness, however limited, is part of our ontology, epistemology, and methodology as well. As humans we are endowed with the ability for critical scrutiny of ourselves and the ability to seek objectivity with regard to our own reasoning processes, even if this ability usually does not come to play in the natural attitude. However, when we undertake phenomenology as a scientific research approach, it seems that we

---

22 In next chapter we will argue that both Merleau-Ponty and Gadamer take up this philosophical thread.

have no choice but to be always drawn toward self-awareness, because it ultimately leads us to consider our constitutive involvement with the phenomena that we investigate and describe (Fink, 1995). It matters less that we can or cannot achieve a pure transcendental position or a pure self-awareness. What matters more is that we realize the importance of taking the first step on the path toward objectivity, that we develop an awareness of the conscious processes that contribute to our understanding of phenomena (cf. Giorgi, 1997). The notion of a beginning point for self-awareness on the path between the opposing positions of transcendentality offers a way for researchers to proceed with the work that needs to be done if we are to begin the changes necessary for a more humanly oriented science (and world).

The next chapter will look at the 'how' of self-awareness, reflection and self-reflection. Accordingly, and against what often is said in descriptions of phenomenological and/or hermeneutical methods, we will argue for the necessity to hold on to the idea of a phenomenological reduction, particularly when formulating methodological principles for human science lifeworld research.

Intersubjectivity

Before we leave the realm of phenomenological epistemology there is one more concept that needs to be illuminated, that is intersubjectivity. Lifeworld theory and phenomenology is about human beings, about humans in the world. When we refer to the human world as the lifeworld, we are implying that as humans we are already in a world context, a world of tradition, a world of history, as well as a world of other humans. This relationship with the world is obvious in Heidegger's (1998) concept "In-der-welt-sein" (the being in the world) and Merleau-Ponty's (1995) "être-au-monde" (being to the world). Prior to any description we might make of our existence, we are already in a world, world with others. In this section on intersubjectivity we shall look at just how we are in the world with others, since this is something that affects openness.

Intersubjectivity is a primordial quality of the human world. To be human and in a world means being-with others, according to Heidegger (1998): "… the world is always the one that I share with Others. The world of Dasein is a *with-world* [*Mitwelt*]. Being-in is *being-with* Others" (p. 155). Even our moments of solitude are affected by others, by their absence:

> Being-with is an existential characteristic of Dasein even when facti-cally no Other is present-at-hand or perceived. Even Dasein's Being-alone is Being-with in the world. The Other can *be missing only in and for* a being-with. Being-alone is a deficient mode of Being-with. (pp. 156–157)

Heidegger's point is that solitude gets its very meaning from the fact that the human world is an intersubjective world. We are alone because someone else is not there. A.A. Milne (1990) illustrates this in a wonderful way in his book about a thoughtful little bear.

> One day when Pooh the Bear had nothing else to do, he thought he would do something, so he went round to Piglet's house to see what Piglet was doing. It was still snowing as he stumped over the white forest track, and he expected to find Piglet warming his toes in front of his fire, but to his surprise he saw that the door was open, and the more he looked inside the more Piglet wasn't there.
>
> "He's out," said Pooh sadly. "That's what it is. He's not in. I shall have to go a fast Thinking Walk by myself. Bother!"
>
> But first he thought that he would knock very loudly just to make quite sure … and while he waited for Piglet not to answer, he jumped up and down to keep warm, and a hum came suddenly into his head, which seemed to him a Good Hum, such as is Hummed Hopefully to Others. (p. 1)

"The more he looked inside the more Piglet wasn't there." The absence of Piglet is directly related to Pooh wanting him to be there. And when Pooh tries to comfort himself with a little song it also is directed to the Others.

van der Berg[23] (1955) gives the complex relation between self and others another dimension by expressing it in this way:

---

23 van der Berg is commonly referred to the Dutch school of phenomeno-logy.

One's fellow man plays a part in the relationship of man and his body. He may make this relationship closer. On the other hand he may also make it more remote, he may increase the distance between my body and myself ... poor valuation of others forms a barrier between one's body and oneself. Wee see ourselves through others' eyes – role-theory recognizes this; the phenomenologist takes it quite literally. When excluded we see ourselves and our bodies as undesirable, unwanted and we cannot inhabit our bodies easily and freely as we would when we feel accepted and confirmed by the other. There grows a split between mind and body, we become embarrassed and ashamed. (p. 55)

It is obvious that the relationship with others affects the being in the world in a general way as well as one's self-awareness. Intersubjectivity is thus a primordial notion of being. But how are we to understand other humans, ourselves, and intersubjectivity? And in particular, how are we to understand and describe the experiences of other people? Those are crucial questions in human science lifeworld research.

Understanding others through indirect appresentation

In the *Cartesian meditations Husserl* (1992)[24] discusses the differences between how things in general and humans present themselves in our consciousness. Earlier, we explicated the function of appresentations in intentionality. We gave an example of seeing a portion of a house from a particular angle yet grasping the idea of an entire house as a whole despite having a vision of only one corner of it. The missing parts of the house were described as appresentations. Appresentations are part of our experience of other humans as well. For example, when we meet another person on the street, initially we see only the approaching side of that person. Nevertheless, we immediately experience what we can see as a whole person. We do not for one minute believe that there is just one surface, a photograph, so to speak, of that person coming toward us. When the appearance of the person presents itself to

---

24 The Swedish book here referred to is a translation of a German edition of *Cartesianische Meditationen* from 1977. However, Husserl held his lecture 1929, and it was published 1931 as *Méditations Cartésiennes*. 1960 it was also translated into English by D. Cairns: *Cartesian meditations*, Nijhoff, The Hague.

our consciousness, it presents as a whole (living) person, even at the moments when we can see only the view we are facing. The parts that we do not immediately and concretely experience are appresented. For Husserl, the notion of appresentation means that perceiving goes beyond what is actually present, and that it could always become present. In the case of objects, or non-humans, the appresentations are usually readily accessible. If we see the front page of a book, we can turn the book around, find the inside pages of it, look at its back cover, etcetera. We are quickly convinced that what we experience as a book really is a book. But for obvious reasons we cannot manipulate humans in a like manner in order to satisfy our curiosity about them. Of course, we could turn the other person around and see the individual from behind, but we can never make directly present the person's interior. We cannot open the person as we can a book. Consequently, we have no direct access to another's emotions, and perhaps more important, we cannot directly experience what s/he is experiencing. The mental and emotional life of others is never directly present to us.

In the course of compiling a phenomenology of empathy, Elliston (1977) analyzed Husserl's *Cartesian meditations*. With reference to Husserl's fifth meditation Elliston suggests that "[t]o perceive others is to take something given, as another self, or to ascribe to this something the sense *alter ego*" (p. 215). In order to understand the nature of this sense and how it is formed, we must "immerse ourselves in our everyday experience of others in order to describe the meaning of what presents itself" (p. 216). Continuing to follow Husserl's Cartesian meditation, Elliston then transforms the philosophical language into everyday expression:

> In the course of my everyday life I empathetically experience something which I take as another self. This empathy is now seen to mean (1) this other *actually exists*, (2) he is a *physical thing*, (3) he *controls his body*, and (4) he *has a world* to which he relates through sensory, cognitive, and affective experiences and upon which he acts. (p. 217)

Elliston details how this experience of others and empathy is possible by referring to Husserl's "sphere of ownness". Husserl claims that when the epoché has stripped the world of all reference to others, what is left is the sphere of ownness. Central in this sphere of ownness is the notion of body. Like Merleau-Ponty (1995) Husserl denies that we exist just as physical body (*Körper*) and affirms that we also exist as an animate organism (*Leib*). Elliston makes clear, that as well an animate organism with its mental acts and processes, we are of an intentional correlated nature. That is, the self as body is a physical thing among others. However, because of having sensations, we are different from other physical entities[25]. Also, we have a direct and immediate contact with the body in a way that we have with nothing else in the world. Finally, self as body differs from other things in the world because it is both subject and object, Elliston says," I not only experience things in the world (self as subject) but that I can experience myself as well (self as object)" (p. 219). Not only can we see and touch other things, we can see and touch ourselves as well.

Elliston claims that the sphere of ownness, described above, is prior to any understanding of empathy as well as to all other higher forms of social consciousness. The sphere of ownness serves as the framework from which to understand another person. Just as our past experience with books is the basis for anticipating the back cover of a book when we see only the front of it, so our own past experience of ourselves provides an analogue for understanding others and their experiences. Elliston says that, "the other is not given to me in exactly the same way I appear to myself ... the similarity is mediated by a kind of *indirect* and counterfactual 'comparison': the other looks not the way I in fact look here but the way I would look if I were there" (p. 223). Thus, there are given similarities between my actual bodily appearance and those of others. However, such similarities are only an approximation of others since our understanding of the inner life of the other never can be directly confirmed. Husserl's answer to this is that we can find an intimate connection between the presumed mental life of others and their behavior, which provides a basis for confirmation of our understanding of them. Still, our understanding of others is never totally certain. "Husserl grants this point by recognizing that the horizon is open, the future is never exhausted, and the process of

---

25 This does not mean that we deny that even animals have sensations. The aim of the statements made here is simply just to argue that humans are more than physical entities.

making evident is never complete", Elliston says. But, and this is important,

> [t]o admit the possibility of being wrong about others because our evidence is always inadequate is not to say that we are wrong or that we cannot tell what is most likely accurate or true. Each experience provides evidence which confirms and/or disconfirms, and the rational person will side with the stronger evidence. (p. 225)

Accordingly, others' mental lives, others' experiences or emotions are never directly presented to us, but only indirectly appresented, as described above. Through imagination, and by comparing others' behavior, expressions, gestures etceteras with how we think that we would be in their place, we come to understand something of them.

It is interesting to note that the current understanding of intersubjectivity, which is based on the ideas that Husserl developed at the beginning of this century, is very similar to research results seen in natural science today. For example, Newton's (1996) analysis of consciousness and understanding has much to say about intentionality that, despite being written in the language of natural science, is closely aligned with phenomenological ideas. Especially interesting is Newton's argument that intentionality plays an important role when we are trying to understand another person. She claims that one understands another if one can understand that person's actions in the same way as one understands one's own actions. When this happens, Newton says, when we understand other person's actions as we do our own, we are "automatically (preconceptually) attributing intentionality to those actions, and hence, to the other. It is in this sense that imagining performing the actions of another is taking the *intentional stance* toward the other" (p. 134). Lacking contrary evidence, one might easily assume that this was written by Husserl himself.

Lived relations with others
For further understanding of intersubjectivity and the possibility of understanding others, we turn to Merleau-Ponty. When attempting to get access to others he starts, as we did above, in Husserl's *Cartesian meditations* and gives credit to the notion of "pairing". Mer-

leau-Ponty (1991) reflects on the reciprocal nature of perceiving another like oneself:

> ... a body encountering its counterpart in another body which itself realizes its own intentions and suggests new intentions to the self [*moi*]. The perception of others is the assumption of one organism by another. ... The behavior of others conforms to my own intentions to such an extent, and designates a behavior which has so much meaning for me, that it is as though I assume it. (p. 43)

When we meet with others, we observe them. We see their behavior and recognize it as something that we also do. When we recognize that the intentions lying behind others' behavior could be ours as well, we can assume that intentions similar to ours underlie the behavior of the others.

Merleau-Ponty (1991a) turned to Scheler (1954), who was a student of Husserl, in order to enrich the understanding of how we move between consciousness of self and consciousness of others. With respect to Scheler, Merleau-Ponty says that while we cannot actually become another person, we can become the other intentionally. He gives us a compelling example:

> [I]n a fire, only the subject who is burned can feel the sensible sharpness of pain. But everything that the burn represents: the menace of fire, the danger for the well-being of the body, the *significance of the pain,* can be communicated to other people and felt by other people. ... the intuition of the feeling (that which constitutes its essentials) is the same for the two consciousnesses. (p. 47)

It is against this background that we can understand Merleau-Ponty (1991b) when he says that "the other ... is a generalized I", and that "my relation to myself is already generality"(p. 138). Others, for Merleau-Ponty, are embodied and lived others. Intersubjectivity is thus, for Merleau-Ponty, intercorporality, meaning that we reach others through our bodily existence, and that,

> ... there would be no others or other minds for me, if I did not have a body and if they had no body through which they slip into my field, multiplying it from within, and seeming to me prey to the same world, oriented to the same world as I. (1991b, p. 138)

We reach others through the body, for example through our eyes or by touch. Together with the others we form a corporeal field, which at the same time is a phenomenal field, that is, a field of meaning. We also reach others through language:

> There is one particular cultural object which is destined to play a crucial role in the perception of other people: language. In the experience of dialogue, there is constituted between the other person and myself a common ground: my thought and his are interwoven into a single fabric. (1995, p. 354)

As bodies we thus share a common world. The reciprocity of intercorporeal communication, or "carnal intersubjectivity", as Merleau-Ponty also calls it, is not

> ... by a mind to a mind, but by a being who has body and language to a being who has body and language, each drawing the other by invisible threads like those who hold the marionettes – making the other speak, think, and become what he is but never would have been by himself. (1987, p. 19)

However, this does not mean that the lifeworld is the same for everyone. Intercorporality forms a common field of action, where we transcend each other's world and thus form an infinite continuance of each other's worlds.

Hermeneutics

Hermeneutics is the philosophy of understanding gained through interpretation, and forms an important part of the basis of human science research. Hermeneutics is not a unified tradition. It is referred to in the plural form by Palmer[26] (1969) who asserts that hermeneutics is a philosophy of understanding that includes different approaches and conflicting perspectives.

The concept of hermeneutics has its roots in the Greek verb *'hermeneuein'*, which means to interpret, and the Greek noun *'hermenia'*, which means interpreting. According to Palmer, hermeneutics has three basic meanings. The first is expressing aloud

---

26 Richard E Palmer has with his book introduced hermeneutics in contemporary philosophy. His contribution is important for the understanding of a scientific hermeneutic.

something with words or proclaiming verbally. Language is, first and foremost, living sound. The second meaning of hermeneutics is explaining something and clarifying it, which involves acknowledging one's particular view of it prior to any logical explanation. Hermeneutic explanation is contextual, providing a background of already accepted meanings. Third, hermeneutics means translating, bringing unknown or foreign text into a language that we understand. The common denominator for all of these definitions of hermeneutics is "to lead to understanding" (Palmer, p. 14). Further, hermeneutics is "the process through which existence is thematized in language" (p. 134), and it is also "a basic theory as to how understanding shows itself in human existence" (p. 137).

The oldest understanding of the word *'hermeneutica'* refers to principles of biblical interpretation (exegesis) and dates from the seventeenth century. As early as 1654 there was a distinction made between the concept of exegesis and the methods and theories that govern it. Gradually the definition of the word *'hermeneutica'* was broadened to include the study of non-biblical literature (philology). With the development of rationalism and the introduction of classical philology in the eighteenth century, the historical-critical method in theology arose. As a result of the Enlightenment, techniques of grammatical analysis were greatly refined, and interpretation was, more than ever before, committed to full knowledge of the historical context of biblical accounts.

Hermeneutics as theory of interpretation

Two hundred years ago, Friedrich Schleiermacher (1768–1834) introduced hermeneutics as a systematic method for interpretation, as well as a theory of how to understand the act of understanding itself. It is still possible, if we look back upon his work, to recognize how epoch-making his writings were. The work of the early Schleiermacher reflects the tension between the religious thought of the Enlightenment, typified by Kant, and Romanticism (Schleiermacher, 1996[27]). In his early writings, Schleiermacher can

---

27   Originally published 1799.

be seen to be affected by the struggle with Kant's philosophy. Schleiermacher refused to accept the duality of the human moral agent, the conflict between emotion and reason, an important idea in Kant's philosophy. According to Schleiermacher, it is not possible to subordinate human actions to rational rules except in a very limited sense. The law of reason can never directly determine our will, he claims. He also found the notion of Kant's "thing-in-it-self" unclear, and maintained his insistence of speaking of the objective world (Crouter, 1996). Hence, in his interpretations of biblical text, Schleiermacher became more systematic than anyone previously had been. As have other philosophical-religious writers such as Kierkegaard and Buber, Schleiermacher speaks at deeply personal levels of human self-awareness.

The later Schleiermacher expanded the theory of interpretation to include any kind of text. As mentioned above, he wanted to examine the act of understanding. According to him, interpretation is analogous with the process of speaking and listening. Schleiermacher considers it just as important to have interpretive methods for the human sciences[28] as it is to have logico-deductive methods for natural sciences. The text, he says, evokes an awareness of the way our partial and fragmented experiences relate to larger, systematic wholes. However, casual, everyday understanding can mislead. That is why we need systematic and reliable methods for text interpretation that is accurate.

Schleiermacher's first rule of methods emphasizes the significance of the context. It is important to understand the author behind a text. Schleiermacher insisted that interpreters set aside their personal context and step into the culture and the time of the author. The second rule can be described as a train of thought between parts (the text) and whole (the context). This movement from whole to parts and back again in the process of understanding is one of the hallmarks of hermeneutic (and phenomenological) research and is commonly referred to as the "hermeneutic circle". Schleiermacher did not, however, introduce the "hermeneutic circle", that was done by Ast[29]. Schleiermacher's third rule requires the interpreter to understand the author psychologically. He refers

---

28 Schleiermacher is most of all concerned with text interpretation, that is, not human sciences in general.

to such an approach as *'Einfülung'*, which means attempts to reach an understanding of the author's mind. The goal is to grasp the psychology of the author[30].

Let us give some examples of the use of Schleiermacher's method: For researchers in the social sciences, who attempt to interpret old legislation or other documents, the first two steps of Schleiermacher's method for interpretation could be useful. The interpretation must then seriously consider the actual context. Literary historians also, from time to time, use Schleiermacher's systematic method. Applied to our efforts to understand a novel by August Strindberg (1849–1912) we must first learn a lot about the culture in Sweden and presumably about the ideal of womanhood in the late nineteenth century. Also important would be knowledge of Strindberg himself and his conflict of opinion with Henrik Ibsen[31]. Then, after knowing something of the context, we can try to understand the meaning of the text by moving between context (the whole) and text (the parts), in accordance with the hermeneutic circle. The final step of Schleiermacher's method would mean that we, by using *'Einfülung'* could "enter into" Strindberg's mind and try to understand what he intended when writing the novel.

Schleiermacher's method for systematic interpretation is, however, generally insufficient and inadequate for doing human science research today. If we want an in- depth understanding of the conditions of being human in existential situations such as, being a parent, being old, suffering from ill-health, and so on, we can better apply an approach of the hermeneutic tradition which was developed during twentieth century, after the phenomenological turning point. We will soon turn to that issue, but we shall first

---

29 Friedrich Ast (1778–1841) is often referred to as a forerunner to Schleiermacher.
30 Almost two hundred years later, it is rather easy to see that Romanticism influenced Schleiermacher. In his interpretive paradigm the author behind a text is implicitly understood as a genius. Readers of a novel or a poem are not, according to Schleiermacher, able to contribute with anything new in their own understanding of the text.
31 Strindberg reacted against Ibsen's, in Strindberg's mind, all too emancipated ideas about women's rights.

look at Dilthey's attempt to establish an epistemological foundation for the human sciences.

A premature idea of lived experience

Wilhelm Dilthey (1833–1911) broadened the horizon of hermeneutics during the latter half of the nineteenth century. In his philosophy of science and research methods he gradually rediscovered meaning, recognizing its importance in the human sciences[32]. The methodology of human science, along with its content, meaning, and intentionality had become of great interest. In spite of his criticism of *'Einfülung'*, Dilthey considered himself Schleiermacher's heir. He was, however, less of a romantic. Palmer (1969) describes Dilthey's writings as an uncritical mixture of the idealist and realist perspectives. Dilthey wanted to establish a non-naturalistic methodology for historical understanding in order to ground the humane studies in a historical and hermeneutical set of ideas and procedures. His recurrent themes were "experience" and "life itself".

Similar to the way phenomenology evolved, Dilthey's hermeneutics was a reaction against the reductionistic and mechanistic perspective of nineteenth century science. Dilthey was the first to search for a method that was adequate for the social sciences. The goal was to depart from the reductionistic and atomistic view of positivism that was blind to meaning, and instead turn to a holistic perspective that could recognize the world of implicit meaning and experience.

In his text, *"Introduction to the human sciences"* (1989[33]), Dilthey tries to demonstrate the need for a foundational science. He saw human sciences as that which is concerned with human beings and their practices. Therefore, he reasoned, psychology is the most important among the humanities and social sciences. Schleiermacher's emphasis upon the psychology of the author thus influenced Dilthey's early work on the hermeneutical problem. He tried to

---

32 Dilthey aimed at hermeneutics as foundation of *Geisteswissenschaften*, a term that commonly is translated as human sciences.
33 Originally published 1883.

give the human sciences priority over the natural sciences by relating them back to general categories of language.

In his later work, Dilthey, however, focused on "lived experience". Accordingly, hermeneutics, and not psychology, became the foundation of the human studies. Dilthey indicated that both the natural sciences and the human sciences have their origin in the life-nexus. The world of the human sciences preserves the reality of the life-nexus in a practical sense; the world of the natural sciences becomes a mere phenomenal construct. This use of life-nexus as a common basis for natural science as well as human science anticipates, according to Makkreel and Rodi (in Dilthey, 1989), Husserl's appeal to the lifeworld for the same purpose.[34]

Dilthey himself preferred the expression "science of man" to describe what he meant by *'Geisteswissenschaften'*. The term *'Geist'*, meaning spirit in English, had a certain advantage relative to Dilthey's task of delineating human sciences from natural sciences; it suggests a clear contrast with nature. The alleged contrast between spirit and nature allowed Dilthey to demarcate two domains in research. His attempts to delineate the natural sciences from the human sciences are based upon epistemological distinctions. According to Dilthey, thinking and questioning must be directed towards life itself. In his preliminary delineation of human sciences, he offers arguments for a relative independence of human sciences vis-à-vis the better established natural sciences. But according to Makkreel and Rodi (in Dilthey 1989) Dilthey relies on the limits of what can be known by means of natural science alone.

In Dilthey's philosophy the human sciences have a more primordial status than do the natural sciences. He distinguishes between understanding, *Verstehen,* and explanation, *Erklären,* as well as immediate knowledge, *Wissen,* and conceptual knowledge, Erkännen. Concerning explanations and conceptual knowledge, the human sciences depend upon the natural sciences. But at the pre-reflective level of understanding and immediate knowledge, Dilthey believes the human sciences have an advantage. In his

---

34 This corrects the usual assumption that Dilthey's only concern was the epistemological foundation of human sciences.

writings, he assumed that psychological descriptions of consciousness would clarify the pre-discursive structure of consciousness, anticipating the philosophy of pre-structures and prejudices, later on introduced by Heidegger and Gadamer, as well as the dialectic of explanation and understanding that was introduced by Ricoeur.

Much of Dilthey's writing was pondering the nature of the act of understanding, which he considered the basis for all studies of human life. He found it important not to separate cognitive structures from feelings and will. He insisted that returning to the perspective that life-is-a-whole is not a mysterious process. Rather, the categories of life are rooted in the reality of lived experience. For Dilthey the key word is understanding. He refers to the human sciences as the understanding of the expressions of life and supports the claim that human studies can envision the possibility of objectively valid knowledge because of the similarities in the structures of feelings and thoughts within the human mind. By using analogy it is possible to understand the expressions of life. The traces left behind by human beings, such as written documents, photos can be decoded by using one's own experiences of life. To gain understanding, the interpreter uses the similarities among human beings. Later, Ricoeur (1976) developed this part of Dilthey's philosophy in an interesting way (see page 81).

Dilthey's broadening of the horizon of hermeneutics is more historical than scientific. Life itself in all its historicality and temporality is in focus, and the purest expression of life is art, Dilthey claimed. "Great literature is rooted in the lived experience of the riddles of life: the why and how of birth and death, joy and sorrow, love and hate, the power and the frailty of man, his ambiguous place in nature" (Palmer, 1969, p. 122). These are the existential questions of life and the subject matter of human science research.

Today we can note, from our vantage point, that Dilthey did not fully succeed in liberating himself from the scientism, of which he wanted to transcend (Palmer, 1969; Lübcke, 1995). After the philosophy of Heidegger and Gadamer, it is clear that Dilthey's efforts to find valid knowledge were a reflection of positivistic ideals, which contradicts historicity and the self-understanding that are so important when we try to understand existential questions. Both Dilthey and Schleiermacher saw understanding as re-experiencing,

Nacherleben. Palmer (1969) elucidates the problem with Beethoven's music and how it is understood.

> For our act of understanding of Beethoven's Ninth Symphony is of course very different in character from the act on Beethoven's part of creating it. The work speaks in its totality of impact; the processes of creating it involve knowledge we need not have in order to "understand" what is "said" in the work. (Palmer, 1969 p. 123)

Hence Dilthey's philosophy is somewhat truncated. According to Lübcke (1995) Dilthey never managed to fully realize his plan. Nevertheless he seems to be the philosopher of the nineteenth century who in the fullest extent influenced the philosophers of the twentieth century. In spite of his premature philosophy, Dilthey's influence on such philosophical giants as Husserl, Heidegger, Gadamer and Ricoeur serves as a concrete example of the historicity of human understanding.

The phenomenological turning point in hermeneutics

Martin Heidegger (1889–1976)[35] was Husserl's student and Husserl himself anticipated him to be the heir of the phenomenology. However, Heidegger moved beyond the epistemological and scientific tendencies in Husserl's transcendental phenomenology. In the project of understanding life in terms of life itself, Heidegger deepened the historical aspect of understanding and exceeded the limitations in both Schleiermacher's and Dilthey's philosophies. He insisted that without an understanding of ontology[36] any explanatory scheme for knowledge is blind. At the time when Heidegger introduced his philosophy, the human science did not readily accept ontology as its starting point. Accordingly, in *"Being and Time"* (1998[37]) Heidegger left the epistemological questions that

---

35 Dates are repeated here for continuity.
36 Ontology, according to The Oxford companion to philosophy, is the science of being in general, embracing such issues as the nature of existence and the structure of reality.
37 Originally published as *Zein und Zeit*, 1927.

were so frequently discussed by Dilthey and Husserl, and turned to the ontological questions of existence[38].

Heidegger asserted that human existence is a more fundamental notion than human consciousness and human knowledge. His philosophy makes it clear that the essence of human understanding is hermeneutic, that is, our understanding of the everyday world is derived from our interpretation of it. All new things encountered in the lifeworld are related to earlier experiences. We do not use a pen without first recognizing it as something to write with, or a knife without understanding that it can cut.

Consequently, the underlying mechanisms of interpretation become of great interest and it is here where we move beyond Schleiermacher's and Dilthey's notions of interpretation. Heidegger's focus upon the pre-structures of understanding goes beyond the older model of interpretation in terms of subject and object. In fact, Heidegger asserts that the concept of pre-structures raises grave questions about the validity of describing interpretation in terms of the subject-object relationship. Likewise, it raises questions about so-called objective interpretation, or interpretation without presuppositions (Palmer, 1969). With the introduction of pre-structures and pre-understanding, Heidegger firmly established hermeneutics upon phenomenological philosophy, and, in particular, the notion of lifeworld. In the history of hermeneutics, this phenomenological "turning point" (Warncke, 1995) was the second revolution, and quite as subversive as Schleiermacher's ideas were when he left exegesis in order to find a system of interpretation that would be valid for all kinds of texts.

As a result of the phenomenological turning point implemented by Heidegger, and later, Gadamer, hermeneutics was converted to an existential philosophy. Existential hermeneutics (Ödman, 1992) is neither a system for interpretation nor a methodology for human sciences. It is an attempt to understand the internal world of human beings just as interpretation and understanding are fun-

---

38 With *Being and Time* it seems that Heidegger broke sharply with Husserl. However, we argue that Heidegger is developing the philosophy of Husserl, "focusing in particular on the ontological dimension of intentionality, not *reversing or abandoning* his account" (Moran, 2000).

damental categories of existence. Existential hermeneutics could rightly be called lifeworld hermeneutic.

Hence, Husserl's lifeworld theory is exceedingly vigorous in Heidegger's philosophy. Instead of using the term lifeworld, Heidegger speaks of being-in-the-world, which means an indissoluble reciprocity between human existence and the world. In his Swedish introduction to Martin Heidegger's thinking, Benktsson (1985) says, referring to the nature of human existence and context, that the world is not the sum of all things but is instead to be understood as an integrated moment in the structure of existence (p. 61). Being is thus central to Heidegger, who seldom talks about mankind in general, referring instead to the everyday environment, being-with-each-other, and our way of being towards one another. The world is "in"[39] one's own existence and existence is "in" the world, in the sense that the world is human and humans are worldly. His term for this relationship is *'Dasein'*. The focus in his philosophy is twofold: Dasein (the being-there of existence) and existence in time. As did Husserl, Heidegger wanted us to understand time holistically. The human being is always on the way: "His dasein is his future" (Benktsson, 1985, p. 19), and it is "human existence itself that makes the different tenses meaningful and of a whole" (p. 21). The human world is always present; as humans, we always live in an existential context.

In our brief discussion of Heidegger here, we have seen that he considers being more basic than human consciousness and human knowledge. Being is the ontological manifestation of the lifeworld and, according to Heidegger, interpretation is the way in which we understand its ambiguity. But interpretation's origin is not human consciousness and human categories. Rather, interpretation arises from the manifestation of the things of the world that meet our gaze and that we experience through wonder and curiosity. Palmer (1969) recalls Heidegger's understanding of phenomenology when he reminds us that it is not we who point out the phenomenon, rather it shows itself to us. Hermeneutics is the phenomenological tool with which we understand being; the hermeneutic process, the process of interpretation, reveals to us that what is hidden.

---

39 "In" is not to be understood as having a spatial meaning here.

Hermeneutics is an ontological process. It is through this process of interpretation that the world shows itself. When we consider the ontology of the lifeworld, the invisible being-in-the-world structures become visible[40]. Understanding is, thus, our participation in the thing that is understood, and as lifeworld researchers, we have an understanding stance with regard to the things that we investigate.

Heidegger's ontological conclusions are still considered challenging and provocative by many researchers. We can easily imagine the disbelief, even outrage within the human sciences (particularly a discipline such as behavioral psychology), as well as in the natural sciences, when Heidegger asserted that there is no certain and objective knowledge. Heidegger's philosophy has, however, inspired many subsequent philosophers. We recognize Heidegger's existential philosophy in Jean-Paul Sartre's *L'être et le néant. Essai d'ontologie phénomenologic*. Hans-George Gadamer is another of Heidegger's heirs who further developed his thinking about historicity in human understanding.

The idea of an open hermeneutic

Hans-Georg Gadamer (b. 1900) is a prominent figure within modern hermeneutics. In *Truth and method* (1995[41]) he investigates the nature of understanding, and in doing so, he challenges the notion of tradition. He does this by linking his inquiry into the history of concepts with the substantive exposition of the theme of tradition. In the introduction of this work he says:

> That conscientiousness of phenomenological description which Husserl has made a duty for us all; the breadth of the historical horizon in which Dilthey has placed all philosophizing; and, not least, the penetration of both these influences by the impulse received from Heidegger, indicate the standard by which the writer desires to be measured, and which, despite all imperfection in the execution, he would like to see applied without reservation. (Gadamer, 1995, xxv)

40 It is important to point out that being in itself is not seen as a phenomenon by Heidegger. Being, like the lifeworld, can never be an object for us, since we are always part of it.
41 Originally published as *Wahrheit und Methode*, 1960.

It is no wonder that this important piece of philosophy often is referred to as Gadamer's *magnum opus*.

The critique of positivism as the prevailing philosophy and methodology of science, is well known. This criticism, which was growing increasingly strong by the end of the 1950's, was primarily inspired by Gadamer, who decried positivism's, and later, all science's adherence to a single method. Positivistic science sought to define the world factually with knowledge that could be verified. The resulting definition of science was formed to suit the method. Verification of its theories and the ability to predict outcomes was its primary goals. Gadamer is adamant that the study of the world, especially not the human world, cannot be reduced to any single method, and certainly not a set of measurements. He maintains that the world is understood through our experience of it in which measured facts are but a part of the whole picture.

Gadamer was not, however, critical only of positivism. He stands firmly with Heidegger as he explicates why Schleiermacher's and Dilthey's search for a scientific method for interpretation proved fruitless. Accordingly, the lifeworld cannot be reached through method, but rather met in an *open* way of approach, which is the natural way in which we belong to the world, the way of true understanding. A researcher looking for guidance in Gadamer's philosophy can observe that Gadamer always returns to *openness*. We must have an open mind if we want to discover anything new, or, as Gadamer puts it, see the "otherness" of something.

The history of effect – Wirkungsgeschichte[42]

The consequence of an open lifeworld approach in hermeneutics is radical in Gadamer's philosophy. Gadamer seems to be conservative, rather, that is what his critics claim. An example of Gadamer's alleged conservatism that is often referred to is his acknowledgment of authority. Gadamer acknowledges that there are good as well as bad authorities, but asserts that the authority of a person is ultimately based upon the recognition that the other person is

---

42 The history of effect, *Wirkungsgeschichte,* is a concept used by Gadamer in order to describe how tradition effects the personal understanding as well as how it effects the society in which people take part.

superior to oneself in judgement and insight, in which case the judgement is given precedence. For this reason this person's judgement takes precedence. Authority in this sense has thus nothing to do with blind obedience to commands. This type of authority can be recognized in, for example, teachers and experts. It is important to note that Gadamer's intention here is not to be normative. He analyzes and describes the immense difficulties inherent in our attempts to "emancipate" ourselves from tradition.

We are less emancipated from values and other pre-suppositions in our society than we would like to admit. Rather, tradition is a very powerful, but nameless, form of authority, according to Gadamer (1995). Now, he is well aware that it is provocative to refer to the authority of tradition. He says:

> The concept of tradition, however, has become no less ambiguous than that of authority, and for the same reason –namely that what determines the romantic understanding of tradition is its abstract opposition to the principle of enlightenment. Romanticism conceives of tradition as an antithesis to the freedom of reason and regards it as something historically given, like nature. (p. 281)

For Gadamer there is, however, no antithesis between tradition and reason.

> The fact is that in tradition there is always an element of freedom and of history itself. Even the most genuine and pure tradition does not persist because of the inertia of what once existed. It needs to be affirmed, embraced, cultivated. It is, essentially, preservation, and it is active in all historical change. ... Even where life changes violently, as in ages of revolution, far more of the old is preserved in the supposed transformation of everything than anyone knows, and it combines with the new to create a new value. (p. 281)

Accordingly, as human science researchers we must understand ourselves as historical beings, always connected with the past. We are always a part of history and can never find a position outside it. Consequently, tradition and historicity is a part of our lifeworld.

The effects of tradition and historicity on lifeworld form our personal historical effect, *'Wirkungsgeschichte'* in Gadamer's mother tongue. Tradition is a foundation in a cultural as well as a personal sense. Society, including family life, upbringing and education, shapes our internal world of understanding as well as of feelings and thoughts. Tradition does not stand over us, but is the institution through which our understanding of the world occurs. All encounters with being, our everyday comings and goings in the lifeworld as well as our more narrowly focused activities as researchers, are thus history-laden. But our history is not evident as such, rather, it appears in the guise of the present, for all past experience is filtered through the present moment. Because meaning is derived from the past as well as tied to the present situation and often enough even to the future, interpretation must take into account the historical context, both past and present. Gadamer characterizes understanding as a movement between the interpreter's past and present in which understanding and creation of meaning emerge incrementally as the back and forth process takes place between parts and the whole.

Accordingly, for Gadamer, understanding means placing oneself within the perspective of a tradition so that the tradition is revealed and the past and the present can intertwine. This, he asserts, is what leads to new insight and new understanding. The illumination of meaning is dependent upon the questions we ask in the present moment from our own position within history. Again, now in the spirit of Gadamer, we must see that it is not possible to find absolutely right or true interpretations. For some time one can be satisfied to have understood the phenomenon under investigation and sufficiently conveyed that understanding with language, but understanding is not eternal. Lifeworld phenomena resist all efforts to explicate them once and for all. What appears true in a certain context at a certain time, may actually be false in another context or at another time.

The understanding of all notions in Gadamer's philosophy, such as authority, tradition and "history of effect", fall back on what he calls "prejudices". Prejudices are the result of the history of effect. Tradition and prejudices appear in the understanding of all new things that we encounter, and stand, consequently, in the way of complete openness. Prejudices nail us to the past as well as to the future, as understanding includes both memories and anticipations. Prejudices are thus as temporal as intentionality itself. Because of our prejudices we are inclined to anticipate the meaning of a thing or a text long before we fully understand it. If a text contains ambiguous messages, we simply interpret it according to our previous understanding of similar texts[43].

Gadamer uses the concept horizon (*Horizont*) in order to describe understanding, the possibilities of understanding, and its limits. The experiences of the world together with the history of effect form a horizon of understanding. If the aim is to understand something in a new way, that is, one wants to look beyond the understanding that is there already, one has to challenge the existing horizons. It is when prejudices are overcome that the horizons of meaning can be expanded.

> The horizon is the range of vision that includes everything that can be seen from a particular vantage point. Applying this to the thinking mind, we speak of narrowness of horizon, of the possible expansion of horizon, of the opening up new horizons and so forth. ... A person who has no horizon does not see far enough and hence overvalues what is nearest to him. On the other hand, "to have a horizon" means not being limited to what is nearby but being able to se beyond it. (Gadamer, 1995, p. 302)

In summary, in Gadamer's philosophy we can recognize that human experience is a happening within, and a meeting with, the world. Human beings and their existence are best understood when they are expressed in gerund form, depicting the essential nature as a dialectic and creative involvement with the world. Human experience is the discovery of how something is, but also the discovery that something is not what it is assumed to be. When we see something in another light, we are changed by this new experience. Sometimes it is uncomfortable to grow and gain new understanding, but as Gadamer points out, that cannot be avoided by anyone who truly seeks knowledge. Meaning is never fixed nor static, but always influenced and derivative, contextual and historical, on a trajectory toward expanding comprehension and understanding. Understanding is not something one *does*, but is the mode in which humans exist. There is no fixed beginning point for understanding; understanding is always already there, within the

---

43 We temporary leave the important notion of prejudices but will return to it in the next chapter. We will discuss the significance of pre-understanding on the basis of a rather implicit but nevertheless radical difference between the natural attitude and the research attitude.

situation. The research conclusion is, that even when a researcher has put an end to the investigation, it is possible for the reader of the scientific report to step in and continue the interpretation.

Gadamer's philosophy, first of all, deals with the conditions of human understanding. Thanks to him we can raise existential, and not just psychological, questions about the internal life of human beings. He does not, however, give us a method for how the scientific process of understanding is best accomplished. As researchers we must find the empirical methods ourselves. We can be sure that Gadamer, least of all, would encourage us to look for *the* method, suitable for all kinds of questions. Nor would he say that human science can understand itself simply by attempting to be free from prejudices.

> Hence in regard to the dominant epistemological methodologism we must ask: has the rise of historical consciousness really divorced our scholarship from this natural relation to the past? Does understanding in human science understand itself correctly when it relegates the whole of its own historicality to the position of prejudices from which we must free ourselves? Or does 'unprejudiced scholarship' share more than it realizes with that naive openness and reflection in which traditions live and the past is present. (1995, p. 282)

We will return to the question of openness in next chapter, but first we will complete the foundational explication of hermeneutics with some notions on the philosophy of Ricoeur and on language.

The dialectic of explanation and understanding

Paul Ricoeur (b. 1912) defines hermeneutics as the theory of rules that govern interpretations of a particular text. In his book *Interpretation theory*, Ricoeur (1976) offers an account of the human language in view of the diversity of function. Ricoeur tries to understand language at the level of such productions as poems, narratives and essays. Hermeneutics has to do with symbolic texts with multiple meanings, or as Ricoeur says, with "surplus of meaning". He believes that even if the text constitutes a semantic unity, hermeneutics has to interpret the complex and equivocal meaning behind the text.

Ricoeur uses Freud's *Interpretation of dreams* (Freud, 1968)[44] as an analogy for the hermeneutic approach (Ricoeur, 1970)[45]. The dream is regarded as a text filled with symbolic images and the interpreter (here, the psychoanalyst) uses an interpretative system in order to bring the hidden meaning to the surface. Hence, hermeneutics, according to Ricoeur, is the process of deciphering which moves from manifest content to the hidden or latent meaning of the equivocal symbols in a text or a statement. Hermeneutics is thus a "system by which the deeper significance is revealed beneath the manifest content" (Palmer, 1969 p. 44). And this is, Palmer continues, a demonstration of distrust in surface or manifest reality. In fact, it is an achievement of Freud's ambition to shatter our myths and illusions. The symbol is regarded as an illusion, which masks a false reality. Consequently the act of interpretation ought to be an act of demystification[46]. There can, however, be no universal canons for interpretation as there are opposing theories concerning the rules of interpretation. Ricoeur's own attempt was to encompass both the rationality of doubt and the faith in the recollective interpretation in a reflective philosophy as a hermeneutical challenge in myths and symbols. In doing so he thematizes the reality behind language, symbol and myth.

In order to make sense of written discourse, Ricoeur (1976) wanted to move beyond the Romanticist hermeneutics of Schleiermacher and the idea of a dichotomy between understanding and explanation set forth by Dilthey. Ricoeur believed that the conflict between these concepts could be overcome if they could be shown being dialectically related to each other. Traditionally, explanation

---

44 Originally published 1900 as *Die Traumdeutung*.
45 We do not believe that Freud's classic psychoanalytic theory is a good example of hermeneutics, especially because it lacks an explicit lifeworld approach. Binswanger's (1963) existential analysis is a better example of psychoanalytic thinking in the framework of a lifeworld perspective. We also believe that Ricoeur might see the same problem here, but simply wants to use Freud as an example where the hidden meaning is disclosed.
46 Marx, Nietzsche and Freud are all, according to Ricoeur, great demystifiers. They all interpreted surface reality as false and put forward a system of thought, which demolished reality. They saw true thinking as an exercise in suspicion and doubt. All three were against religion, and they were all asking for a new system to interpret the manifest content of our words (Palmer, 1969).

finds its paradigmatic field of application in the natural sciences. When there are external facts to observe, it is possible to use a hypothetical-deductive procedure in order to explain general laws for covering the facts found in research. Understanding, on the other hand, finds its field of application in the human sciences.

> It relies on the meaningfulness of such forms of expression as physiognomic, gestural, vocal or written signs, and upon documents and monuments, which share with writing the general characteristic of inscription. The immediate types of expression are meaningful because they refer directly to the experience of the other mind which they convey. (Ricoeur, 1976, pp. 72–73)

It is through a dialectic of understanding or comprehension (*verstehen*, in Dilthey's hermeneutical tradition) and explanation (*erklären*, in the same tradition) that Ricoeur develops his interpretation theory. In this theory, understanding and explanation tend to overlap and to pass over each other. The range of propositions and meanings is explicated or unfolded in the phases of explanation. Understanding emerges out of the chain of partial meanings moving toward a whole in an act of synthesis and it relies on the meaningfulness of expressions such as gestural, vocal and written signs. "The immediate types of expression are meaningful because they refer to the experience of the other mind which they convey", as Ricoeur (1976, p. 73) states. The less direct sources are no less significant, but they convey the other mind's experiences indirectly. "This continuity between direct and indirect signs explains why "empathy" as the transference of ourselves into another's psychic life is the principle common to every kind of understanding, whether direct or indirect" (p. 73). Ricoeur suggests a distribution of the concepts of understanding, explanation, and interpretation as mutual forms of understanding relying on the same sphere of meaning. In oral conversation, for example, the transfer into a foreign psychic life finds support in the sameness of the shared sphere of meaning. The dialectic process has already begun. "To understand the utterer's meaning and to understand the utterance meaning constitute a circular process" (p. 74).

Ricoeur describes the dialectics of interpretation, first, as a move from understanding to explanation, and then, as a move from explanation to comprehension. The first understanding is a naive grasping of the meaning and the second a sophisticated mode of understanding supported by explanatory procedures. Ricoeur further asserts, that in the beginning understanding is a guess, that we simply have to guess the meaning of a text if the author's intention is beyond our reach. We can understand an author better than he understood himself. An intentional form of explanation appears as the mediation between the different forms of understanding. Causal explanation, isolated from the experiential and dialectic process, is a mere artifact of methodology, but intentional explanation is not, according to Ricoeur.

Language

Language has an important hermeneutic function and in the hermeneutics described above the importance of language is emphasized. Language is the tool in all dialogue and all questioning and it makes possible the interaction through which the lifeworld is shared. In fact, it is this shared understanding that constitutes the world and language opens our lifeworlds to each others. Consequently, language is as primary as understanding.

The issue of language was essential in Schleiermacher's attempts to find a methodology valid for all kind of interpretations. Without words, thoughts will remain unfinished and indistinct (Schleiermacher, 1996). According to Dilthey (1991), the connections between perceptual contents, spatial arrangements and temporal succession form one of the most important epistemological issues, which are expressed in language. He states, "It is the 'this' to which we can point and which is expressed linguistically only by means of representation and a word that is capable of expressing several things" (Dilthey, 1991, p. 414).

With Heidegger came an ontological understanding of language. He states, "The intelligibility of Being-in-the-the-world ... *expresses itself as discourse.* The totality-of-significations of intelligibility is *put into words*" (Heidegger, 1998, p. 204). Gadamer (1995) is also clear on this point and says that "*the whole process* [of understanding] *is verbal* ... Language is the medium in which substantive understanding takes place between two people" (p. 384). The emphasis on discourse is important to Gadamer, who asserts that we cannot always find an understanding of a phenomenon in the individual words, not even if we use the entire stock of words in a language. Instead, "the truth of things resides in discourse" (p. 411). Although language is a tool for human sciences, it is not language per se that is important. Rather, what we make use of is the message that language conveys. Language, its statements, expressions, concepts, and words can never be meaningfully separated from its existential roots. Words have in themselves a hermeneutic function; they help bring the phenomenon that we are investigating into the light to disclose itself.

Heidegger (1998) devotes much attention to language and speech in his philosophy. He distinguishes authentic discourse and idle talk. "Idle talk is the possibility of understanding everything without previously making the thing one's own" (p. 213). The groundlessness of idle talk is a danger in a scientific understanding of language, it "perverts" the act of disclosing (Heidegger, 1998). Idle talk seems to paralyze the open and seeking attitude and it thereby prevents an authentic meeting with meaning, Benktsson (1985) clarifies. Benktsson expresses the notion of authentic discourse, that "it creates an understanding relationship to that which is spoken about" (p. 53). Implied in the notion of authentic speech is true understanding, which comes from an openness to that which is spoken. Idle talk, which may be recognized in the jargon that accrues around any established ideas, is a hindrance to real understanding and is thus something to be avoided in all research.

Gadamer (1995) emphasizes the fact that every meaningful conversation presupposes a common language. It is meaningful conversation and the dialectic of question and answer that can create a common language. Here, in the structure of hermeneutical experience, which is tied to language, we may gain a deeper insight into what Gadamer means when talking about "the historically effected consciousness". "[T]he fusion of the horizons of understanding is actually the achievement of language" (p. 378). According to Gadamer, language is in fact so near our thinking that it seems to conceal its own being from us. Understanding of the subject matter must then take the form of language. Gadamer continues:

> It is not that the understanding is subsequently put into words;
> rather, the way to understand occurs-whether in the case of a text or
> a dialogue with another person who raises an issue with us-is the
> coming-into-language of the thing itself. (p. 378)

For Gadamer, as well as for Heidegger, language, being, and history
are not only related but overlap one another. We have earlier
examined the temporal aspects of understanding, and here we can
see how the tension between now and then effects the role of language. Time helps us understand – or misunderstand. Time makes
the unimportant disappear and allow hidden meanings to appear
with greater clarity.

When language is used it has a reference, says Ricoeur (1976). A
text or speech actually gives meaning. The "utterance meaning" is
the objective side, and the "utterer's meaning" is the subjective
side. In a lexical definition of language signs only refer to other
signs within the system. But, according to Ricoeur, language is
directed beyond itself. Language has a reference only when it is
used, and performatives are exhibited by every class of speech act.
Besides verbalizing something, the "utterer" is doing something by
saying and yields effects by saying it. All aspects of language are of
importance in the act of interpretation. When we turn to the world
and the things themselves in order to communicate the lived experiences of research informants and understand their meanings, we
have to be aware of language, both its advantages and limitations.

Phenomenology and hermeneutics – no separate magnitudes

We have so far in this chapter elucidated phenomenology and
hermeneutics for the purpose of explicating a human science
research methodology. For the sake of clarity, phenomenology and
hermeneutics have been presented as two different philosophical
traditions, despite our stress of commonalities instead of the differences. In this chapter we have also tried to stay as close to the original philosophical ideas as possible. We believe that it is important to have the philosophical foundation clarified before begin-

ning a research process. However, our purpose is not to do philosophy, but to engage in empirical research analysis. In the next chapter we will proceed in illuminating certain philosophical standpoints by explicating the empirical aspects. It is from an empirical formulated epistemology that conclusions about methodological principles can be outlined.

But before we turn to this issue there is one more thing to do. It is not our intention that phenomenology and hermeneutics, these important parts of western philosophy, are to be understood as separate or unrelated traditions. Therefore, we will end this chapter by highlighting some of the ideas that have been presented earlier in the chapter and show them as unifying themes that run through both philosophies.

The lifeworld perspective

It is often argued that the existential aspects of the lifeworld did not come until hermeneutics entered the philosophical arena. The lifeworld perspective is important in hermeneutic philosophy as well as in phenomenology. Despite Husserl's introduction of the term and the theory of the lifeworld, we cannot say that his philosophy was a lifeworld phenomenology. His philosophy, rather, is a transcendental phenomenology. Nevertheless, he wrote extensively about the lifeworld and lifeworld theory is of great importance in his philosophy, especially the final parts of it. There is a lifeworld phenomenology, however, defined by Merleau-Ponty. We have selected and earlier presented some of what we consider to be his most illuminating passages about it.

Merleau-Ponty, Heidegger, Husserl (in his lifeworld theory) and Gadamer (in his essay on the enigma of health), all express similar views of humanness. Their common view is that individuals and their living conditions can never be completely understood if they are not looked upon as living wholes. The significance of such a view is that what we refer to as objective signs: laboratory results, x-rays, and externally identifiable symptoms, examination scores and grades, all make important contributions to health care, and to learning, but are of limited value when the purpose is to illuminate the human being and the lifeworld. The picture of those for whom we care or educate (or, of those who care and educate) is always incomplete without taking into account their own understanding of themselves, their lived bodies, and the meaning that their life situations hold for them.

The issue of pure description

In its narrowest sense, the difference between phenomenological and hermeneutic philosophy lies in phenomenology's emphasis on transcendence and pure description, and hermeneutics' emphasis on pre-understanding and interpretation. Both Husserl, as a representative for phenomenology, and Heidegger, as a representative for hermeneutics, acknowledge the existential and ontological reality of phenomenology as a face-to-face meeting with being. Heidegger proceeded, however, along his own lines to develop phenomenology as a philosophy of human existence. He introduced a concept that Husserl's philosophy had not broached, namely, interpretation. Whereas Husserl exhorts us to go to the things themselves in order to understand, Heidegger, as well as his followers, saw that once we are there, understanding depends on recognizing what we bring with us, namely, our pre-understanding and interpretations. Whereas Heidegger maintained that phenomenological understanding requires recognizing one's own pre-understanding and interpretive function, Husserl put a parenthesis around those epistemological aspects, and emphasized instead a transcendental or "pure" consciousness as the key and necessary factor for phenomenological analysis.

Descriptive phenomenologists, often regarded as Husserlian, aim for pure description in which past knowledge about a phenomenon is bracketed, allowing the phenomenon to been seen "precisely as it presents itself" (Giorgi, 1992, p. 121[47]). Helenius (1990) says of the phenomenological reduction, that when the phenomenologist has "freed himself from theoretical and empirical fastenings" he can go "to the thing" (p. 49). In descriptive phenomeno-

---

47 Giorgi's approach to phenomenological research will be more thoroughly presented in chapter 5. Here we allow us to just briefly mention some of his accounts for the purpose of furthering the discussion.

logy, reduction means that one sets aside theories of reality as explanations of the phenomenon. The aim is to be as open as possible for the phenomenon in question.

Interpretively oriented researchers, frequently referred to as Heideggerian phenomenologists, see bracketing as a misnomer for the reflexive processes occurring in interpretive research, and reject the idea that one can step outside of one's unique viewpoint in order to see a phenomenon apart from the encumbrances of one's experience of it. Hermeneutical researchers often insist that objectivity, or neutrality, is unachievable, even undesireable, because of the impossibility of freeing oneself of involvement as a member of the lifeworld.

These conflicting viewpoints are frequently debated, often dividing researchers into two opposing camps. But this battle gets no support from philosophy. Husserl, in his theory of intentionality (see p. 51 above, Husserl, 1970a), accounts for a phenomenon's hidden aspects that consciousness supplies in order to complete the picture according to our understanding of the whole of what we experience. Phenomenological philosophy acknowledges that act of completion and, moreover, insists that we examine it in order to understand our position in regard to the phenomena that we research. Such epistemological insistence parallels hermeneutics' demand that researchers delve into and unfold the historicity of phenomena. In neither phenomenology nor hermeneutics is there pure description per se. Both phenomenology and hermeneutics acknowledge the fact, that we always experience the world *as something,* the world is always presenting itself to us in the form of *meaning.* In this respect, Husserl's notion of appresentations completing the picture is comparable to the pre-structures and the implicit knowledge that Heidegger (1998) and Merleau-Ponty (1995) speak of, or the pre-understanding and prejudices of which Gadamer (1995) speaks. Heidegger insists that pre-understanding is a condition for new knowledge. Gadamer notes that pre-understanding is an unavoidable, even necessary, pre-condition for understanding and acquiring knowledge, but, as Husserl maintains about appresentations, Gadamer states that we have to be aware of pre-understanding and suspend it, that is, question it, to prevent its negative influence on understanding.

Accordingly, pre-understanding and appresentation are both intentional structures[48], and form our pre-theoretical, non-critical, taken-for-granted knowledge about something which we acquire as residents of the lifeworld. Normally, this is not a problem as long as the natural attitude is the satisfactory approach for encountering the world. However, when the purpose is to propose or question knowledge, upon which, for example, health care and education decisions are made, the natural attitude must be exchanged in favor of a more critical attitude. In this attitude, openness is of crucial importance. As human science researchers we want to adopt an attitude that the world, in all its complexity, can show itself to us. Both phenomenology and hermeneutics emphasize such openness as the first step of critique. Both philosophies give such detailed epistemological principles that, following either phenomenology or hermeneutics, it is clear that our research results must not depart from the original research data. Conclusions derived from analysis should be clearly seen as originating in the data rather than in any external structures such as theory, or the researcher's prejudices and pre-understanding. Furthermore, both phenomenology and hermeneutics give an epistemological basis for emphasizing the importance of researcher self-awareness for the purpose of maintaining a scientific openness.

As we see it, hermeneutics as a framework for human science research would be a less than adequate research approach had it not been for the phenomenological turning-point. It is the phenomenological understanding of the lifeworld and the crucial notion of intentionality that makes modern hermeneutics a valuable foundation for human science research. Similarly, thanks to the hermeneutic turning-point in the phenomenological movement the complexity of the lifeworld is amenable to our investigative efforts.

---

48 The idea of appresentation or apperception in Husserl and the idea of pre-understanding in Gadamer are, from a philosophical perspective, not identical. For the purpose of empirical research this difference is, however, less important than the similarity.

3 An open lifeworld approach

The epistemological focus of this book centers on phenomenologi-cal and hermeneutic philosophy. Despite the differences between these two philosophical approaches, important for our purpose here is their common epistemological understanding. We have chosen to explicate this epistemology as a lifeworld approach to human science research, which needs a method to describe the phenomena of the world, the everyday world of humans, that is the world as it is experienced, by humans. The phenomena that human science researchers explore and describe are studied in their most original meaning, as events of the lifeworld.

Within the realm of the lifeworld, phenomenology looks not simply at objects and events as such, but at the way that they are experienced, as phenomena. The philosophers that we basically draw on, Husserl, Heidegger, Merleau-Ponty and Gadamer, are uni-fied on this point, life manifests itself in experience. Phenomeno-logy seeks the patterns of experience, the principles, in order to grasp the meaning of the phenomena in question, which is then described as faithfully as possible. The discovery of patterns of experience sets us on a path different from that of traditional posi-tivistic science's processes which conveys the notion that we are separate from or unconnected to the things that we observe, explore, and manipulate. Phenomenology makes clear that we as researching embodied consciousnesses are participating in the rela-tionship between ourselves and the world that we experience. Our residency in the lifeworld places us in the position of creative con-tributors to the meaning of the world. At the same time, as researchers, we have to be aware of our contribution to the under-standing and describing of the meaning of the world. Lifeworld research that is based on phenomenological philosophy, with its theory of intentionality and notions on transcendentality, makes our relationship with the world of particular importance, and gives us information about how we are connected to the phenomena that we study.

Previously, intentionality was described as a central theme of the lifeworld approach. "The thing" as Husserl called it, the focused upon object, is always understood as something, carrying an implicit and/or explicit meaning. The goal in all lifeworld research is to discover, analyze, clarify, understand and describe that meaning. Most often the goal is to find and illuminate the essential, the most invariant, meaning of the phenomenon being explored. In order for meanings to be seen and understood clearly, a certain scientific attitude is needed. Rather than formal steps or protocols, the necessary approach for lifeworld research is characterized by a striving for openness, a concern for elucidation, and a purposeful leaving aside of expectations and assumptions so that the phenomenon and its meaning can show itself and, perhaps, surprise us.

We begin with a general description of openness and its challenges, which includes notions of openness as immediacy, that is, openness as a close and direct relationship with the phenomenon. Openness is further explicated by relating it to the notions of inter-subjectivity, meaning and uniqueness. Openness will also be explained in relation to two important concepts, pre-understanding and self-awareness.

Openness

Phenomenology as a research approach is made up of two basic components. The first component is the phenomenological turn to "the thing" being studied, the phenomenon, and the second, the demand for sensitivity to "the things" (Bengtsson, 1991). This means the researcher must engage in an openness to the phenomenon that is necessary in all lifeworld research[1]. Going to the things themselves involves turning to the experienced reality with the aim of understanding that which is of interest as a phenom-

---

1 Openness is crucial for research in general, as Capra (1991) has noted regarding modern physics. However, we are concerned here with lifeworld research rather than research in general.

© Studentlitteratur

enon. Instead of taking scientific theory, common sense, theories or any perspectives at all as given, as lifeworld researchers we try to do justice to the object of examination, that is, we try to be clear about what it means to be open and sensitive in approaching the phenomenon.

A metaphor may help here. Just as craftsmen, who from necessity must choose their tools depending upon what object is to be formed, so must researchers chose their tools with care. Making the best choice demands a basic understanding of the phenomenon's specific character. The methodological tool must be well selected and formed so that the desired knowledge is accurately and effectively obtained.

Openness thus means that as researchers we make ourselves available to the world, to the phenomenon of interest, as it presents itself (Husserl, 1970b; Heidegger, 1998; Merleau-Ponty, 1995; Gadamer, 1995). Such an attitude of availability is not easily accomplished because of our natural tendency to see events or objects as something that already has meaning. Openness is required in order to see the events or objects of the world in a new way. Cultivating the ability to sustain an open stance is crucial for research. It requires thoughtful vigilance over one's approach to the phenomena of the world.

An open stance

More than simply an aspect of the method, openness is the expression of a way of being. It is an attitude; an open and discovering way of being that stands in direct contrast to a dogmatic approach. The significance of this way of being is that if the person who seeks knowledge maintains an open position then the phenomenon will show us how it can and should be studied and how it is. Openness is the mark of a true willingness to listen, see, and understand. It involves respect, and certain humility toward the phenomenon, as well as sensitivity and flexibility. To be open means to conduct one's research on behalf of the phenomenon. Consequently, as Palmer (1969) emphasizes, openness is a criterion of objectivity[2].

2   See foot note 5, chapter 2.

In his analysis of the development of modern hermeneutics, Palmer makes explicit the central position of the lifeworld theory in this movement. Within the general theory of lifeworld, phenomenologists and hermeneutisists stand outside the subject-object distinction and offer "the objectivity of allowing the thing that appears to be as it really is for us" (Palmer, 1969, p. 179).

For researchers, openness means having the capacity to be surprised and sensitive to the unpredicted and unexpected. Heidegger (1998) describes an open position as "curiosity" (p. 214) and talks of a "desire" to see, to understand (p. 215). Through the researcher's open stance, the events and objects of the lifeworld may disclose themselves as different than they were earlier assumed to be. The ability to be open stems from a natural attitude to the world and is shown by this quote from Heidegger (1998):

> Dasein's openness to the world is constituted existentially by the attunement of a state-of-mind. And only because the 'senses' [die "Sinne"] belong ontologically to an entity whose kind of Being is being-in-the-world with a state-of-mind, can they be 'touched' by anything or 'have a sense for' ["Sinn haben fur"] something in such a way that what touches them shows itself in an affect. (pp. 176–177)

It is a well-known problem that as researchers we do not always see what is there, and sometimes we are lured into seeing something that does not exist. Therefore, we must always maintain a reasonable doubt about our experience. As Heidegger says, there is always the possibility that some being shows itself as something that it actually is not. When we have adopted an open stance we are more likely to develop the ability to discriminate, that is, to see and think clearly and critically in regard to our prejudices which increases the likelihood that we will be sensitive and responsive to the phenomena that we study.

The principle of openness is thus central to phenomenology as well as to the hermeneutical tradition. Both of these traditions are concerned with approaching phenomena as they present themselves to us instead of imposing on them pre-conceived ideas or hypotheses. But it is one thing to uphold "openness" as an ideal or as a guiding principle that can be clarified conceptually and epistemologically, and quite another to practice openness as a researcher. It is not just that "being open" is difficult when one is undertaking a particular study but that the very meaning of this idea is ambiguous. It entails both assuming a stance of vulnerable engagement with a phenomenon while maintaining a disinterested attentiveness. Despite its inherent ambiguity, we can find clear evidence of openness in everyday life. For example, an individual can engage another in a receptive and accepting manner making it possible for that person to take a more objective look at a troubling situation.

Openness as an open and immediate mind[3]

The notion of openness has been discussed recently in some detail by two Dutch theoreticians and researchers, Ilja Maso (1995) and Adri Smaling (1995). Maso argues that excellent qualitative research requires trifurcate openness: openness to the research situation, the research question, and to oneself. These three dimensions can best be construed as interdependent. The first involves becoming aware of how the phenomenon at hand reveals and conceals itself to the researcher as a function of his or her approach and personal character. This recognition allows the researcher to make whatever adjustments are feasible and desirable so that the phenomenon may be revealed to the greatest extent possible. Openness to the research question means that one attempts to carry out the research in such a way that the basic question can be answered fully using the most appropriate methodology and by reviewing the relevant literature. It also includes keeping in mind the way in which the question directs and limits the inquiry. Finally, openness to oneself requires that one take into account one's own contribution to the research, in terms of one's personality and style, for instance, and the way in which one is affected by the research project. This kind of openness to one's own experience means that along the way one is likely to experience disorien-

3   A part of this section was presented at the International Human Science research Conference, Long Island, US 2000: Dahlberg, K. & Halling, S. *Human science research as the embodiment of openness: swimming upstream in a technological culture.* This paper will also appear in Journal of Phenomenological Psychology, 2001.

tation and confusion as one is caught up in initial impressions and vague hunches and is trying to make sense of what is still unfamiliar.

Similarly, in his discussion of openness, Smaling (1995) addresses the question of what role openness could or ought to take in the social sciences. (He leaves to others to describe the role it actually plays.) Smaling too thinks in terms of three kinds of openness: open-mindedness, open-heartedness and dialogical openness. The first, open-mindedness refers to the receptivity of the researcher to the subjects and the subject matter. An immediate openness exists when a researcher is able to engage with a participant, establishing trust and confirmation and a level of nearness that allows the possibility of disclosure. Here, Smaling has in mind Heidegger's notion of hearkening as a "goal-free" listening. When hearkening, the researcher is listening in a way where there occurs a giving-over of her/himself to the intersubjective relationship. Heidegger (1998) makes clear that this form of listening is something that involves more than just one's ears:

> Being-with develops in listening to one another [Aufeinanderhören], which can be done in several possible ways: following, going along with, and the privative modes of not-hearing, resisting defying, and turning away.

> It is on the basis of this potentiality for hearing, which is existentially primary, that anything like *hearkening* [*Horchen*] becomes possible. Hearkening is phenomenally still more primordial than what is defined 'in the first instance' as "hearing" in psychology – the sensing of tones and the perception of sounds. Hearkening too has the kind of Being of the hearing which understands. (pp. 206–207)

In the moment of listening, the researcher belongs to the world, to the phenomenon, and to the research data and, instead of mastering the situation, allows herself/himself to be mastered by it. This is what engagement with the phenomenon means.

This close research relationship, is also described by Popper (1988), who says that we can find ourselves in "an intensive mental condition and, at the same time, completely forget ourselves but always with the ability to reflect about ourselves at a moment's notice" (p. 231). This is a condition that, according to Popper, marks both intellectual and artistic work. He says that, "[i]n such a condition we can forget where we are – always an indication that we have forgotten ourselves" (p. 231).

Open-heartedness (Smaling, 1995) refers to self-disclosure by the researcher of some of his or her thoughts or personal experiences, and thus, open-heartedness suggests that the researcher is self-revealing or self-disclosing. It is important to have a clear under-standing of what this entails because it can so easily occur inappro-priately. The relationship between researcher and informant is one of imbalance. In every research situation the power rests with the researcher, who decides when, where, and how the investigation takes place, which questions are asked, and which answers are legitimate. This imbalance can be mitigated by researchers' willing-ness to be open and to share some of their own personal experi-ences. The effect of such openness is that the researcher may be perceived as genuine and trustworthy, thus leading the way for the informant to relax and talk. In addition, a researcher's capacity for open-heartedness – an ability to engage with others – models self-disclosure for informants. But a caveat is offered here regarding two potential results of open-heartedness, one ethical and the other methodological. The ethical issue may arise when an inexpe-rienced researcher shares too much of her/his own personal experi-ences. Informants may then accommodate in a like manner and reveal so much of their private world that they ultimately feel exposed, or exploited as a result of the interview. Similarly, when participants are immersed in the experience which is being recalled and explored they may reveal their innermost existential life prob-lems, even to the extent of, for example, sharing suicidal thoughts which they may have had[4] (Dahlberg & Wenestam, 1990). It may be frightening to novice researchers when an interview leads to the revelation of disturbing thoughts such as suicide. But Perls (1969) reassures the researcher that s/he can always trust in a person's capacity to decide when to let go of psychological defenses and experience her/his innermost thoughts. That such a decision is made during an interview is an indication of the trust that a informant has in the interviewer as well as his or her own self-

---

4   When this happens it is important that support is provided following the interview so that the interviewee can integrate the expanded understand-ing that has resulted from the interview.

trust. Nevertheless this concerns aspects of research that must be thought trough from an ethical perspective.

Another methodological issue of open-heartedness is that injudicious disclosure from the researcher may ultimately influence a informant to corroborate the researcher's ideas and expressions instead of relating her/his own experience. When this occurs, it is not necessarily the informant's lifeworld that is revealed in the interview, but the researcher's. Finally, a researcher's objectivity can be compromised by unanticipated emotional intensity which unrestrained self-disclosure can precipitate. The goal for lifeworld researchers is to engage with participants in a way that suggests how to self-disclose without breaching limits beyond which objectivity and integrity are compromised.

Thirdly, for Smaling (1995) dialogical openness refers to conversations with other researchers and, within the constraints required by research, with informants. Ideally, Smaling argues, openness should be characterized by a dialectical and balanced relationship that enables the research to proceed at a higher level of objectivity. For instance, dialogical openness in the form of discussions with other scholars may help the researcher place in a new perspective the often compelling emotions and impressions resulting from a stance of open-mindedness.

As a way of further framing this exploration of openness, and of considering the researcher's experience from a more explicitly psychological perspective, we draw upon Schachtel's (1959) classic discussion of the development of focal attention and the emergence of reality. While Schachtel's presentation of the development of perception and thinking in children is out-dated with respect to some of its specifics, his characterization of the qualities of focal attention is astute and helpful. By focal attention, Schachtel means our capacity for fully centering our attention on an object so that we can perceive or understand it from many sides (p. 251). As a result we can genuinely discover something about its various facets by viewing it narrowly in relation to urgent concerns or preoccupations, be they biological or psychological in nature. Focal attention, Schachtel emphasizes, excludes the rest of the field whereby making it an act of concentration.

Concentration or attentiveness is the researcher's capacity to be bodily and mindfully present, here and now, in the research situation. The researcher is thus "immersed" in the phenomenon that he or she is exploring. We might think of an interviewer who is fully attuned to an informant and screens out background noises. Thus it is evident that the other side of attending to and being genuinely interest in something, as Maso and Smaling also acknowledge, is a closing off or exclusion of other topics or phenomena. Similar to excluding surrounding phenomena, but of a temporary nature, is the act of setting aside preconceived questions or theories that would obscure one's vision of the phenomenon. The aim of concentrated focus is to stay with the situation as it presents itself.

Even if Schachtel's theory of attention is in many ways a parallel both to Husserl's theory of intentionality and to Gestalt psychology (which Schachtel also mentions), it does present some ideas that are distinctive. Schachtel emphasizes that focal attention presupposes a certain freedom from internal or external demands that create significant anxiety for the researcher. Successful focal attention is more likely to occur if the perceiver feels relaxed, safe, and free from pressure. Schachtel says:

> Just as the completely need- or fear-governed action (and the instinctual action) never really encounters the object, so the thought which is under the pressure of either too much fear or anxiety, or under the pressure of too urgent or narrow a goal, does not do justice to its object. Only thought which is sufficiently free from the pressure of urgent needs or fears can contemplate its object fully and recognize it in relative independence from the thinker's needs and fears – that is, as something objective. Thus focal attention is incompatible with severe anxiety. The starving person does not think about what he eats, but grabs at anything.

> But even outside the sphere of urgent biological needs, it can be shown that too strong need pressure interfere with productive thought. In thinking about a problem one is usually successful only if one does not press too hard for a solution; that is, one is more likely to be successful if the thought is truly object-centered, free to contemplate the object from all sides, than if the thought is goal-centered, under the pressure of *having* to produce a solution immediately. (p. 273)

Every researcher recognizes the problem that Schachtel describes! But nevertheless, though we see his wisdom, we so often press ourselves to find the right solution at once. Instead, from a perspective of openness, taking Schachtel's advice frees us to pause and think, "to wonder and to explore" and thereby "devote" ourselves to the object of study (p. 274). Schachtel emphasizes the importance of a thoughtful approach, pointing out that when we are dealing with human beings, our "[f]ocal attention is slower and longer in developing than focal attention to other objects of the environment" (p. 275). Schachtel is reminding us of the complexity of intersubjectivity. Deeper understanding between persons, no matter the nature of the relationship, happens when the persons involved take the time to learn from each other. For example, playfulness and creativity, which are so essential for the emergence of a deeper understanding, require a relaxed attitude. Open-mindedness is neither an enduring state nor a trait. In practice, researchers are never free from procedural concerns that can interfere with availability to participants and the phenomenon. All of us have to reckon with the reality that sometimes we are close-minded and may need assistance in dealing with the psychological and situational within a given research project.

As we have seen, Schachtel asserts that focal attention is not to be construed as a single or uniform act of attending to an object, or a topic. Rather, it is a series of varied approaches. He postulates that focal attention may be construed both as a passive, reactive phase as well as a more active phase in the exploration of the object. Likewise openness has phases and makes different demands on the researchers at various points in the process. That is, since self-reflection is integral to openness[5], researchers find that at times it becomes necessary to step back and take stock of their own mental processes in order to not get lost in a particular manifestation or understanding of the phenomenon in question.

Examples of openness in the conduct of research

In what follows we will examine issues relating to openness more concretely by discussing specific studies.

Coenen's (1986) study of the movement, perception and expres-

5   We will discuss this issue later in this chapter.

sion of deaf children's interactions provides a thorough and candid account of one researcher's effort to remain open as he becomes increasingly involved with the subjects whose lives he wants to understand. It also shows how tricky this process can be.

In many respects Coenen (1986) exemplifies the dimensions of openness that have been discussed so far. He specifies his theoretical assumptions and presents in detail the way in which he comports himself as a participant observer of the way that deaf children interact with each other at their school. Coenen describes his initial experience of being an outsider in the situation because he was a foreigner in the United States and did not know sign language. He also describes how at first he had little sense of the implicit structures and patterns of interaction in the school and how the children gradually accepted him and subtly drew him into their world. His conduct as a researcher exemplifies what one might call "pliability" in the sense that he carefully and patiently accommodated himself to the situation that he was studying. Eventually, he sees the deaf children's distinct features of a highly evolved and sophisticated form of communication and interaction, and he describes this using terms like "fluid" and "incorporation".

The study offers a glimpse of what happens when a researcher's attitude of openness is compromised. Coenen describes a visit by the deaf children to a school for hearing children. The teachers at the hearing school are seen by Coenen as insensitive to the deaf children and he is, very understandably, troubled and angry. Now, the problem is not that he reacted with feelings or anger, or that he became deeply involved with and fond of the deaf children, but rather, the problem is his one dimensional portrayal of the hearing children's teachers. Further, Coenen characterizes the patterns of hearing communication as rigid, rule-bound, and coercive, without also acknowledging that verbal dialogue is in its own right a sophisticated and creative form of communication. In short, he is depicting communication in the world of the deaf as normative and faulted verbal communication for its failure to be like deaf communication. Coenen states that before beginning his study, he had assumed that the deaf children were handicapped. By the end of the study, however, he has gone beyond simply correcting a misperception and questions if verbal dialogue might not be the deficient form of communication.

Our intention is not to minimize the value of Coenen's study but to indicate the elusive character of openness and to emphasize openness can have various meanings at various stages of a research project. Shifting from one stance of openness to another can be exceedingly difficult. Coenen's experience beautifully exemplifies his receptiveness and openness to discovery that made it possible for him to enter into, in a manner of speaking, the world of the deaf children, and to collect rich data. But it was this availability to new experience that eventually obscured his vision and left him unable to step back and consider the situation more dispassionately. Our criticism is that in his study there is insufficient reflection on his own participation and experience that would have allowed another perspective to emerge. It is an accepted maxim in field research that "going nature" is one of the pitfalls of participant observation.

In the context of psychotherapy, Lawner (1981) introduces an interesting principle when he makes a seemingly contradictory statement, "I needed enough distance to get close to it" (p. 307). This enigmatic statement points to the fact that it is the combination of presence and pliability that is ultimately productive. What Lawner is getting at, in general terms, is that our relationship with the phenomenon we are studying prevents our seeing it from a more clarifying perspective. For example, the phenomenon may have become so familiar to us and so intimately related to us that it has become impossible to see it any other way. The problem in Coenen's study is that he had become so appreciative of the world of deaf communication that it became the lens through which he construed the world of hearing communication.

Whenever we invest time and energy to learn about a topic that we are exploring, we develop a certain possessiveness about it, it becomes familiar, our own pet project so to speak. Because we are close to it and invested in it, we may loose our curiosity about it. The temptation is to end the search for other possible points of view. As researchers we need to be close to the phenomenon that we are investigating in order to be open to it. But the inherent danger of proximity to the thing that we are studying is that we run the risk of loosing openness as well as objectivity. At the same time we strive to engage our informants and establish a direct and close relationship, a reflective distance must also be maintained. Thus,

106

we constantly move back and forth between nearness and distance in order to avoid immersion in, for example, the interview situation to the extent that objectivity about the interaction as well as the content of the interview is lost. This is the dance of lifeworld research. Its holistic nature is characterized by opposites such as immediacy and distance, and human science researchers know that productive research requires attention to both.

It has been suggested that "closing off" is the implicit background of openness, that focusing on one thing excludes other things. Closing off one's attention presupposes a certain freedom from anxieties and concerns as Schachtel (1959) suggests. If we look more specifically at the phase of research commonly referred to as data collection (which misleadingly indicates a dispassionate gathering of facts or an everyday task) it becomes apparent that remaining open to that which is of fundamental interest is no simple matter. Whether participant observer, as was Coenen, or engaged in interviewing, in order to get in-depth interviews, one has to be receptive and sensitive. Effective and meaningful interviewing is necessarily personally demanding, especially when it comes to difficult subject matters, or informants who are naturally reticent. This is evident, for example, in Davidson's and his colleagues' (1995) study of the experience of patients who were discharged into a community from a mental hospital. Although the patients preferred living in the community where they have greater autonomy and more privacy, their lives were described by the researchers as filled with quiet desperation and hopelessness about their future. Understanding their predicament had a great impact on the researchers, who stated that they were "troubled by the tragic nature of these people's lives" as they bore "witness to their suffering" (Davidson et al., 1995, p. 131). Our point is that experiencing others' pain is the lot of the researcher who enters into the lives of others in order to understand them. What must be bracketed, then, is much more than presuppositions and values, difficult as that is. In truth, remaining open is always more than an intellectual task. It demands an alert awareness of one's entire intellectual and emotional response to the situation and to those who have let us into their lives. We do not get in-depth data by just staying distant.

Let us look at another example, this one from research in health care. Consider what it means to interview a patient with an illness, for instance, cancer. Listening in the manner needed to grasp an account of life and illness is to open oneself to the suffering of the other, and in doing so, gaining a heightened sense of one's own mortality and vulnerability. This is embodied listening. It brings home the fact of death as more than cognitive knowledge. This example reminds us rather forcefully of Gadamer's (1994) assertion that knowledge in the human sciences always has something of self-knowledge about it. In the face of such anxiety provoking situations, the researcher potentially closes off, fails to listen, and fails to be receptive, at least at times. The question is not how do we remain open (as if we could attain such a state continuously) but how can we maintain some degree of openness even as we find ourselves turning away. The back and forth movement is forcefully presented in Robinson's (1998) phenomenological study of women who cut themselves. While interviewing these women and in reflecting on the stories she collected, she found that she was continually disturbed, shocked and distracted from the material at hand. Recovering some degree of equanimity and balance was no easy matter for this researcher who dealt with a subject matter that would evoke profound uneasiness in any of us.

The experiential and psychological dimensions of moving back and forth, between being open or closed, between nearness and distance, is generally not acknowledged in the literature, but it is something that researchers acknowledge unofficially. The remedy, if that is the right word, must include opportunities to share among colleagues and others the struggle to remain open.

Finally, we need to mention another significant and related challenge to openness that arises for researchers, namely, how to remain open when in the midst of dealing with the unknown, when one simply does not understand what is happening in an interview or what to make of the data that have been collected. During an interview one may be unsure how to understand and respond to what is being said, or how to take the interview to a deeper level. The same uncertainty or confusion often arises as one seeks to find meaning in the descriptions, field notes, or transcripts that one has collected. Lawner (1981), whose article we referred to previously, has written on the experience of the unknown in psychotherapy. Many of his points are relevant to research. He writes, "As therapists [and, we would add, as researchers], we often move in darkness in which nothing can be seen." (Lawner, 1981, p. 306). Lawner goes on to emphasize the importance of tolerating this experience of darkness and trying not to force sense or meaning to emerge. To force meaning is to foreclose the emergence of a deeper level of understanding. This experience of "being in the dark" is one that is especially hard for relatively inexperienced researchers to tolerate; the fear is that one will never get out of a situation of not knowing. This is a most unpleasant prospect if one is working against a deadline for a publication, or the completion of a dissertation. The critical question, then, is what can support the researcher who is in the dark? First, one can remember that one is not totally in the dark with respect to what one is studying – rather, it is only an aspect of the whole that is unclear or unintelligible. Just as therapists might say to themselves, "I don't know what is going on with this person right now, but I have some sense of who the person is generally," so the researcher might say, "I have no idea as to how this aspect fits but I have some sense of the phenomenon overall." Secondly, we can speak of faith in the process of discovery. Admittedly, it is difficult to sustain faith if one has little experience. Those colleagues or research supervisors who are more experienced can advise one to stay focused on what is apparently incomplete until one starts to see glimpses of light and the whole picture starts to emerge. As Lawner (1981) reminds us, it is helpful to keep in mind that in seeking understanding there are bound to be alternating periods of darkness and light, that this is the very nature of the process. Beware of the researcher who thinks that he or she is always in the light! Third, while one is in the dark, one can improvise. When an inexperienced pianist hits the wrong key, he or she stops playing and starts all over again, thereby losing the harmonic whole. An experienced musician uses the mistakes and adds a series of tones to create a new harmony that the listener understands as a skillful variation of the tune. Finally, the lifeworld researcher's adage might well be: confusion is good because it means that we are still open to the phenomenon.

Openness as an antithesis to "method"

We have been discussing openness along the lines of Gadamer's (1995) description of scientific openness. Gadamer speaks of openness as a wish to see, a wish to understand something in a new way. Along with Husserl, Gadamer points to an openness and a sensitivity towards the things as a methodological principle. However, Gadamer also explicitly warns us against following a method, which presents a methodological problem. If one has a principle that requires openness and sensitivity towards the things under investigation, is this not a methodological principle? The problem here is how to practice openness in a way that does not become a routine procedure, a method which evolves into a set of automatic steps to which we become bound. How can a researcher be both scientific and systematic, while at the same time avoid following a particular method?

What Gadamer (1995) warns against is conceiving of method as "following a marked route", which he points out as the original Greek meaning of the word. If a researcher follows "a marked route", that is, adheres to a previously determined method step by step, then openness is at stake and the possibility of truly understanding the phenomenon is seriously undermined. In Gadamer's mind method does not lead the researcher to the truth. Instead, he says, if there is anything such as a truth it must be found through a dialectical process. Gadamer's rejection of method stems from his understanding of the priority of the lifeworld and our belonging to it. Gadamer's principle of method is summarized by van Manen (1990), who considers Gadamer to be saying "that there is a way to deal with methodological concerns that is decidedly unmethodological in a purely and technocratic sense" (p. 3). Palmer (1969) also describes the open alternative for understanding a text:

> Methodologically this means that one does not seek to become a master of what is in the text but to become the "servant" of the text; one doesn't so much try to observe and see what is the text as to follow, participate in, and "hear" what is said by the text. Gadamer plays on the relationship between listening and belonging and serving which the word "belongingness" ("Zugehörigheit") suggests. (p. 208)

To be a methodological servant means avoiding research restrictions and a rigid, lockstep use of method. Openness instead means having the patience to wait for the phenomenon to reveal its own complexity rather than imposing an external structure on it, such as the dogmatic use of theories or models. Openness in lifeworld research means entering the world of a person and leaving behind any structures that would shape one's expectations for what will be found.

Rather than being defined by any sort of formal steps or protocol, what is essential for researching human experience is an unrelenting striving for openness and an ongoing concern for moving beyond initial assumptions and preconceptions so that the phenomenon and its meaning can show itself in a way that we did not expect it to. As we have stated, engagement with a phenomenon is demanding work. At the very least, researchers must grasp epistemological concerns and have developed personal skills. Further, openness requires that researchers endure periods of chaos where there seems no clear way to proceed. In short, we must resist any approach to research that demands absolute certainty and order. Openness in research stands in opposition to the established notion of research as an unvarying procedure. Another maxim of lifeworld research might easily be: messiness is allowed.

There is a paradoxical character to openness since, on the one hand, discipline is demanded, but on the other, to be open is not a matter of "will." Or, as Farber (1964) writes, "one is not always willing to do what one wills." Thus, with respect to openness, we see how human science research is *not* primarily a technological enterprise. This difference is especially important since there is a widespread fascination with and faith in techniques that are understood as rapid, replicable, and ostensibly objective and reliable ways to produce knowledge. In contrast, Marguiles (1982) discusses creativity in the practice of phenomenology, psychoanalysis and art, and asserts that "[t]he investigatory methods, by their very nature, should resist routinization. They are self-renewing for observational novelty" (p. 1025). And, what is true of the methods is equally true of the researcher who embodies these methods.

Intersubjective openness

In the paragraphs above on openness as an open and immediate mind much is being said also about the researching intersubjectivity. In order to be explicit about the emphasis on openness we also want to make some further notions on the intersubjective encounters that in some way or another happen in lifeworld research. Intersubjectivity is the matrix of caring practice and of pedagogy. In the encounter between caregiver and patient, teacher and student, the primary concern is growth in the other person. Intersubjectivity is important in research as well, but there is difference. The encounter between researcher and informant has as its primary goal the development of knowledge. However, accompanying the goal of knowledge is a general ethical concern for a fellow human being, which may be the goal of the research.

In every research endeavor there is an experiencing subject, the individual who has agreed to participate and thus becomes an informant in the study. Just as the notion of intersubjectivity is important for the relationship between caregiver/teacher and patient/student, the same is true for the collaborative relationship between researcher and informant in human science research. In such research, attention is given not only to the information that the individual conveys about the phenomenon being examined, but also to the way in which s/he experiences being a part of the project. Human science researchers strive to make the research relationship an equitable one, cognizant of having entered a private domain, the informant's experience.

If the research approach is to be understood as open the researcher must be aware of the intersubjective influence on the research situation, either it is an interview or an observation. First of all, both the researcher and the informant should be able to grasp the phenomenon. Secondly, contrary to the common everyday situation, this intersubjective sharing is not equal. The researcher shall hold her/his own experience of the phenomenon back as much as possible in favor of the experience of the informant. Even if this is an obvious scientific claim it might be that the research situation is influenced by an everyday manner. One example: the natural attitude of framing a "good" encounter and sharing opinions in the way people do in an everyday way, may affect the researcher who "understands too well", so to speak, that is, the researcher understands more than is really being explicitly stated in the research situation. In such a situation the natural attitude has taken priority over the scientific attitude, and the pre-understanding has been given a too free role. In a scientific approach the claim of openness demands from the researcher an awareness of what happens in an intersubjective encounter, so that the unequal relationship is formed in favor of the informant. Openness is thereby directed towards the phenomenon and the informant

Meaning

"Because we are in the world, we are *condemned to meaning*", says Merleau-Ponty (1995, xix). Being in the world thus means that we cannot avoid meaning. This fact is the starting point for phenomenological research. When we are open as lifeworld researchers, we are open to meaning. An open, lifeworld approach to research puts one in touch with deeper levels of meaning, not as an attribute that we bring to our research, but rather as a means of discovery of meaning

When we are trying to understand phenomena through research we aim at finding meaning. Meaning is directly related to the understanding of phenomena. Heidegger (1998) says:

> When entities within-the-world are discovered along with the Being of Dasein – that is, when they have come to be understood – we say that they have *meaning* [*Sinn*]. ... Meaning is that wherein the intelligibility [Verständlishkeit] of something maintains itself. (pp. 192–193)

The aim of lifeworld research is to make the phenomenon appear in a clear and comprehensible way. When the phenomenon becomes clear it is because of the continuous search for meaning.

Husserl was concerned that the basis of scientific research be founded in the world as it is experienced, before theories are devised to explain, or measurement is conducted. In all of his works, Husserl continually reminded the scientific community to begin with the "things" of experience. The things of which he spoke, the phenomena which science studies, are always, first of all, experienced as something, that is, bearing implicit meaning that can be explicated and clarified. Gadamer (1995) expresses this Husserlian idea:

> The intention and fulfillment of meaning belongs essentially to the unity of meaning, and like the meaning of the words that we use, every existing thing that has validity for me possesses correlatively and by virtue of its nature an 'ideal universality of actual and potential experiencing modes of givenness'. (p. 244)

Meaning has thus to do with givenness, how things are given to us for consciousness, or, in other words, how the things present themselves for us. The goal of research within a lifeworld paradigm is clarification of meaning as it is given. In Husserl's (1977) words, it is about the still mute experience, which we are concerned with leading to the pure expression of its own meaning. Accordingly, we should be aware that the meaning that we discover belongs to the phenomenon, and we should avoid supplying the understanding with a meaning that does not belong there. Here is where the phenomenological concept bracketing becomes interesting. As researchers we have to restrain our pre-understanding, in the form of personal beliefs, theories, and other assumptions that otherwise would mislead understanding of meaning[6]. The importance of seeing through the context when aiming at describing the meaning of a phenomenon is outlined by Natanson (1973), who says that with the reduction,

> the materiality, causal nexus, values and meaning-for-others of the 'object' are bracketed. What remains is the object as meant, regarded purely in terms of its givenness to the precise extent that it is given and solely in the manner in which it is given. (p. 85)

Also Giorgi (1985, p. 45) emphasizes the importance of being "present to what is given precisely as it is given". It is not the researcher who gives a phenomenon its meaning. Instead the meaning is disclosed in the researching act that takes place between the rese-

---

6   The meaning of pre-understanding and bracketing will be further explicated later on in this chapter. The problem of restraining one's pre-understanding in research will also be dealt with in chapter 4 and 5.

© Studentlitteratur

archer and the phenomenon. Natanson (1973) says that meaning is found in an act "through which common sense locates its objects and events as pointing beyond their bare surface features to some intentional schema in which they find their grounding" (p. 108). The search for meaning is thus a question of diving below the surface and finding the deeper underlying and intentional meanings.

From a lifeworld perspective, however, meaning is never finally complete. Meaning is always contextual and recognized as expandable and expanding (Merleau-Ponty, 1973, 1995) and the possibility for understanding is infinite (Gadamer, 1995). Therefore one cannot say that a meaning is described once and for all. Meaning emerges in the relation to the lifeworld, and when the lifeworld changes, meaning changes as well.

In order to understand meaning we must focus upon the role of language. Being is "wordly", Heidegger (1998, p. 204) says. When we describe our research informants' lived experience and understand their meanings, we have to be aware of language, both its advantages and disadvantages, contributions and limitations. Language is the vehicle that communicates meaning and allows us to understand the lived experience, but it always falls short of the lived experience itself. Furthermore, language is not just verbal. Language is also non-verbal, which at first may seem contradictory. One's bodily gestures convey meaning that we understand in a language way, that is, the meaning of the gesture is labeled as such and such. Similarly, we understand the meaning of a picture through language: we have a silent conversation with ourselves as we gaze upon it. That which is non-verbally communicated is then more or less "translated" into verbal language in the research process. With respect to openness this means that whenever we communicate in the encounter with the informant, in one way or another, we have to deal with language.

Merleau-Ponty (1991a) concludes a philosophical discussion of language by saying, "... language makes thought, as much as it is made by thought" (p. 102). The meaning of words and the thought expressed by them are always in a dynamic relationship. In the midst of this we are always directed toward meaning. Meaning is never complete, but is always open to an analysis that aims at expansion of meaning. It is not the form, the symbols themselves that are of importance but their meaning, that is, the thought that is expressed in various forms, including words. Or, more precisely, "... we would find that it is the intention to unveil the thing itself and to go beyond what is said to what what is said signifies" (Merleau-Ponty, 1991b, p. 102). Language cannot be separated from thought, and it is not merely the expression of thought that is already formed. Rather, thought is discovered through its expression in language (Merleau-Ponty, 1991a,b).

Uniqueness

When we are open we can see the unique. Seeing the unique requires an ease with complexity. In his Merleau-Ponty study, Bengtsson (1987b, 1993a) says that the world in which we live is by no means characterized as an objective and definitive system, but should be understood as an open whole. In order to understand this world we have to pay attention to concrete, lived reality, especially its internal dialectic and many-sidedness, its dimensions and layers. Merleau-Ponty speaks, thus, of a scientific sensitivity to the complexities of the lifeworld.

In opposition to an approach where all differences are controlled and reduced to a common denominator which can be measured and quantified and thus generalized, an open lifeworld perspective signals instead an interest in prioritizing the unique individual or what is unique in a situation. In research, uniqueness refers to an understanding that the individuality of participants takes priority over their position as representatives of a larger group. Lifeworld researchers are not interested in controlling, as potential bias, the unique perspective of individual participants. However, that lifeworld researchers regard participants as unique does not mean that generalization is to be avoided. Generalization in lifeworld research takes the form of essences. The essence of a phenomenon is discovered through description of implicit experience, that is, the direct experiencing of the lifeworld before any attempts at causal explanation. The essence of a phenomenon are those invariant structures without which the object or event would cease to exist as itself (Merleau-Ponty, 1968). Descriptions of such experience should be instantly recognizable, expanding and enriching the store of knowledge about the lifeworld.

Uniqueness and sameness is a paradox of lifeworld research. Participants are at once both unique and irreducible, and similar to others with whom they share consensus about the lifeworld. Uniqueness is irretrievably coupled with sameness; humans are at once both much more alike than different (Sullivan, 1953) and, singularly, themselves. We share sameness insofar as we all exist as humans but we are unique through our choices about how to live that existence (Sartre, 1998). A characteristic of lifeworld research is that its researchers are comfortable with paradoxes such as simultaneous sameness and uniqueness, and the continuous negotiation between the stances of immediate immersion in experience and the distance of objectivity. Acceptance of, and ease with, the ambiguity of multidimensional, noncausal, nonlinear thinking is a distinguishing feature of such research and of the researcher as an intentional being. The capacity, even proclivity, for thinking in paradox, and integrating opposites, characterizes lifeworld research and demonstrates its holism, making it possible to see and explore both visible and invisible phenomena (Merleau-Ponty, 1968), bringing them to life through elegant description.

Pre-understanding

Openness can never be absolute. Absolute objectivity, however desirable as it may be, is an unreachable goal. There exists no scientific *tabula rasa*, no researcher is a "blank document", and there exists no "uncontaminated" place from which to start a research project. Researchers, as all other living persons, have lifeworlds that are the inescapable contexts for their research. This is the point which many phenomenologists, who consider themselves followers of Husserl, are critical. Like Gadamer, they object to Husserl's theory of transcendence, the attempt to stand outside the lifeworld. Gadamer (1995) states that the "world horizon is a presupposition of all science as well and is, therefore, more fundamental" (p. 247). He further claims that Husserl's phenomenology must regard itself as included in the lifeworld. We want to make clear an important distinction here. We have no argument with Gadamer's assertion that phenomenology itself belongs to the lifeworld. But we do think it is important that Husserl's aim is broadly understood, not only from a philosophical standpoint, but also from an empirical. He sought a way to free intentional consciousness from any doubts about what it sees. His insistence on what we might call a 'removed view' which is detached from intruding prejudices and assumptions was to give the phenomenologist the confidence to trust in the reality of what is seen when everything else has been bracketed aside for the time being. In *Truth and Method* Gadamer (1995) has the same kind of goal of being open to the phenomenal world, but *within* the lifeworld approach. Here we cannot escape pre-understanding, but must learn to keep it in check, to bridle it, reflect over it, and understand the implications of it. Otherwise it is impossible to confront "the otherness" of a phenomenon in the process of research[7].

Openness is always constrained by pre-understanding. In all research, quantitative as well as qualitative, we have to deal with our pre-suppositions in order to remain open throughout the whole process of inquiry. Pre-understanding, as presuppositions or prejudices, stand in the way of complete openness. In all types of research it is important to be aware of how pre-understanding affects the process of research: how the problem to be studied was chosen, how it is defined, how the research questions are formulated, the choice of method, and so on. Further, in descriptive phenomenological research, it is important that pre-understanding is recognized and restrained during the search for meaning and essences. Likewise, in interpretive (hermeneutic) studies, researchers must recognize and reflect on their pre-understanding and its influence upon the interpretations being made. If we are not aware of our pre-understanding, and neglect its associated problems, we risk obtaining results that are primarily a reflection of our past experience or unrecognized beliefs. Then, we merely confirm what we already know, and no new understanding occurs.

---

7   This discussion is not meant to oversee the fact that reaching a description of the transcendental ego was Husserl's ultimate goal. What we want to do, however, is to show an understanding of this struggle that is of great value for empirical research.

For the purpose of explicating openness and its limits we need to understand the intentional structure of pre-understanding and its effects upon research. There are several questions to be contented with. One question is, can a person, researcher or not, be fully aware of his or her pre-understanding? A tentative answer to this question is, probably not. There are good reasons to believe that some parts of the pre-understanding are unconscious or subconscious and therefore difficult to reach. This does not, however, diminish the need for reflections concerning the structure of pre-understanding and its influence on research. Another question is, what is the nature of this pre-understanding? Other questions are, how is it possible to gain increased openness by being more aware of one's presuppositions? How is it possible to better understand one's pre-understanding and its effect upon understanding? These questions are being addressed in the next sections of this chapter.

In chapter 2 we described that part of the philosophy of hermeneutics that belongs to the foundation of this book, thereby also briefly describing pre-understanding as a main path in Gadamer's philosophy. Here we will further explicate the nature of pre-understanding and its history.

The idea of pre-understanding

During the early 19th century, Schleiermacher saw that misunderstanding is a natural form of understanding. About fifty years later Dilthey introduced the term "pre-understanding" when he posed the question, is it possible to really understand the author behind a text? Dilthey suggested that when we are reading a text we understand it in relation to our pre-understanding, and that, rather than consider understanding as scientific, it should be thought of as historical. The world can only be understood through reference to life itself in all its historicality and temporality (Palmer, 1969).

When Heidegger wanted to analyze the being that understands its own being, he found that interpretation is the foundation of all human understanding. Our interpretations are however not direct reflections of the "real" world; rather, they are emanations from the pre-structures, or for-meaning, (*vorhabe, vorsicht, vorgriff*) found in our internal world. Because of this, Heidegger (1998) insists, interpretations free from presuppositions are impossible. The pre-structure of understanding goes beyond the traditional model of interpretation as a dynamic between subject and object. In fact, Heidegger believed that the notion of pre-understanding raises grave questions about the basic validity of describing interpretation in terms of the subject-object relationship. Likewise questions are raised about what is meant by so-called objective interpretations, or interpretations without presuppositions (Palmer, 1969).

Although he was not the first philosopher who thought about pre-understanding and its importance concerning everyday thinking as well as scientific studies, it is Gadamer (1995) who has made significant efforts to reflect on and illuminate the nature of pre-understanding, or as he prefers to call it, prejudices. The concept of prejudice is central in Gadamer's philosophy. As did Heidegger, Gadamer talks about understanding the fore-meaning that precedes every phenomenon that we try to understand. He declares that pre-understanding, as fore-meaning or prejudice, is an intentional structure which is already activated when we regard something *as* something. It is crucial to understand this. Without pre-understanding, Gadamer claims, there can be no understanding. On the other hand, he makes clear that we cannot allow pre-understanding to take over and hinder understanding. The primary hermeneutical task is "to be aware of one's own bias, so that the text can present itself in all its otherness and thus assert its own truth against one's own fore-meanings" (Gadamer, 1995, p. 269). This approach implies the "foregrounding and appropriation" of one's pre-understanding. As a matter of fact, says Gadamer, this process is what makes the scientific endeavor "secure," thereby agreeing with Heidegger.

Typically, in discourse about phenomenology and hermeneutics we find that followers of Husserl accept his lifeworld theory but reject his idea of the transcendental, including the epoché. We concur; a lifeworld perspective is incompatible with the idea of a pure, transcendental point of view. Like other followers of Husserl's philosophy, Gadamer is convinced of the thoroughly grounded "worldliness" of our existence, that is, that we can never go beyond the lifeworld, nor its tradition, a very important concept in Gadamer's philosophy. Gadamer (1995) says about the unconquerable pre-understanding:

A person who believes he is free of prejudices, relying on the objectivity of his procedures and denying that he is himself conditioned by historical circumstances, experiences the power of the prejudices that unconsciously dominate him as a vis a tergo. (p. 360)

Referring to Husserl's discussion of transcendental subjectivity, Gadamer (1976) also asserts: "Clearly, he himself, as the one who engages in transcendental reflection, is surrounded by this horizon of the world without ever questioning it" (p. 189). Aware of it or not, we are always in a world that supports us with horizons of pre-understanding. However, instead of totally dismissing or disparaging Husserl's notion of transcendence, Gadamer (1976, 1995, 1998) takes seriously upon the problem and suggests an approach to pre-understanding that is in line with his emphasis on a scientific openness. In an open frame of mind, we are more likely to recognize prejudices that govern our understanding. Of particular importance is discovery of prejudices that silently inform our judgments and making us see what we "would like to be" (1998, p. 31).

Husserl's philosophy does not include an explication of pre-understanding, but in his theory of intentionality, he presents a foundation for understanding the phenomenon of pre-understanding. The theory of intentionality, as mentioned earlier[8], was part of Husserl's plan to create an epistemologically for the natural attitude. There is always an intentional relationship with the things that make up our everyday lives; we understand the meaning of the things that we use and that we see around us as the things and places that belong to and signify our world, according to Husserl. Accordingly, intentionality also involves filling in the partially accessible qualities or characteristics of an object which are not directly presented but which nevertheless are there in our conscious experience of it. These partially accessible characteristics that contribute to our experience of the thing as something, which are not immediately presented to consciousness, but nevertheless exist in our consciousness, are what Husserl named apperceptions or appresentations, or, the object's horizons. Husserl's notion of appresentations can be compared to the pre-understanding of

---

8   Some ideas here are repetitions of chapter 2, but reiterated for this chapter's clarity.

which Heidegger (1998), Gadamer (1995) and Merleau-Ponty[9] (1995) speak[10]. Accordingly, when we understand something *as* something we already are using a kind of pre-understanding – even if we do not use the label of pre-understanding for this implicit act. In the texts of the above named philosophers, pre-understanding is conveyed as an unavoidable[11] and necessary precondition for being able to gain knowledge. Both pre-understanding and appre-sentations are to be understood as our pre-theoretical, non-critical, taken-for-granted knowledge about something that rules, espe-cially, the natural attitude. If we want to be certain about what really presents itself to us we have to adopt a scientific approach to pre-understanding.

In our reading of Husserl as well as Heidegger, Merleau-Ponty and Gadamer we have found that they all, in a complementary way, deal with the multifold question of restraining pre-under-standing in human science research. Husserl emphasizes the need for methodological reduction, that is, bracketing all pre-supposi-tions, in the search for meaning and phenomenological essences. But he does not make clear the meaning and content of pre-under-standing. Heidegger, Merleau-Ponty and especially Gadamer eluci-date pre-understanding and its underlying mechanisms. However they are much less clear about how to manage pre-suppositions and prejudices, which is needed for a productive understanding of the process of scientific work.

The need to influence pre-understanding

We claim that Gadamer aims at outlining an epistemology of open-ness that serves both philosophy and research[12]. The challenge for

---

9 Merleau-Ponty does not explicitly use the term pre-understanding, but he uses the term implicit understanding with a similar meaning.
10 See footnote 48, chapter 2.
11 At the same time Husserl, of course, aimed at avoiding this condition by the idea of transcendentality.
12 Gadamer should first and foremost be understood as a philosopher. How-ever, in his later writings, for example the excellent analysis of the enigma of health (1996), he shows a deep interest into contemporary science and its research.

such a methodological discussion is to show how pre-understanding can be an obstacle to understanding, and how it can be restrained while at the same time emphasizing its contextual function. Such an epistemology leads to the openness that makes it possible to see "the otherness" of the world's phenomena. Gadamer (1995) describes openness to new experiences like this:

> The truth of experience always implies an orientation toward new experience. That is why a person who is called experienced has become so not only *through* experiences but is also open *to* new experiences. The consummation of his experience, the perfection that we call "being experienced", does not consist in the fact that someone already knows everything and knows better than anyone else. Rather, the experienced person proves to be, on the contrary, someone who is radically undogmatic; who because of the many experiences he has had and the knowledge he has drawn from them, is particularly well equipped to have new experiences and to learn from them. The dialectic of experience has its proper fulfillment not in definitive knowledge but in the openness to experience that is made possible by experience itself. (p. 355)

Most people can probably agree with this ideal and will probably agree that researchers should be seasoned in this way. But how can it be achieved in the context of research? How do we allow for the world to show its otherness to us? How do we adopt that open stance?

Here is the proper place for the phenomenology that Husserl proposed, or more exactly, for what he calls the phenomenological reduction. As we said earlier in chapter 2, Husserl (1998) wants us to step out of the natural attitude and "parenthesize" parts of the world from our consciousness and let a reduction take place in order to be present to the true givenness of phenomena of the world. It is important, however, as Giorgi (1997) reminds us, that we modify philosophical ideas for the purpose of empirical scientific analysis. For researchers, the phenomenological reduction means that in order to be fully present to the world's otherness, past knowledge about the actual phenomenon must be set aside, or "held" in abeyance. In empirical research performing the phenomenological reduction means "that no existential claim is being made for the description" (p. 244), that is, that we temporarily place into doubt what we assume we understand about the phenomenon, instead, describing the meaning of the phenomenon, as it is experienced.

Merleau-Ponty (1995) gives a clear account of the natural attitude and our presuppositions:

> It is because we are through and through compounded of relationships with the world that for us the only way to become aware of the fact is to suspend the resultant activity, to refuse it our complicity (to look at it *ohne mitzumachen*, as Husserl often says), or, yet again, to put it 'out of play'. Not because we reject the certainties of common sense and a natural attitude to things–they are, on the contrary, the constant theme of philosophy–but because, being the presupposed basis of any thought, they are taken for granted, and go unnoticed, and because in order to arouse them and bring them to view, we have to suspend for a moment our recognition of them. (p. xiii)

Ashworth (1996) argues that Merleau-Ponty thereby gives Husserl's idea of bracketing the meaning of "set[ting] aside theories, research presuppositions, ready-made interpretations, etc. in order to reveal engaged, lived experience" (p. 9). It is obvious that, for researchers such as Giorgi and Ashworth, bracketing refers to the adoption of an open researching attitude to the world as it presents itself, the most central idea of phenomenology, which is implicit in its very name. It is also obvious, that they leave aside that meaning of bracketing that involves a transcendental ego.

Contrary to what many of their followers say, both Merleau-Ponty and Gadamer hold on to ideas that correspond with the reflective openness of phenomenological reduction. Merleau-Ponty (1964) says:

> ... [the philosopher[13]] must suspend the affirmations which are implied in the given facts of his life. But to suspend them is not to deny them and even less to deny the link which binds us to the physical, social and cultural world. It is on the contrary to *see* this link, to become conscious of it. It is "the phenomenological reduction" alone which reveals this ceaseless and implicit affirmation, this "setting of the world" [*thèse du monde*] which is presupposed at every moment of our thought. (p. 49)

Aware of that we are anchored to a world, Merleau-Ponty does not even try to go beyond it. Still, he emphasizes a phenomenological

---

13 Could also be read "the scientist".

124

reduction, and for him that is a reflective stance that does not withdraw from the world. Reflection, Merleau-Ponty (1995 says,

> steps back to watch the forms of transcendence fly up like sparks from a fire; it slackens the intentional threads which attach us to the world and thus brings them to our notice; it alone is consciousness of the world because it reveals that world as strange and paradoxical (xiii).

For Merleau-Ponty, as well as for Gadamer, as we soon shall see, scientific openness to the phenomenon is of crucial importance.

Gadamer lays out for us the process of hermeneutics and acknowledges the difficulty for scientists that pre-understanding presents: "Understanding begins ... when something addresses us. This is the first condition of hermeneutics. We know now what this requires, namely the fundamental suspension of our own prejudices" (1995, p. 299). He further explains this idea:

> The fundamental elimination of prejudices that science requires of its researchers may well be a laborious process, but it is always easier than overcoming the illusions that constantly arise from one's own ego (that of an individual, group, people, or culture to which the person belongs and listens) in order to see what is. (Gadamer, 1998, p. 31)

Gadamer depicts a position of distance in the process of understanding. By distancing ourselves we see better, is his message. Keeping in mind that the discovery of meaning is infinite, "distancing", Gadamer (1995) says, "lets the true meaning of the object emerge fully" (p. 298).

A distancing and reflective attitude is thus crucial in our scientific work. It means a balancing act where we want to keep a scientific openness at the same time as we are aware of our worldliness. For Gadamer (1995) the meaning of this balancing endeavor means, that we have to "distinguish the true prejudices, by which we *understand*, from the *false* ones, by which we *misunderstand*" (p. 299). This is a tricky business. It is hard to "separate in advance the productive prejudices that enable understanding from the prejudices that hinder it and lead to misunderstandings" (Gadamer, 1995, p. 295). Self-awareness is especially problematic because there is so much of our interior life that is beyond our conscious reach despite our willingness to look inside. That is what we learn from psychoanalysis. But we cannot rest in an assumption that suspending our presuppositions and adopting self-awareness is a complicated procedure. Gadamer (1995) gives guidance: "It is impossible to make ourselves aware of a prejudice while it is constantly operating unnoticed, but only when it is, so to speak, provoked" (p. 299), he says. Thus we have to provoke our pre-understanding and, as Gadamer says, put it "at risk" (p. 299). Gadamer asserts this is done with questioning.

Questioning the pre-understanding

Gadamer (1995) states, that openness and suspension of prejudices requires questioning, "… all suspension of judgments and hence, a fortiori, of prejudices, has the logical structure of a *question* (p. 299). Asking a question puts one in a position of openness: we must await the answer. When we are seeking to uncover a phenomenon and open up our pre-understanding, we must ask the right questions. Gadamer reminds us that the essence of questioning is to open up possibilities and keep them open. Tradition as well as all pre-understanding must be challenged, must be put at risk. We have to question tradition and our own particular history including the beliefs and practices that we take for granted because they have for so long been a part of our lives. We must put questions to our pre-understanding in a way that makes us see more clearly how our prejudices are formed and how they effect our approach to the world. But any questioning is not sufficient. Gadamer prefers true, authentic questions, which are nothing other than questions of openness.

A question always has a "sense of direction" (Gadamer, 1995, p. 362). Questioning points consciousness in a certain direction. When a question is asked, it always circumscribes an area within which it is possible to find an answer. Therefore an answer is never just any-old-answer, but it is always shaped by the question's content and meaning. An incorrect question will give an incorrect answer and an unclear question will give an unclear answer.[14] Gadamer (1995) says that contrary to what is generally understood, it is

14 This is important for the discussion of validity in scientific research.

the question that takes priority over the answer. Confusion often arises not so much from answers that are unclear, but from the question that prompted the answer. Gadamer stresses the basic condition for authentic questioning and says that, "in order to be able to ask, one must want to know, and that means knowing that one does not know" (p. 363). To form a true question means, therefore, understanding that one does not know, and understanding this, that one seeks insight. To understand that one does not know means having placed in doubt all cherished beliefs. A true and real question has no given answer. A rhetorical question is thus not a true question, but one that seeks confirmation of beliefs. A rhetorical question is not an open approach. Questioning as Gadamer understands it, must be practiced by every researcher who wants to adopt an open stance in human science research, which demands that its practitioners learn the art of questioning.

What, then, is pre-understanding? Gadamer (1995) gives an answer: It is mainly tradition. Tradition works as an authority that "always has power over our attitudes and behavior" (p. 280). He stresses the point that, *"Understanding is to be thought of less as a subjective act than as participating in an event of tradition,* a process of transmission in which past and present are constantly mediated" (p. 290). As humans, we are situated within tradition; we are part of tradition and tradition is part of us. All scientific understanding, as Gadamer says, "is *addressed* by tradition" (p. 282).

Gadamer's standpoint is thus precise and unambiguous; our presuppositions derive from the tradition in which we participate. Tradition does not stand over against our thinking as an object of our thoughts. Instead it is the horizon within which we conduct our thinking. Put in that way, pre-understanding is a way of expressing one's involvement in the lifeworld, hence, pre-understanding can never be fully objectified. Because we cannot completely objectify our pre-understanding, we need an epistemology that complements our position as always already involved with the phenomenon we study. Such an epistemology conceives of understanding as a dialectical process between the things encountered and the self that encounters them. Consequently, this epistemology emphasizes self-understanding as an important part of the task of opening up pre-understanding. With its focus on history and tradition, hermeneutics implies just such awareness of self.

Pre-understanding emanates from tradition and forms a context with which the researcher is familiar. Of course, this is aslikely to constrain as to facilitate understanding. Pre-understanding can be a preconceived meaning or common prejudices related to the studied phenomenon. As researcher, one can have emotional attachments to a phenomenon or simply be used to the phenomenon as an ordinary part of life, and thus fail to see anything other than a familiar landscape. Pre-understanding may also include one's favorite theories or thought models which become part of, or worse yet, the starting point for the research. Research that blindly follows a theory or a thought model is not open. Popper (1988)[15] warns us for example against the dogmatic use of theories, since that seriously limits our possibilities to see objectively. Popper sees psychoanalysis and Marxism as examples of theories that are dogmatic and used dogmatically. Even other human science theorists, such as Giorgi (1989a), Glaser and Strauss (1980), argue against having a theory as a point of departure for research. They emphasize instead a more unconditioned and open approach. There is, however, a place for theories and thought models after data have been allowed to speak on their own. This will be further explored in a succeeding chapter.

In summary, what we have learned from Husserl, Heidegger, and Gadamer, and Merleau-Ponty, is that in order to be open and receptive to the world we have to look at and question our pre-understanding. But how is this done? How can a researcher be open and undogmatic? We believe, that by developing a sensitivity for self-awareness and by investigating the structure of one's pre-understanding, a researcher can increase the possibility of openness in research. To this end we turn now to an investigation of the cognitive, social, and emotional aspects of pre-understanding. Various frameworks from cognitive and social-psychological and psycho-

---

15 Popper's reason for arguing against certain theories is their weakness in relation to the possibility of falsification, which is an epistemological argument that does not belong to the philosophy of this book. We think though, that his idea per see, that dogmatic theories obscure openness, is import.

analytic theory will be examined[16]. We will examine some theories in light of Gadamer's "history of effect", and discuss the possibility of increased openness in research.

The cognitive aspect of pre-understanding

Even if we accept the assumption that we cannot have a full and unobstructed view of our emotions, most of us would like to claim that we at least know our thoughts, as well as the views and opinions behind them. Piaget's theory concerning the development of cognitive and conceptual structures suggests, however, that we are not fully aware of how we form an opinion, or why we interpret our environment in a particular way. According to Piaget (1980), we are dependent upon biological and environmental factors when encountering and understanding new situations. Consequently, researchers cannot be certain that their interpretation of new situations is necessarily the result of an open mind and logical thinking.

Cognitive psychology addresses the issue of pre-understanding indirectly. According to Piaget (1980) a child gradually emancipates from fantasies and intuition, and, as the ability to generalize and discriminate develops, eventually acquires the capacity for logical thought. It is in this context that Piaget introduced the term "accommodation." In acts of accommodation, children radically change their presuppositions about what they encounter in the course of daily living. "Assimilation," on the other hand, refers to the way that children incorporate the new way of thinking. Thanks to the gradually increasing capacity of the brain, around the age of six, children abandon magical and intuitive thinking in favor of increasing contact with reality. We can assume therefore, that the structures of assimilated thoughts comprise an aspect of pre-understanding.

As adults, however, we are less inclined to radically change our existing interpretations of the world. By adulthood, we have a relatively fixed cognitive structure, which, in cognitive theory is called a "schema" (English & English, 1958). The schema shapes the way

---

16 Doing this, we are aware that those theories, compared to phenomenology, have somewhat different ontologies or different starting points. The aim is, however, not to use these theories within a phenomenological framework, that is, as phenomenological theories. Instead the aim is to simply use these theories to explore the nature of pre-understanding.

we experience and react to new things that we encounter. English and English describe the consequences of a cognitive schema; "one step follows another not merely because one knows by feedback that the body is in position for such a move, but because the whole series has established or activated a pattern or schema" (English & English, 1958, p. 478).

Hence, cognitive psychology suggests that the cognitive side of pre-understanding is pre-conscious and pre-reflective. Upon examination of the concept of schema, it becomes obvious that a great deal of human understanding stands outside explicit and critical reflection. However, by paying attention to the fact that such schemata exist we move closer to more expanded and effective self-awareness.

The social aspect of pre-understanding

A British citizen holds a different opinion about personal responsibility in crimes of passion than does a French citizen. Society in general does not believe in witches in the 21th century, but did so in the 17th century. Despite today's emphasis on social and political equality between the genders in the western world, it is still fair to say that women are more likely than men to place their children's welfare ahead of professional success. Examples such as these illustrate the differing values and opinions of various social groups and we would not be remiss in speculating that the pre-understanding of the individuals in these examples differ as well.

Social interaction begins in early childhood. During the process of acquiring self-awareness, a child becomes a spider in its own web, gathering the necessary language and social skills that make it possible to create a systematic and complex apprehension of the world. In G. H. Mead's (1934) theory of social interaction, socialization requires access to "significant others" (e.g. parents) as well as "generalized others" (people in the society, playmates, teachers etc). Consciousness of the self makes it possible to reflect upon ourselves as objects as well as subjects. Mead refers to these two dimensions as "I" and "me." The development of this capacity requires an environment with access to stimuli, which affect the sender and the receiver in the same way, for example, children's mimicry of their parents mannerisms, and parents' imitation of the child's expressions. Essentially, the child tries on the role of the parent in order to understand the world as the parent experiences it. Along the way, as the child imitates adults, surrounding objects become bearers of meaning; they are represented by symbols that the child learns. Important symbols that the child learns are those of the world in this first form of communication.

Because of our proclivity for symbols, we are not simply passive responders to a reality that imposes itself. Rather we actively create and recreate the world in which we live and act. We name, remember, categorize, perceive, create abstractions and new ideas and transcend space and time and ourselves- all through symbols.

Blumer (1969) carried on Mead's work and developed the theory of symbolic interactionism, which sheds more light on the social aspect of pre-understanding. Blumer's theory holds that meaning is created in interaction with others and that symbolic interactionism

> ... does not regard meaning as emanating from the intrinsic makeup of the thing that has meaning, nor does it see meaning as arising through a coalescence of psychological elements in the person. Instead ...the meaning of a thing for a person grows out of the ways in which other persons act toward the person with regard to the thing. (p. 4)

Only through interaction with others is meaning established for objects (an object in the language of symbolic interactionism is anything that can be indicated, or referred to, and includes persons as well as things). There is no pre-established meaning assignable to things other than the meaning that is the result of human interaction. Because symbolic interaction requires interpretation to arrive at meaning, it is constituted as a flexible, open, contingent process. Its meaning is dependent on nothing fixed, but is dependent solely upon its own evolving, dynamic qualities that constantly undergo change. Consequently, society is always in a state of change because it is comprised of individuals whose interaction requires interpretation. Symbolic interaction is restricted to what happens between people. It is relevant as well to what happens within a person.

Because our attitudes often lie outside of conscious choice, symbolic interactionism is primarily concerned with perspective rather than attitude. Symbolic interactionism sees humans as acting in a world that they consciously define through choices made when assessing their actions and those of others, and then redirecting themselves accordingly. Human interaction gives rise to symbols, language and perspectives, which in turn lead to interpretations. Perspective, as a component of pre-understanding, is generally held to be dynamic and conscious because it is defined through interaction with others and can be consciously chosen. We form our own perspective by examining the perspectives of those with whom we interact, the societies with which, and in which we communicate. Over time, with succeeding interactions, our definitions may change, influencing our interpretations and perspective.

The emotional aspect of pre-understanding

All understanding is embodied (Lakoff & Johnson, 1999). Embodied understanding necessarily includes emotions. There is abundant empirical research to support the notion that meaning is created via our bodily and imaginative apparatus (Lakoff & Johnson, 1999). Long before we express our understanding in symbolic form with language, we implicitly understand with our neuromuscular systems. Gendlin (1962, 1978) depicts the idea of emotional pre-understanding with the expression "felt sense", the bodily experiencing that precedes verbal expression of an experience. Based on his empirical research with psychotherapists and their patients, Gendlin proposes an idea that can be referred to research, and illuminates the meaning of learning to recognize the changes that take place in our bodies during, for example, interviews. First of all it is important to recognize the bodily and emotional reactions that we have, because they can say something about one's pre-understanding. Thus the reactions have to be verbalized, for example when going through what happened during the interview, either for oneself or together with an adviser. Putting the emotional reaction into words is experienced as relief because what was, heretofore, only a felt sense of something that eluded words is suddenly captured and articulated. The frustration of being unable to identify, understand, and articulate experience is relieved when the bodily sense of the problem is captured in words. Even if the original problem, for example, a troubled relationship with an interviewee or a research, remains, being able to name a particular aspect of it that had only been dimly perceived, brings a sense of relief that is experienced bodily.

132

For Gendlin (1962), another way of expressing felt-sense is "experienced meaning," by which he intends to convey that meaning arises from our bodies before it is expressed in language. Clearly, what Gendlin, and others have seen, that understanding begins at an implicit, feeling level, parallels the philosophical notion of pre-understanding. Just as in the cognitive and social/psychological forms of pre-understanding, the emotional aspect of pre-understanding mirrors all of our history: our past development as individuals, as well as the culture and the society in which we live.

Klein (1989) deals with unconscious feelings and their influence upon pre-understanding. In her theory the internal world affects and even determines understanding of the external world. Klein's work is within the field of psychoanalytic psychology. However, she reduces the importance of the classical idea of our fundamental instincts, thereby dismissing it as the main point in traditional psychoanalysis. Instead she emphasizes the importance of interpersonal relations during early childhood. According to her theory, it is during the early time of life we create the foundation of unconscious parts of the internal world, and, consequently, important aspects of our pre-understanding.

Klein's recognition of the significance of interpersonal relations during infancy is important in her approach to understand children. According to object relation theory, our internal world is populated. A child is initially totally dependent upon adults, especially its parents. Consequently, parents usually become internal objects of high significance. We can recognize this when adults relate to their babies in quite the same way as their own parents related to them, in spite of lacking conscious memories of their own early childhood. Hence, the early construction of the internal world is a reflected image of the children's interpretations of their nearest surroundings. This process is most vivid during early childhood, but it is of importance during our whole lives.

This theory, quite alike but more in depth than the theory of interactionism (Mead, 1934), explains why we usually talk about Americans, Russians, Italians and Scandinavians as genuine different in personality, in spite of the lack for biological explanations concerning these differences. Hence, if we, for example, adopt an infant from the south of Europe to parents in the north of Europe the child as adult will probably understand the world more like a North-European than a South-European. The theory of internal objects explains why.

Klein's theoretical framework also includes assumptions concerning "splitting". A small child creates this primitive psychological structure to be able to handle chaotic impressions. The mother is for example, from time to time, experienced as *either* good *or* bad. Consequently the internal objects are also, from time to time, divided in *either* good *or* bad, and the world is experienced as *either* kind, acknowledgeable and satisfactory, *or* evil, threatening and dangerous. If splitting dominates the pre-understanding of adults, and for example researchers, it will serve as a severe obstacle for openness. We can recognize the mechanism of splitting when an adult suddenly and totally changes his or her attitude. The reason for this is trifling and, for example, other people cannot understand why this person unexpectedly forgets about good and trustful interpersonal relations, because of disappointments or frustrations. A researcher, who's pre-understanding is characterized by such an emotional dichotomy, risks being one-eyed when trying to understand a phenomenon. In such circumstances, the research report will be a contribution to a simplified debate rather than a nuanced and objective description of the life-world.

The historical nature of understanding and pre-understanding

All pre-understanding is, whether we are aware of it or not, a history of effect[17]. Gadamer (1995) claims that in order to acquire methodological consciousness we must better understand ourselves and our positions in history. To this end, we have looked at the cognitive, social and emotional aspects of pre-understanding as understood in the empirical sciences. In all of the theories we found the power of tradition as Gadamer conceives of it with the term historicity. Even cognitive schemata are developed within a tradition

---

17 For many this is an awkward translation of the German original, *Wirkungsgechichte*, but because it is the term generally used in translations to English we also use it here.

(Lakoff & Johnson, 1999). The cognitive, social and emotional aspects of pre-understanding and their coherence with tradition and history of effect can be conceptualized in the following way.

The suffering that accompanies health problems is an area of interest in health care research. Most people have some kind of personal experience of illness. For a researcher these experiences may be conscious or unconscious but they will assuredly affect the process of inquiry. If, for example, a physician, psychologist, or nurse, as a child had parents who provided them with loving care during childhood illnesses, this caring attitude is the model of caring for them as professionals.

When, in vocational training, we are confronted with a suffering person, our natural reaction is to provide the sort of care that we experienced as a child. Students who had positive experiences of loving care in their own families are likely to take a similar approach to their patients. We hold colleagues who are perceived as kind and caring persons as models for ideal caregiving. But these childhood experiences, reinforced in vocational training, constitute an historical effect which later can play a subtle part in the research that we choose to conduct. It is not uncommon for individuals who have suffered with disease or injury to enter a health care profession. Further, it is not uncommon that we are drawn to that familiar area of suffering in our research. But if our childhood experience and vocational training aren't recognized as part of our pre-understanding, our research can be influenced in unforeseen ways. In research, a caring relationship in and of itself will not elicit true phenomenological data that allows a researcher to see something new. Researchers must recognize and set aside their own beliefs in order to hear what interviewees are telling them and to see the "otherness" of life experiences that do not match their own.

To be able to "go the things themselves" in an open way the researcher has to avoid projective interpretations, that is, letting one's pre-understanding govern understanding of something. Every time we try to see tradition clearly and openly in terms of its own meaning, we must query its historical effect. Posing the right questions to one's historically influenced perspective is the hallmark of understanding and a necessity for methodological consciousness. "To ask the question means that we are recognizing that understanding becomes a scholarly task only under special circumstances and that it is necessary to work out these circumstances as a hermeneutical situation," says Gadamer (1995, p. 306).

To be historically aware means having the insight that self-knowledge is never complete. "Our need to become conscious of effective history is urgent because it is necessary for scientific consciousness. But this does not mean it can ever be absolutely fulfilled" (Gadamer, 1994, p. 301). Aware that we can never fully grasp the historical nature of our consciousness, we can, however, aim at developing our scientific consciousness as much as possible. We are suggesting here that by considering psychological and sociological theories, crucial aspects of historicity can be examined, and, at least to some extent, understood. The theories that we have briefly outlined above reflect traditional western thought only, but nevertheless illustrate the power of tradition, which lies beyond rational logic where it determines our attitudes. Further, that which has been sanctioned by tradition has an unspoken authority that we experience as historical effect. All upbringing and education depend on the authority of tradition. Even when we outgrow our parents and educators we never completely become our own master apart from tradition.

When we are aware of historical effect we run less risk of asking questions based upon a narrow perspective. In addition, when we examine aspects of our pre-understanding we understand ourselves better, thus increasing the range of vision from our particular vantage-point. The task for the researcher is to answer what lies behind and beyond, through the horizon of the question that we pose to the phenomenon, thus opening up new horizons.[18] A researcher must find the right horizon of inquiry for the questions evoked by the encounter with tradition. Gadamer (1995) explains: "To acquire a horizon means that one looks beyond what is close at hand – not in order to look away from it but to see it better, within a larger whole and in truer proportion" (p. 306).

18 Since Nietzsche and Husserl, the concept "horizon" has been used to characterize the way in which thought is tied to its finite determinacy and the way one's range of vision is gradually expanded. "A person who has no horizon does not se far enough and hence overvalues what is nearest to him" (Gadamer, 1997, p. 302).

Increased knowledge of pre-understanding explains why we ask the questions that we do in a given area of research. The process of inquiry requires the researcher to be reflective about the methods being used and the meaning of the data that are gathered. We are in accord with Gadamer's and Husserl's insistence that researchers control their natural attitude in order to discover something new that does not already exist in their pre-understanding. Gadamer's claims are implicit and Husserl's are explicit. Husserl calls control of the natural attitude "bracketing," while Gadamer's term "questioning" is more subtle. Ashworth (2000) expresses a similar notion as giving "due weight to the creativity of consciousness – its originary productivity – and to the connectedness of awareness to the events of the world" (p. 13). Congruent with researching open-mindedness, Ashworth is critical of the dualism that is present in most theory and in particular, of the empiricism and intellectualism that phenomenology so elegantly balances. If we want to optimize openness in research we have to face the fact that we are forever in the position of a pre-scientific, pre-given world that is meaningful to us. But we also have to include the fact that consciousness is capable, to a certain degree, of understanding itself and investigating intentionality. Ashworth (2000) puts it this way: "Openness is to be secured both in the sense of immersion in a meaningful world and also in the sense of being aware in a creative manner with the capacity to responsibly construe and re-construe these meanings" (p. 13).

As human science researchers who strive to develop scientific knowledge, we cannot afford to ignore the enigmatic character of the human world and simply mirror our own pre-understanding. "We must confront the *fait accompli* that we are conscious in less-than-fully open modes, weighed down by illegitimate baggage" (Ashworth, 2000, p. 14). The scientific adventure of questioning and restraining pre-understanding in research is an act that requires knowledge, patience, discipline, and not least self-awareness.

Self-awareness, self-reflection and reflection[19]

Human science research, attuned as it is to openness in moments of immediate intersubjective presence and search for the meaning of unique experience as well as general structures, requires of the researcher self-awareness. Considering the power of pre-understanding, it is obvious that researchers need to develop a self-critical stance in order to optimize the possibilities of openness, and thereby, objectivity. In the above discussion of pre-understanding, we saw how heavily burdened we are simply by being in the world. We do not, therefore, aim at absolute objectivity, because, however desirable it may be, it is an unreachable goal (Merleau-Ponty, 1995, 1968). Bracketing with the aim of a total phenomenological reduction is impossible. The reflexive activity that a suspension of pre-understanding signifies, however, is essential to all phenomenological research. Reflexive consideration of one's experience with the subject matter of any scientific research project is essential for the validity of that research.

To focus on reflection is to perform the most basic phenomenological act – "the phenomenological method operates exclusively in acts of reflection," (Husserl, 1998, p. 174). The reflective act presents the issue of the phenomenological reduction, which is a matter of dispute among phenomenologists. While some hold that reflection implies transcendence, others argue that transcendence is humanly impossible. Our position is that the gulf between those who dismiss transcendence as an impossible goal and those who insist that it can be accomplished is less problematic than it might appear. What is important for human science research, however, is to understand that the capacity for self-awareness, however limited, is part of our ontology. As humans we are endowed with the ability for critical scrutiny of ourselves and the ability to seek objectivity with regard to our own reasoning processes. It seems

---

19 The originally Latin word reflection was originally used in the context of optics, and means then to bend or turn backward. Gadamer (1996) gives us to understand that it was the Stoic philosophy that first had some notions on optic reflection and "the mystery of light" (p. 146).

that we have no choice but to be always drawn toward self-aware-ness when we undertake phenomenology because it ultimately leads us to consider our constitutive involvement with the phe-nomena that we investigate and describe. It matters less that we can or cannot achieve a pure transcendence or a pure self-aware-ness than that we realize the importance of taking the first step on the path toward objectivity, developing an awareness of the con-scious processes that contribute to our research and understanding. The notion of a beginning point for self-awareness on the path between the opposing positions regarding transcendentality offers a way for researchers to proceed with the work that needs to be done if we are to begin the changes necessary for a more humanly oriented science and world. However, like most philosophical con-cepts, reflection is a complex concept of which there are subtle var-iations. We hope to explicate what it means to be self-aware before turning to method.

Self-reflection

The term self-awareness conveys a general sense of keeping a criti-cal eye on oneself. Self-awareness can be perceived as self-reflec-tion, that special act of pondering one's own thought processes. With reflection, then, consciousness is directed upon oneself and one's actions. Human consciousness can never become an object in the same sense as the things of the world. An object in general, as soon as it is known by a consciousness, "loses its power of resist-ance, is conquered and becomes disposable", as Gadamer (1996, p. 53) elegantly puts it. This is not the case with consciousness itself.

Reflection is inherently paradoxical. We can never put total trust in its adequacy to disclose the world's phenomena since we tend to forget that our act of reflection, undertaken in order to discover an object's meaning, is part of the consciousness that gave the object its meaning in the first place. Reflection always has a blind spot that cannot be seen or explicated (Merleau-Ponty, 1968). Further, when we are in the natural attitude and a phenomenon presents itself to us, it is always infused with meaning. In this initial encounter with a phenomenon, there is a basic kind of reflection of which, generally speaking, we are not aware. However, from an epistemological or methodological perspective, we do not refer to this first level as reflectivity. Rather, it is simply the intentionality of the natural attitude, which could also be referred to as ontological interpretation.

So, we have the natural attitude with its uncritical and self-unaware position from which the world is ordinarily understood. But there is another approach, a critical one. This approach involves calling forth processes of reflection of which we are aware. Through reflection, consciousness, which is directed towards the world, turns toward the self and establishes a distance from the world and from the natural attitude, and thus from the approach within which we take for granted that the way that we understand the world is the way that it is (Bengtsson,1993b, 1994). We call this self-reflection.

Both Natanson (1973) and Fink (1995)[20] propose that when Husserl discusses transcendentality he implies self-reflection and self-awareness. Accordingly, we use the term self-reflection to convey the human capacity for transcendence, the ability to think about and reflect upon our own consciousness. Gadamer (1996) echoes this idea, "Reflection, the free process of turning in on oneself, appears as the highest form of freedom that exists at all. Here the mind is properly in its own element in so far it relates solely to its own content" (p. 50). Gadamer points to this ability as an essential aspect of humanity. Self-reflection, the critical and considered approach to one's usual immersion in the natural attitude, has as its object the process of reflecting itself. Husserl (1998) states.

> Any mental process which is not an object of regard can, with respect to ideal possibility, become 'regarded;' a reflection on the part of the Ego is directed to it, it now becomes an object *for* the Ego. The situation is the same in the case of possible Ego-regards directed to the components of the mental process and to its intentionalities (to that of *which* the mental process may be a consciousness). In turn, the

20 It is also worthwhile to note that Sartre (1998), whose task it was to examine consciousness in-the-world and by no means agrees with Husserl's basic notions of the epoché, still seems to be in a mundane harmony with Husserl stating that it is possible to distance oneself from the world and thus achieve a reflective awareness in which we can see ourselves in the constitutive acts of understanding meaning.

reflections are mental processes and, as reflections, can become the substrates of new reflections; and so on ad infinitum as a matter of essentially necessary universality. (p. 174)

Fink (1995) captures and elucidates the essence of Husserl's transcendental phenomenology with the notion of the "phenomenological onlooker," who is, at once, both the one who looks as well as the subject who sees him/herself looking. "The theory of method is, therefore, nothing other than the process of that subject's self-objectification" (p.13). We might think of the phenomenological onlooker as the researcher. Fink compares the reflections of the phenomenological onlooker to all human reflective activity: prior to any reflection there is consciousness of the self. Also Merleau-Ponty (1995) notes that it is the nature of consciousness to be aware of itself and its acts, and states, "self-consciousness is the very being of mind in action (p. 371). We might thus conclude that practicing self-reflection is a given for the conscious mind.

The suspension of pre-understanding indicates the mental procedure of distancing oneself from immediate involvement with the phenomenon under investigation. To be open and sensitive towards a phenomenon, we must, as researchers become conscious of what we already know and think we know about the phenomenon in question. Put simply, the suspension of pre-understanding is a maneuver that aims at scientific objectivity and openness to the world, and the phenomenon, so that it can show itself to us. In phenomenological terms, self-reflection, the suspension of pre-understanding and openness mean maintaining touch with one's intentionality, one's intentionality or one's unique perspective of the phenomenon under investigation.

Gadamer (1996) borrows an example from Köhler's research on monkeys to illustrate the idea that self-scrutiny begins when something is amiss:

> The frustrated desire for a banana leads to a certain 'thoughtfulness', that is, when the desire remains fixed on its goal it leads to an indirect recourse to something else, to something that is not itself a goal, but rather a means to an end. But such a 'means to an end' is not really itself an object of attention, any more than one's hand becomes an 'object' when it is unable to reach what is desired simply by stretching out. Rather, this 'attention' and the thoughtfulness which is both directed towards attaining the goal and yet turned

away from it are expressed in the action of achieving the goal; once the goal is achieved the means which were formerly 'at hand' are cast aside. The disturbance requires the removal of what is causing the interference, that is, it requires the eventual disappearance of attention to oneself. (p. 54)

If Köhler is right, the process of self-reflection is naturally awakened by events that halts one's research because something is wrong. As scientifically aware researchers we also learn to stop and check ourselves when something is going right!

Self-reflection with the goal of self-understanding is the hallmark of psychotherapy. But the idea of self-reflection as a necessary component of research methodology is not as familiar to or accepted by the scientific community. It is therefore important to stress the difference between the act of reflecting that looks at the thinking "I" and its processes of consciousness, and grasping the significance and the implications of doing so. We can be self-reflective without being self-aware. We can reflect on our actions and behaviors, our decisions and so forth, and yet remain unaware of the significance, the subjective meaningfulness that influences our actions. Self-awareness is not an elusive something that only a few learn to possess, but is always a potential capacity that can be developed. Self-awareness is something which we cannot escape (however much we might like to!). Because self-awareness is inescapable it demands attention and explication, particularly by those of us who investigate and describe the lived experience of others. Researcher self-awareness is methodologically and ethically paramount to valid phenomenological research.

Professional and scientific reflection

In addition to self-reflection, there are other reflective actions that are important in the conduct of research. In his analysis of reflection, Bengtsson (1993b) identifies two types besides the reflection of self: professional reflection and scientific reflection. Professional as well as scientific reflection are modes of self-reflection that one is usually engaged in with one's fellow researchers. In this way, self-scrutiny is understood as an intersubjective activity. As Heidegger

(1981) says: "Knowing oneself (*Sichkennen*) is grounded in Being-with" (p. 161). Consequently, intersubjectivity is prior to subjectivity. Benktsson (1985), a Swedish interpreter of Heidegger's philosophy, puts it in this way:

> The subject's relationship with the own self, this primordial characteristic of the human existence, is thus not a relationship that exclude others but on the contrary includes others. It is not about an isolated subject, that secondarily establishes a relationship with others, but in this existential typical relationship with one's self, the human is also related to others. (p. 49)

Much of the reflective and critical examination of the research procedures is a solitary chore for researchers. However, the presence of another who can listen and discuss unconditionally, makes the reflective process easier. For research students especially, it is crucial to have the assistance of a more experienced researcher who can foster, and take part in the reflective process. Typically, research colleagues regularly examine and discuss their common or collaborative work and in the process develop knowledge that would not have been possible without the generative function of dialogue. Through dialogue, we develop what could be called a professional or collegial knowledge (Bengtsson, 1993b). In human science research praxis, researchers[21] step away from their natural attitude, where one is lost in the doing, and, through dialogue, make themselves, their knowledge, and their own actions an object for study.

Science, which is nothing other than the systematic and methodical use of experience (Merleau-Ponty, 1995; Bengtsson, 1993b), is itself a series of distancing steps that call for reflection. Ultimately, scientific results are read and critiqued by others. Practitioners use scientific research results as they evaluate and improve their caring and teaching skills, all of which require distancing from and reflecting upon everyday actions.

The knowledge that we acquire through science becomes, through reflection, an object for consciousness. Merleau-Ponty's words, "to slacken the threads of intentionality", convey Husserl's notion of distancing from something without negating it. To put

---

21 Or, for that matter, professionals such as caregivers and educators.

slack into the threads that connect us with the phenomena we perceive. It implies that we can strive for objectivity by examining what we believe we know about them – always with the understanding that we are part of the lifeworld and cannot step outside of it in order to study it. In a similar way Bengtsson (1993b) suggests reflection as a way to make visible such knowledge that is normally hidden from us. We need to remove ourselves in order not to be locked into the immediate happenings, in order to examine the actions that are being carried out and to learn from that which is happening. When such immediate involvement has been halted, we can view a phenomenon from different perspectives until the essential aspects of the thing are seen. Instead of being immersed in the natural attitude, we distance ourselves and focus more critically upon the phenomenon of interest. Distancing in this context does not mean, as it might seem, a dissociation, which leaves something behind. Rather, as we have noted earlier, distancing in a thoughtful way helps us to come closer and really see the phenomenon.

Openness requires the ability to be reflective. Reflection is a form of distancing, which Ricoeur (1976) suggests as a way for researchers to critically examine their method and its use. Through reflection lifeworld researchers consider their scientific approach and research methods critically. To think critically about one's approach and methods means that one's thought processes, understanding, and knowledge are systematically and impartially scrutinized for influence on the research process and the outcome of the study. To be reflective about the lived world means making a shift away from immediate, concrete involvement with a phenomenon, into a reflective stance where the researcher can view both the phenomenon in question and the research procedures that are in progress, for example during an interview investigation.

Reflection is relevant for the informant also. In an interview, for example, we know that openness has worked when we notice that the interviewee begins to reflect about something that is in focus. In the best of interview situations we notice that for the interviewee the reflection is of a completely new sort. Perhaps the individual has never before reflected in this way, or perhaps never before has been given the possibility of reflecting in this way.

Finally, reflection is necessary in the description phase of the study when the result is presented. It is here that theory could be consulted as a way of enlarging the possibilities of understanding. However, the danger exists that uncritical reliance on theory can erode openness. Theory should always be used cautiously so that the phenomenon directs how and where the theory is used.

4 Methods for lifeworld research – data gathering

Concrete phenomena in the world, such as a book or a coffee percolator, and even more complicated things such as computers, are relatively easy to explore and examine. They are also easily measured. But this approach is not possible when we are trying to understand complex and abstract phenomena such as human experience. Health care, social care as well as learning and pedagogy are areas of human experience that do not allow themselves to be quantified and measured. Phenomena such as suffering, meaning, learning, remembering, understanding, caring and teaching have no concrete existence in time and space. They are phenomena only within a lifeworld perspective; there is no other meaning, or suffering, or learning than that which we experience. Lifeworld elements are, in one way or another, tied to the human beings that experience them. Consequently, human science and lifeworld research require methods and research techniques that can meet the characteristics of human being data, that can meet the lifeworld.

In lifeworld research, gathering of data is steered by three factors; the research question in its context, the nature of the phenomenon and the aim to go to the things themselves, that is, to be open and sensitive to the phenomenon of study. The emphasis on research openness and sensitivity includes the understanding that data gathering is affected by the intersubjective researcher-informant[1] relationship, the aim to be close and immediate, and the search for uniqueness and meaning. In the midst of the lifeworld and its complexity we are aware of our own lifeworld positions and our own basic function in the world, our own intentionality, as

---

1   In research literature there are several terms for the person who provides with data. In this book we have chosen to talk about this person as an informant, alternatively, a research informant.

well as the research informants', and, not least, the pre-understanding that is a part of every human being's lifeworld. There is thus a need for scientific scrutiny[2].

Giorgi (1997) points out three criteria necessary in order for, as he says, "a qualitative scientific method to qualify itself as phenomenological in a descriptive Husserlian sense" (p. 235). These criteria are; description, phenomenological reduction, and the search for invariant meanings[3]. The first step, descriptions, is a necessary starting point for lifeworld research. In order for the world to reveal itself as phenomena we need descriptions of lived experiences from others. These descriptions should come from the natural attitude, that is, we do not want a construed, interpreted or otherwise thematized description. Giorgi puts it this way: "What is critical is that the description be as precise and detailed as possible with a minimum number of generalizations or abstractions" (p. 243).

The phenomenological suspension of the pre-understanding, called the phenomenological reduction[4] by Giorgi, means a

---

2   Here in a more concrete part of our attempt to describe a human science research methodology it is obvious that we draw upon the philosophical understanding that we described in the previous chapters. However, at this point we leave, so to speak, the philosophical level and enter the scientific research level. As human science researchers our primary aim is not doing philosophy, but research. This does not mean that philosophy is left in behind. On the contrary, we still keep it as the foundation from which the research actions are directed. But by undertaking research we are taking a scientific approach rather than a philosophical one. One could say that we transform the philosophical ideas into scientific research practice.

3   We want to clarify that even if Giorgi's approach mostly is understood as a method for analysis in qualitative research, we mean that it is useful as a general framework for data analysis as well as data gathering.

4   In chapter 3 we discussed the meaning of the Husserlian concepts reduction and bracketing. A problem with these concepts is that they imply the notion of transcendence and a pure ego, the goal of Husserl's philosophical work. We are aware that Giorgi does not adopt that meaning of the concepts, but give them an empirical use that harmonizes with our understanding of a phenomenological scientific research approach. Nevertheless we have chosen other words in order to illuminate the important task of reflecting over and restrain the pre-suppositions that researchers live with and bring to their studies. In general, "reduction" is changed to "suspension", a word that Gadamer uses to describe a scientific strife for openness within a framework of the inescapable lifeworld. Instead of "bracketing" we use several words, depending on the context, but words as restrain, keep in check, and bridle or curb, describe the aim of not letting the pre-understanding be.

147

researching stance that breaks from the natural attitude. Even when we are data gathering we have to be aware of the requirements of the lifeworld approach. To aim at a suspension of one's pre-understanding means to step back and describe the things experienced as presence, according to Giorgi (1997). This is what it means to investigate "things" in the world as phenomena. Giorgi emphasizes, that "the only claim that the researcher will make is that the concrete experience is an indication of what the subject was present to, and not necessarily that the description is an objective account of what really took place" (p. 244).

Despite our general pre-understanding of the world we have to stay with "the things" as phenomena, as they are experienced by the informants of a study. This is important, for example, describing the lifeworld of severe mentally ill people. The possibility of understanding their everyday life increases if we put stress on the lived experience of it.

Employing descriptions within the attitude of the phenomenological suspension of the researcher's pre-understanding further means, "that a person must withhold past knowledge about the phenomenon he or she is researching in order to be fully present to the concrete instance of the phenomenon as presented by the subject's description" (Giorgi, 1997, p. 244).

As researchers we have to keep in check everything we know beforehand about the phenomenon in order to be open to that which presents itself. If we let theories or personal experiences of the phenomenon take part in the data gathering we might end up having a beautiful description of the phenomenon, not the research informant's – but our own!

Finally, when we are gathering data in a phenomenological way, we must keep in mind the goal of understanding a phenomenon's invariant meanings. Giorgi (1997) stresses that while philosophical essences are universal, that which he calls "scientific essences" always are contextual and also dependent upon the perspective of the discipline (pp. 244–245). When gathering data, the mind of the human science researcher is already directed towards meaning. One consequence of such mindfulness is, for example, that we might ask for clarifications, exemplifications in order to deepen our understanding of the phenomenon from the informant. That is, we do not simply want conventional opinions or general standpoints about the phenomenon, since that kind of descriptions will be of little worth in illuminating meaning.

There are no phenomenological or hermeneutic research methods or techniques for data gathering per se. In a project that is based on a lifeworld perspective, the researcher can make use of all the types of data gathering techniques found in everyday life and in other research approaches, although, some types, such as questionnaires, are of limited value. Because the aim is to find lived experience, interviews and written narratives are the most valuable data sources, but observations and drawings are techniques that also are useful in lifeworld research. Most of all a combination of methodical procedures of data gathering meets the criteria of openness. The success of the technique chosen and how it is best managed depends on the research question that is asked, the context in which the question is asked and the data that are found, as well as on the creativity and abilities of the researcher. And, of course, it must meet the above-described conditions.

In order to describe ways of working with research data we draw upon the epistemological assumptions that have been described in the first chapters, but also upon our own lived experience as researchers. We describe narratives, interviews, drawings, observations and fieldwork as methodical means, which are suitable when qualitative phenomena are to be examined. One or more of these techniques can be the main component(s) in a study that is carried out within a phenomenological or hermeneutic lifeworld approach. They can also be parts of a bigger project.

Narratives

A narrative is a description of a lived experience. It is written or recorded by the research informant within the natural attitude. It focuses on an episode in the informant's everyday life experience, which in some way illustrates the phenomenon that is the topic of study. It is always personal experience that is focused upon in the narrative, and the telling of it is relatively undisturbed by the researcher[5]. Narrative in the form of anecdote is described by van Manen (1990) as "a usually short narrative of an interesting, amusing, or biographical incident"[6] and, "secret, private, or hitherto unpublished narratives or details of history"[7] (p. 116). He also refers to an anecdote as "a minute passage of private life". All descriptions fit our understanding of narratives in research.

The main reasons for collecting data in the form of narratives are to obtain data that are optimally undisturbed by the researcher, and to get a limited description of a certain event. In all kinds of research that involve informants the researcher, in one way or another, affects the data. In their study on the use of narratives in nursing research, Frid, Öhlén and Bergbom (2000) emphasize that narratives are created relationally. According to them, there is always an actual or imaged receiver of the narrative. At the very least, the data are influenced by the questions asked and the invitation proffered the informant. The use of this kind of narratives is however called for, when researchers want to obtain a description without getting involved in an interview dialogue or other kinds of methodical means that require the immediate presence of the researcher. As soon as the researcher and informant have come to an agreement, the informant who is supposed to reveal a narrative is then left relatively undisturbed by the researcher, who is absent when data are being developed. Researchers may also wish to limit the amount of information that is gathered. Giorgi (1989a, 1997) often uses narratives, and his method of analysis is developed to suit the use of narratives, that is, a limited amount of data.

Narratives are a powerful form of human communication. There is reason to believe, that narratives were passed along between generations long before proof of them were found on stone, clay, or papyrus. Narratives preserve accounts of lived experiences for succeeding generations, or different folk groups. A concrete example will illustrate this. A colleague of ours went to India. She told us a colorful story about the trip and several complications there

---

5   In the section on interviews we will also describe the use of narratives within interviews, but in this section we concentrate on narratives as monologues.

6   van Manen refers here to the Oxford dictionary.

7   van Manen refers here to the Webster dictionary.

including the toilet problem. In the part of India that she visited, it is the custom that during daytime women are not allowed to act in such a way that suggests they use toilets. There were two options, our friend told us, either to save this business till dark fell, which the native women did, or doing it in such a way that the doing was not observed. Our friend learned pretty quickly to dress in long skirts and could occasionally be found squatting down, looking at flowers or engaged in some other equally innocent activity. The story told us a lot about her hardships in a foreign country, but it also told us something important about the situation of women in that country.

Narratives can be either written or spoken. In the case of a verbal narrative, a tape-recorder of some kind is essential. van Manen (1990)[8] emphasizes the art of writing in human science research. "Writing fixes thought on paper", he says and points to the benefit of writing in the sense that it makes explicit experience that in some sense has been primarily internal (p. 125). This is a familiar occurrence in everyday life. One can have a letter clearly in mind so long as it is in the thought stage. But when one sits down to write the letter, all of a sudden it becomes problematic, requiring much pondering. But in the very act of writing, thoughts are loosed, and begin to solidify and become clear.

When a research informant is asked to write or tape-record a narrative, instructions given to the person must be carefully thought through, because there may not be an opportunity to request a second version. Informants should be directed to write as concretely, precisely and with as much detail as possible about the lived event, avoiding vague generalizations and the temptation to theorize. What is wanted is the lived experience, precisely as it is lived, no more, no less. For this reason, writing the narrative in first person captures an experience as lived more emphatically than third person.

Giorgi (1985) was interested in the phenomenon of learning, something that everyone experiences in their everyday world. He asked some people to describe, as carefully and in as detailed a manner as possible, a concrete situation where they had learned

---

8   van Manen's strong emphasis on writing in a way that makes it constitutive falls outside our understanding of writing.

something. One of Giorgi's research informants described how he had learned to ride a bicycle, another how she had learned how to make yogurt. From these narrative accounts of experience, it was possible to find a general description of learning.

Another example is a study that focused on nursing students' experiences of holistic health care (Dahlberg, 1992). Both interviews and short narratives were used to get data. Before writing their narratives the informants received the following information: Tell about an event within health care that you experienced as holistic care, for example, an episode when you were aware of yourself practicing holistic care. A variety of different descriptions resulted, all focusing on the lived experience of holistic health care, but within various contexts. A number of the narratives originated in district nurses' work in the patients' home environment, while others described the students' own experiences as patients or relatives of patients.

Narrated data can also be in the form of a diary. In this case the informant makes a note, for example, daily or weekly, about a certain phenomenon or event. An example where diary notes were used is a study of students' experiences with educational drama and its effects on their supervision during nursing education (Lepp, 1998). The students wrote a note after each weekly session, describing what they had experienced, how it had affected them, what they had learned, and their reflections during the actual session. These descriptions were analyzed with the intent of discovering what it means to participate in educational drama as a nursing student. When diary narrative are used, the researcher gets a series of written or taped notes or small stories from each informant. The quantity of data collected with diary narratives can be of the magnitude of data from interviews.

Narratives are often the preferable form for gathering data about critical situations. Critical incidents are those situations that remain as vivid and detailed memories over a long period of time. A good description of a critical incident is often more illuminating than any other type of description. An effective way to elicit such description is to ask the informant to describe a positive and/or a negative situation. For example, Drew (1986) asked patients to describe one positive and one negative experience with caregivers. Similarly, Sundström (1996) wanted to know how students experience confirmation during nursing education. The students were asked to write one detailed account of a concrete situation in their education when they had felt confirmed and one account when they had felt excluded rather than confirmed. Both studies resulted in a number of narratives in which the phenomenon of confirmation and its negative opposite were illuminated within a variety of contexts. Both studies produced descriptions of informants' experiences that were rich with recalled thoughts and emotions.

Useful narratives can be found outside the research arena. van Manen (1990) cites biographies as an excellent source of information about human experience. Although biographies are usually written to be entertaining as much as informative, they often contain such a wealth of detail that they are applicable as data for scientific analysis. A well-written biography offers as extensive a collection of data as that found in an empirical study. Because of the time constraints of full-time education, students can quite justifiably turn to literature for their data. For example, nursing students interested in how patients experience different forms of illness and accompanying health care have made use of non-fiction literature such as *Heartsounds*, (Lear, 1980). In addition, there is a plethora of autobiographies in which celebrities describe their illnesses as well as other accounts of the diseases for which there is currently no cure, such as HIV syndrome, AIDS, ALS, and Alzheimer's disease.

Fiction is an additional source of information. Classics such as Tolstoy's *The Death of Ivan Ilych*, or Dostoevsky's account of the phenomenon of human guilt are examples of data about the human condition. Novels that depict differing roles for men and women, or stories about life passages and particular historical periods are easily obtained. Almost any human experience such as silence, peace, rest, loss and loneliness have been described in fictional work.

Finally, narratives can stimulate dialogue about a particular topic. The tacit knowledge underlying professionals' response to violent patients was the focus of a recent study (Carlsson, Dahlberg & Drew, 2000). As an introduction to the interviews that followed, the research informants, psychiatric personnel were asked to describe an encounter they had with an aggressive patient that had ended positively for both of them. The recalled incidents, some having taken place as much as ten years earlier, had great impact on the informants. The narrative accounts of these encounters served as a warm-up to the subsequent interview, facilitating the informants' recall of emotions and thoughts. In this way the interview proceeded in the natural attitude to explore lived experience.

Interviews

In the introduction to his book on interviews, Kvale (1996) asks, "If you want to know how people understand their world and life, why not talk to them?" That is a good question. The desire to know how people experience their world is reason enough for research interviews. The scope of subject matter for interviewing is limited only by the researcher's and informant's hesitancy to embark on a particular topic.

Narratives enhance interviews, adding to their substance. There is, however, an important difference between a narrative that is produced solely by the informant, and the narrative from an interview. Because it is the result of a dialogue, the narrative of an interview is directly influenced by the researcher. Consequently, interviews are considered collaboratively produced narratives, a mutual product of researcher and informant, regardless of efforts by interviewers to minimize their impact on informants' responses. Still, even when a narrative is the result of solitary writing by an informant, it is subtly influenced by the researcher who requested it.

Research interviews are not unlike everyday conversation. However, our everyday conversations may or may not be open. When we engage in conversations with the intent of persuading others to change their opinions, or to try something new, we stand firmly within our own viewpoint. Such conversations are not open in the way that is necessary in research. Conversation that is open

> ... is a process of coming to an understanding. Thus it belongs to every true conversation that each person opens himself to the other, truly accepts his point of view and valid and transposes himself into the other to such an extent that he understands not the particular individual but what he says. What is to be grasped is the substantive rightness of his opinion, so that we can be with each other on the subject. (Gadamer, 1995, p. 385)

154

Lifeworld researchers go to "the things themselves" by way of interviews and turn to the research informant's lifeworld in order to explore a phenomenon of common interest. Lifeworld interviews are the means of listening to the voice of the lifeworld and at the same time strengthening it. The researcher's task is facilitating interviewees in telling their stories, and, as Gadamer said above, to "be with" the informant. Both interviewer and interviewee should understand the phenomenon better as a result of the interview. Comments such as, "I had not understood this so well before," and "This is funny, I have not thought about this in such a way before," are evidence that the interview was a success. Participating in a true lifeworld conversation has the effect of bringing interviewees closer to their own experience, expanding awareness and understanding.

The interviewee is engaged subjectively and is given a chance to express her/his unique experiences of the phenomenon of interest. The focal point of the interview is the way that the interviewee experiences the phenomenon and expresses its meaning. Nevertheless, the primary interest in lifeworld research is not just the person as informant, but the phenomenon. Gadamer (1995) explains:

> Where a person is concerned with the other as individuality – e.g., in a therapeutic conversation or the interrogation of a man accused of a crime – this is not really a situation in which two people are trying to come to an understanding. (p. 385)

Thus, if an interview is to be an authentic and open research conversation, the interview questions must be directed towards the phenomenon. Otherwise, if one is more interested in the informant as a person than the experience that the individual is trying to communicate, the ensuing conversation is not an authentic research activity, according to Gadamer. An open interview may be characterized in much the same way as a sporting event, where the emphasis is not on the players, but on the game itself. As a game, an interview takes place in and through us (Gadamer, 1995). In such an open interview there is abundant opportunity for reflection. The interview can move here and there, back and forth, but all the while guided by the rules of the game.

In lifeworld research an interview is considered dialogue, even common conversation, yet the researcher's questions are important. The questions and the way they are posed are crucial for research that seeks genuine insight into a person's experience. A true question is one that does not presuppose a particular reply, but reflects the questioner's awareness of not knowing the answer (Gadamer, 1995). The likelihood of discovering a true question is increased with a researcher's awareness of what s/he considers important and is able to see the assumptions contained therein. When such self-awareness is clear, the question that is formulated to guide the research is more likely to lead to genuine knowledge. Lifeworld researchers, understanding that they lack insight about the way that other people experience the world or a special aspect of it, craft research questions that open up that experience. Such questions, because they are authentic, allow for unexpected answers to emerge.

The reflective dialogue

The goal of a phenomenological interview is to get the interviewee to reflect on the phenomenon. Usually, the phenomenon is part of the interviewee's experience in some way or other, but without conscious deliberation; lacking articulation or explication as a "gestalt" it resides in the background of the individual's life (cf. Wertheimer, 1961). In order for the requisite reflection to occur, the two partners in the dialogue must have a common interest in deepening the subject. Kvale (1996) expresses this by saying that the interview should be an inter-action, a continual sharing and discussion of the different views of two people towards a common topic. This is the true meaning of the term interview (inter-view). In a research interview, however, the two perspectives are not of equal interest. It is the interviewee's perspective that has priority, and the interviewer's role is to support the interviewee's attempts to reflect.

Throughout an interview, as researchers we make a concerted effort to direct the informant's intentional consciousness. This means facilitating the individual's attention toward the phenomenon of interest and directing the interaction toward deeply anchored meanings, rather than superficial attitudes or commonly held beliefs. Meaningful reflection requires an interviewer to take nothing for granted, instead, persistently questioning and responding in such a way that facilitates and encourages the interviewee toward ever deepening layers of meaning.

A research interview, which aims at establishing a dialogue in which to reflect on a particular phenomenon, must be optimally open. In other words, researchers must learn how to manage their interviews so that they can monitor their own openness to the phenomenon, as it is expressed by the interviewee. Here optimal refers to finding a balance between a completely unstructured and a structured interview. Interviewing for the purpose of establishing a reflective dialogue is best unstructured, avoiding a designated question and answer format. Instead a researcher's task is to cultivate productive dialogue that addresses the phenomenon as deeply and thoroughly as possible. With this goal in mind, questions and comments should be a matter of the researcher's spontaneity and engagement during the interview.

Limitations of an interview as dialogue

The open interview has, however, limitations. A research dialogue means that the researcher and the interviewee do not participate under the same conditions. An interview dialogue differs from everyday dialogue since the interviewer maintains the initiative and controls the interview. The interview cannot be about just whatever comes up. The researcher is not interested in the interviewee's whole world of experience, only that of a particular phenomenon. In an interview, researchers are not either as willing to share their opinions about the phenomenon in question as they might during an everyday conversation with colleagues. Furthermore, researchers typically decide when an interview will take place, where it will be, how long it may last, etc.

To pretend that research informants are on the same footing is not, according to Theman (1979), advisable. He says, that in a dialectic relationship where the initiative and the superior knowledge of the issue, and the control of time limits and economical benefits, all end up in the hands of one person there exists no equality. "As a matter of fact", he says, "not being a genuine person, in a situation where this is demanded, means missing the point, that is, the level of reality claimed for" (p. 15). Steps can be taken that reduce the disparity between researcher and interviewee, but the researcher always has the final word. Even if researchers ask informants to indicate preference about time and place for the interview, they still remain on unequal footing.

Sequence of the interview

In order to engender an open dialogue an interview needs to have some form of focus. Even so-called unstructured interviews are not totally bereft of structure in the way that a casual conversation is; one or the other person leads.

At the beginning of a research interview the interviewer has the initiative. At this point the sphere interest is revealed and limited by the *opening question,* which ideally is a balance between structure and openness. The question should be simply and clearly worded so that the interviewee feels invited to reflect and competent to begin describing her or his world. Since many lifeworld interviews are about everyday life situations in some way or another, an example of a suitable opening question might be: "How is a day in general for you?" Such a question is common place for most people and at the same time there is a suggestion included, that the interview will be about lived experience. Subsequently, a more focused question might be, "What is it like to live with diabetes?" Any life experience can be substituted, for example, the experience of living alone, or chasing a partner. The goal here is to direct the interviewee's intentional thought toward a certain area of interest. As the interview proceeds, several sub-areas may need to be explored. Each time a new sub-area emerge, a new, directing opening question is asked, "What is it like...? However, a warning here for lifeworld researchers: avoid any sort of rigid adherence to protocol rather than spontaneous engagement that will, in the end, despite any detours or digressions, elicit description far better than an overly calculated approach.

Once the beginning phase of an interview is over, or a sub-area is introduced, the initiative is handed over to the interviewee. Skilled interviewers know that at this point their role is to follow the lead of the interviewee, to support and encourage self-disclosure with matter-of-fact, non-reactive responses to whatever the interviewee divulges, and if necessary providing assurance that there are no right or wrong answers. The questioning now should be for clarification, or for the purpose of inviting expansion, for example, "Can you say some more about that?" or "Can you give me an example?" Always the goal is to facilitate deepening reflection and articulation. To be avoided is any sort of conventional conversation about expected subjects in expected ways. Initially, informants may want to give us what they think we are after in an interview, or may echo prevailing social clichés or jargon. An experienced interviewer learns how to redirect informants to authentic responses that arise from lived experience.

Accordingly, during this data-gathering phase, nothing new is introduced. Instead the strategy is responses that lead to in-depth exploration of the interviewee's recollections and disclosure, as well as the manner in which they are expressed, that is, clarifying and attending to the informant's emotions that accompany disclosure. The goal is to move towards the unexpected, the unknown, and unreflected, in order to reflect upon and disclose the phenomenon. The interviewer's task is to devise questions and directions that facilitate the deepening and clarifying of thoughts and ideas, thereby assisting informants in revealing their experiential life.

Due to our own experience of conducting interviews in lifeworld research, we want to emphasize the productive tactic to ask for clarification of informants' understanding. Even leading questions, if used judiciously, can be of use as Kvale (1996, p. 151) demonstrates with an excerpt from Shakespeare:

HAMLET: *Do you see yonder cloud that's almost in shape of a camel?*

POLONIUS: *By th' mass, and 'tis like a camel indeed.*

HAMLET: *Methinks it is like a weasel.*

POLONIUS: *It is back'd like a weasel.*

HAMLET: *Or like a whale?*

POLONIUS: *Very like a whale.*

HAMLET: ... *(Aside) They fool me to the top of my bent.*

(Hamlet, act III, scene 2)

By way of his questioning technique, Hamlet does not learn much about how Polonius actually experiences the cloud, but he discovers that Polonius' statements are not to be trusted, which was the real goal of the interview. Sometimes as researchers we must test informants' understanding. We may offer alternative ideas as a way of challenging their statements, inviting correction or expansion. The goal of such an exchange in an interview is to clarify the underpinnings of the interviewee's beliefs or opinions. In so doing, we increase the likelihood that we will understand the interviewee's intentions, which in turn increases our understanding of the phenomenon we are investigating.

With the exception of the first opening question, with which interview is commenced, both of the phases just described, the request for reflection followed by support of disclosure, occur repeatedly throughout the interview as new themes or ideas appear. Less experienced interviewers may feel unsure of their ability to create an effective balance between structure and an open forum. A useful tactic in this case is a list of prompts to which the interviewer can refer to ensure that important areas are not forgotten. However, prompts serve only as help for one's memory; they are not intended as a list of questions to be asked verbatim. In keeping with the principle of engagement and spontaneity, actual questions asked during the interview dialogue are formulated in the moment they are asked.

Immediacy in interviews

In chapter 3 we specified openness as a close and immediate relation to the informant. Researchers who are able to infuse their interviews with a sense of immediacy are more likely to engender the openness that is necessary for gathering in-depth data. An interview has this immediacy when both persons are present to each other in the deepest sense, each concentrating on the phe-

160

nomenon, as well as what is going on between them. Immediacy in an interpersonal relationship has the same quality as the "here-and-now," to borrow a phrase from Gestalt therapy, or group therapy lexicon. There is an intensity about their exchange, which arises from the authenticity of the dialogue. An immediate, here and now atmosphere in an interview precludes the use of any of the second-hand thinking of clichés and faddish speech. Maintaining this sort of concentration, however, is not easily done. Inexperienced interviewers frequently find themselves distracted with the decisions needed to keep the interview on track, or by the intrusion of outside noises, interruptions by others, and other such distractions. For whatever reason, when immediacy is diminished, openness is jeopardized.

If immediacy pervades the interview, an informant is more likely to follow the interviewer's request/direction to recall and ponder aloud the phenomenon of interest, which in turn increases the possibility that meaning will develop and expand. This is what we want to happen, but sometimes interviews digress into minutia or into peripheral topics, which can present interviewers with the difficult decision whether or not to redirect the interview. The best course of action is to listen carefully and judge the relevancy of the digression. Sometimes in order to make a particular point, an individual must begin with a story, but just as likely an interviewee, uncertain what to say, relates whatever comes to mind. The interviewer's task then, becomes weighing the benefits of following the stream of associations, or limiting the interview to the designated topic. An atmosphere of immediacy facilitates the decisions that must be made about the progress of the interview. Decisions are made more spontaneously and naturally as a result of the mutual support that comes from two individuals who are present for each other.

Dramatized interviews

There are various ways to deepen an interview. One that we have already mentioned is asking an interviewee to relate a particular incident, an incident of lived experience. However, sometimes this directive is not enough. For many reasons simply talking about a particular experience does not adequately convey its significance. An approach that draws on the information from the subjective body is needed; dramatizing recalled events is such an approach to interviewing. Psychodrama, created and developed by Moreno (Fox, 1997) is one form of dramatic enactment as is educational drama (Lepp, 1998; O'Toole, 1992). Gestalt therapy (Perls, 1969) uses a similar technique. Dramatic techniques, borrowed from psychodrama, have been described by Drew (1993), and by Carlsson, Dahlberg, Drew and Lützen (2001).

Re-enactment interviewing is most commonly done with two persons, the interviewer and the informant. In some instances a full psychodrama may be produced if the informant has friends or acquaintances who agree to act as auxiliaries. In either case, once the action portion is completed, auxiliaries have been thanked and dismissed, the interview proceeds in the typical format as a personal, face-to-face interaction in which the events just portrayed serve as a beginning point for the dialogue between interviewer and interviewee.

Re-enactment begins with "warming-up" and "setting the scene" (Drew, 1993). The warm-up period and subsequent scene-setting expedite recall by activating feelings and thoughts associated with a particular event, for example, an encounter with an aggressive and threatening patient (Carlsson et al., 2001). Once the informant is immersed in scene of the recalled event, the directive should always be to "show" what happened rather than to permit the informant to simply talk about it: "What do you want to show me about this moment?" At this point, it is important to keep the re-enacted dialogue in the present tense, which increases the intensity of the experience. Instead of, "I did thus and so..." the informant is directed to say, "I am doing thus ....". Thoughts and feelings are more intense in the 'here and now' action of reenactment, because they are being directly accessed in the body, which is a repository for memories and emotions. As informants soliloquize about the recalled event they often are startled to find themselves experiencing memories and emotions of which they were previously unaware.

Re-enactment interviewing was used in the study of caregivers' successful encounters with aggressive patients mentioned above (Carlsson et al., 2001). Re-enacting past events helped the inter-

162

viewees to remember in great detail what transpired between themselves and their threatening patients. The caregivers in this study stated that re-enactment brought up feelings about the event in such as way that they once again experienced the encounters. For example, in the moment of re-enacting the bodily movements with which they protected themselves, the feelings of that moment were aroused, and the internal dialogue that they had had with themselves in the moment were suddenly relived. Subsequently, in the seated portion of the interview, these feelings were easily expressed and described.

Psychodramatic re-enactment provides a highly effective way to ground phenomenological interviewing by recreating the context in which the phenomenon appeared. When conducted by a skilled researcher, preferably experienced in the use of re-enactment, this method brings forth a rich panoply of detail about the physical setting and the interactions that took place, as well as bringing into the present moment the emotions that the informant experienced (Drew, 1993). Re-enactment interviewing provides access to the embodied memory and enhances the engagement and immediacy necessary for generating meaningful data. It is a method that allows us to collect intensely rich and comprehensive data by tapping into the wisdom of the body. In research that has a lifeworld approach, methods that emphasize the subjective body are immeasurably effective for capturing the phenomenon of interest. Yet such interviewing is commonly neglected, in part, because special training is necessary for using re-enactment interviewing techniques. It would behoove us to find ways to promote and support training for interviewing in human science research that incorporates human bodily expression. Interviewers who are interested in acquiring such skills can seek training through the established psychodrama certification organizations in both Europe[9] and the United States.

---

9   In Europe, it may be easier to get the actual training in educational drama
     workshops.

Other supportive sources

As researcher one has to be open and flexible, allowing experiences and phenomena to show themselves in forms that suit them best. Another interviewing strategy, often used in Gestalt therapy, is making use of informants' visual art works (Perls, 1969). For some individuals it is easier to express themselves in a drawing or a painting than in language. Such is often the case with children. A drawing is an effective beginning point for understanding the meaning of an event for a child. Typically, a drawing will lead the interview dialogue directly into a lived event, thus giving the child as well as the interviewer access to the lifeworld. One could say that a drawing is the midpoint between the lived experience and its verbal expression. The same can be said for poetry or music, which can be more expressive of everyday life than prose. As in the use of dramatization, the interview proceeds in the traditional seated, face-to-face manner following the presentation of art work, poetry or music. The interviewer strives to deepen the interview and to get rich descriptions by way of the supportive sources of data.

Preparations for an interview and its after-work

Since the interview is understood as a dialogue, a research conversation, the questions that are asked do not follow a prescribed format. However, the same content must guide the formation of questions, that is, the same phenomenon must direct the dialogue of all interviews in one study. To assure that the same information is requested in all interviews, an interviewer memorandum can be prepared, which lists a few question *areas* that are of interest. The actual questions that are asked come from the interviewer's spontaneity of the moment. Again, we caution that adhering to an overly detailed memorandum has a deleterious effect on openness and immediacy. Instead of being free to be open and engaged with the interviewee and the phenomenon, the interviewer finds her or himself concerned instead with following the schedule of questions.

In any case an interviewer should have a fairly clear conception of the phenomenon before the interviews begin. A too vague grasp

164

of the phenomenon and the main areas of focus can lead to an interview that is about everything under the sun. The importance of a carefully crafted opening question cannot be over stated. In addition, researchers must have a good grasp of their own pre-understanding of the phenomenon, and of the suspending procedure. "What has been my experience of this phenomenon and what do I know or don't know about it?" What is it that I want to know?" A personal journal is especially useful for reflecting on one's pre-understanding, as well as documenting the experience of the study. As we have said, a total bracketing of one's pre-understanding is not possible. But self-reflection done with the idea of restraining one's pre-understanding is an important help in separating one's experiences from the research informant's. As such, self-reflection enhances the study's validity claims (Drew, 1989).

Good sound equipment is important. An audio tape recorder should have conference capability so that voices are captured from any place in the interview room. This is especially crucial for re-enactment interviewing where participants move about, or when voice volume falls with intense emotions or at moments of uncertainty. Well-equipped researchers will bring pencils, crayons, and paper if drawing is anticipated. Additional items are drinking water and tissues. Interviewers who are trained to do re-enactment may want to include some common props such as pillows, blanket, cardboard boxes, etc. as accessories for dramatization.

Regardless if interviewees enter a study through telephone contact, or letter, or direct contact with the researcher, they must be given the information that participation is voluntary. They have to be assured that their privacy will be guarded, that the researcher will keep in confidence information that would reveal their identities. This is done by pledging that transcriptions will contain no proper names, addresses, etc. and by destroying the tape recordings after transcription. Equally important for patients or students who participate in research is that their future health care or academic standing will not be influenced[10].

---

10 We want to emphasize that institutions have different rules for conducting research. Researchers have responsibility for understanding and adhering to these rules and restrictions.

The setting for an interview is at the discretion of the individuals involved. Sometimes it is advantageous for the researcher to come to the interviewee's home, where s/he feels safe and comfortable. This was the case in a study of visually handicapped (Wenestam & Dahlberg, 1990). In an educational study (Dahlberg, 1992) students were interviewed at the colleges where they were enrolled. In any case, the primary consideration is the comfort and convenience of the interviewee. Secondary considerations are extraneous noise and disruptions.

Transcribing recorded interviews

A research interview is usually audio-taped and transcribed into text so that data are more accessible to analysis. Good transcribing technique includes non-verbal information, such as periods of silence, sighing, coughing, laughing, crying and hesitations. However, meticulous transcription of this sort can be very expensive. Typically, researchers train their transcribers regarding the extent of inclusiveness that they want in the transcriptions. If a researcher's budget for transcriptions is limited, the non-verbal nuances of the interview may be omitted. In this case, the interviewer should listen to the tapes while reading the transcripts and note the aspects of the interview situation that were not captured in language. One way to accomplish this is to instruct the transcriber to leave an empty column at the right side of every page which can be used for notes[11]. Double spacing between the interviewer's and the participant's comments is also helpful. The transcript should appear much like the dialogue of a novel, with each new statement beginning at left margin.

Giorgi (1989a) has pointed out that research data are always less than the research situation. No situation can be totally captured in language. Even with video-recording, the actuality of the lived interview is diminished:

> Recording a conversation on a sound tape is better than memory, and recording on videotape is better because body language is

11   This space is also used for analysis notes.

included, but one should not be deceived into thinking that one has everything. What becomes data is only an aspect of the situation. (Giorgi, 1989a, p. 43)

Kvale (1996) discusses the interview and its transition to text. In a similar manner to Giorgi, Kvale points out the inherent failure of language to impart the entirety of a lived situation. Such loss is due in part to the limits of language as a means of depicting lived experience, as well as the human limitations of the transcriber who can only approximate a situation that s/he was not involved in originally. Kvale cites a study in which one tape recorded interview was transcribed into several differing versions of the actual event, and advises that the best arrangement is that researchers do their own transcribing. If this is not feasible, then transcriptions should be read by the researcher while listening to the tapes, as soon as possible after the interview.

Ethical reflections on interviewing

Inexperienced researchers may be startled by the intensity of informants' emotional reactions during an interview, especially when re-enactment is used. Anticipating that tears, anguish, fear and anger may arise during an interview, researchers are well-advised to be prepared to stop and wait supportively, as the individual experiences the feelings and makes some sense of the moment. It is not unusual that interviewees appreciate an interview as the first time that they have had an opportunity to express certain thoughts and ideas that are important to them. In the study of sight-impaired persons (Wenestam & Dahlberg, 1990) interviewees expressed just that feeling. Despite painful emotions that resurged during the interview, they were glad for the opportunity to talk to someone who was willing to listen about the experience of being visually handicapped in our society. Although emotional relief and insight are not the primary purpose of an interview, it nevertheless offers the possibility of working through the feelings and memories associated with past experiences. Perhaps not surprisingly, many interviewees in healthcare studies report that even though they have received extensive healthcare over a long period of time, the research interview was the first time anyone had asked them how they felt about the illness and its effect on their lives. That an interviewee talks about experiences that they have shared in everyday conversation, indicates that an open and immediate engagement was established between themselves and the researcher.

This said, the ethical principle "do no harm," or non-maleficence, poses the questions: Is it likely that interviewing someone about a painful experience will harm them? How should the researcher handle such a situation? Perls (1969) offers some advice: People often have strong psychological defense mechanisms that have protected them in some fashion, but which also create problems. In favorable circumstances, when we no longer need them, we can let go of those defenses. But, Perls reminds us, every person maintains these defenses as long as they are necessary. Therefore, as researchers, we can trust in every person's ability to choose whether to maintain or to let go of a defense. Indeed, experienced researchers know that no amount of persuasion will entice a reluctant interviewee to talk about something that feels too dangerous to open up. This reluctance is to be respected.

One way to handle a situation, in which an interviewee comes up against a fearful or painful topic, is to make the observation to them that they have hit upon something, which seems of importance. The researcher may suggest that returning to it at a different time or with a different person is alternative. Giving an interviewee permission to withhold thoughts about something intensely important to them acknowledges their sovereignty as human beings. It may also convey a sense of hope for eventual relief of painful feelings. This notwithstanding, it is the researcher's responsibility to provide support for as long as necessary while the interviewee is disturbed or distressed. The researcher should be sure that the interviewee has regained composure and a measure of control before the interview concludes. It may also be necessary to refer the interviewee to a counselor following the interview.

Fieldwork and observation

Openness and sensitivity towards, and thus a nearness to, the phenomenon being studied characterize the lifeworld approach. This means, among other things, that the research method and the questions that are asked can never be decided beforehand. Sensitivity to "the things themselves" demands that the nature of "the things" influences the design of the research questions and choice of method(s). Such is the case if the phenomenon belongs to a mixed field that includes the intersubjective in any respect, and perhaps a number of different situations and contexts. Interviews and written descriptions might not be adequate to capture the phenomenon fully. Instead the search for the phenomenon may extend to a larger area, and, for example, a ward or a classroom must be included in the study. This approach is commonly referred to as participant observation and fieldwork, a research method originally developed by anthropologists and ethnographers.

Anthropology and ethnography[12]

The methodologies of anthropology and ethnography (and ethnology sometimes) are often used in healthcare and educational research and are regarded by some as synonymous. Some theoreticians see anthropology as the metatheoretical and theoretical framework for ethnography, which in turn includes the empirical research methods (Ploug Hansen, 1992). Recent branches of anthropology and ethnography in healthcare are referred to as ethnocaring (Leininger, 1985, 1991), healthcare anthropology (Sachs, 1992a, b), and healthcare educational anthropology (Pilhammar Andersson, 1996).

According to an encyclopedia (Nationalencyklopedin, 1989) the term anthropology comes from the Greek 'a'nthropos', which means 'human', and 'logi'a', which means 'teaching', 'science', which in turn comes from 'lo'gos', which means 'word'. In other words, it is the teaching and science of humankind. Traditionally,

---

12 For deeper descriptions of anthropology and ethnography we recommend the reader to search for specialist literature in that field.

anthropology includes the study of mankind's development and physical characteristics, as well as the study of the world's different cultures and societal types. In the American tradition, archeology and linguistics belong to anthropology. Anthropology is also found in the lexicons of theology and philosophy, for example, in Luther's and Hegel's anthropologies. It also appears in pedagogy (Kullberg, 1996) and medicine (Sachs, 1992a). Other influential anthropologists have been Mead, Malinowski, Boas, and Durkheim, to name a few.

Ethnography is a recently coined term for what was earlier known as cultural and social anthropology that examines social and cultural structures and processes. During the 1980's ethnography was increasingly used in healthcare and educational research. The term ethnography comes from the Greek 'e'thnos', which means 'folk', and 'graphia', which means 'description', and comes from 'gra'pho', 'write'. Leininger (1985) defines ethnography as: "The systematic process of observing, detailing, describing, documenting, and analyzing the lifeways or particular patterns of a culture (or subculture) in order to grasp the lifeways or patterns of the people in their familiar environment" (p. 35).

Anthropology, as the study of the biological, historical, cultural, and social aspects of humans, has made a unique contribution to the human sciences with its research methods and theories (Ploug Hansen, 1992). Ploug Hansen regards it as a basic science about society and culture, both globally and locally. She considers it a primary research approach for any culture regardless of its locale. Once thought of as a research strategy for foreign cultures, anthropology is now an accepted and respected research mode for limited studies in familiar cultures. This comes as no surprise. One's own culture has as much research value as a foreign culture. Thus, the cultures of both healthcare and education are suitable and interesting fields for anthropological studies.

The choice of research strategies depends upon the nature of the culture to be studied. In a foreign culture researchers are strangers, continuously bombarded with new impressions and experiences as unfamiliar phenomena appear, are experienced, and analyzed. In this case, the art of research involves moving in for a close look to gather information for subsequent research, and concomitantly, distancing oneself from the flow of information in order not to be

170

drowned by it. Additionally, researchers in a foreign culture do not share the same pre-understanding with the culture's native citizens and this can be a source for misunderstanding.

Researchers who study their own culture typically have contextual knowledge even if specific knowledge about a certain area is lacking. An example of contextual knowledge is the nurse researcher who wanted to investigate a physiotherapeutic area of care in which she had no prior experience. In order to acquire a certain amount of contextual pre-understanding she registered as a patient at the institution and attended for several months before beginning her research (Dahlberg, 1997b).

In one's own culture the phenomena are often as self-evident and natural for the researcher as water is for a fish. So, in addition to conceptually "stepping back" from the topic or problem in order to gain perspective on the situation, researchers must restrain their own past experiences of the phenomenon. However, often we are not clear what needs to be bracketed. Therefore, we must look for something that has been outside our immediate awareness, so-called tacit or practical knowledge that we have heretofore taken for granted. But these hidden and tacit parts of our experience do not lend themselves to easy detection.

Anthropological research, especially within one's own culture, gives us the clearest example of the elusive task of remaining at once both integrated and removed from the phenomenon that we study. Because the natural surroundings of the research object are also the researchers' natural surroundings, anthropologists and ethnographers often find it easy to get in touch with the informants and the phenomena of study. At the same time they learn to distance themselves from the object of study in order to scientifically analyze and understand it. Accordingly, anthropologists and ethnographers have to learn how to examine their own participation in and understanding of the field they are studying. Such a delicate balancing process quickly teaches one that the field of study is never fully grasped.

The complexity of anthropological and ethnographical research is not diminished by the fact that it lacks an explicitly expressed research methodology. It is often described as practical research in which the consequences of ontological and epistemological assumptions are left unacknowledged. According to Kullberg

(1996), this lack of attention to ontology and epistemology is the legacy of a field in which research methodology was self-taught and passed along to other researchers, who then carried out their own studies based on the earlier self-taught models. Aside from its invisible epistemology, there is no standard for the field's methodological processes, resulting in great variations of methodological descriptions in published reports. Kullberg comments, that even nowadays the methodological sections in many anthropological and ethnographical works are treated summarily, and she gives a preliminary explanation as to why this is so:

> An experience I had when I began working with ethnography was exactly what the two English sociologists Martyn Hammersley and Paul Atkinson (1987) express, namely that ethnography uses reality's own methods and techniques, but refine these to use them in systematic knowledge seeking. I experienced in my ethnography training, that I could use my experience from my years as an active teacher. (p. 15)

The quote above is illustrative of the common approach of anthropology and ethnography to the minimal methodological difference between the practical and the professional, in this case, educational versus scientific methods.

In Ploug Hansen's (1992) understanding, anthropology is described as being composed of both a "thought space and a method space" (p. 490). The thought space, she says, refers to the understanding and description of the universal as well as the particular or unique in the human's social and cultural life. Ploug Hansen stresses the point that it is important to keep a kind of tension between the knowledge of the universal and the knowledge of the unique. The thought space has been gradually composed of anthropology's accumulated knowledge, the theories as well as the afore-mentioned self-understanding. This frame of knowledge supports anthropological fieldwork.

Fieldwork

The essence of anthropological and ethnographic research is fieldwork. But what does the term field mean? In this discussion, field refers to the intersubjective, that is, more than one subject. Further, field means a social context of some sort, that is, the subjects in the field are socially connected. For example, a field could be a health care unit, or a classroom, or any other of numerous social institutions. Every field has cultural attributes of some type (recall the chapter on paradigm theory). In order to understand a field a researcher must understand its cultural attributes. A field could therefore also be understood as a "culture." For our purposes here, field and culture are interchangeable terms.

As in other lifeworld research, fieldwork is never commenced with hypotheses or specific theories. On the contrary, the central tenet of field research is to begin as free of, and unprejudiced by, theory as possible. As we have pointed out before, however, no researcher can approach a research area completely "empty" or "pure." Everyone has some form of pre-understanding of the research area, including researchers in the field. There are always meta-theories as well as general theories such as health care knowledge, psychological, sociological, medical, and/or educational knowledge, that influence the researcher's world view, the worldview of the sciences, as well as the ordinary persons who are the focus of the research.

The first part of fieldwork is thus unstructured. A fieldworker does not know immediately exactly what should be studied, because within any field there are countless phenomena to be considered. It is only after some time spent in the field that interesting and relevant questions could be formed and formal data collection can begin. This means that researchers themselves are their most important tools. By participating in the field to be studied, the conditions for studying are created. As Ploug Hansen (1992) expresses it, the researcher stands "always between her/his data and reality" (p. 489). In addition to emphasizing the researcher as subject, Ploug Hansen also puts forward the idea that data are something created by the researcher. Data do not exist ready-made, "out there in reality", for the researcher to gather in as if picking flowers[13]. Instead, the field that the researcher observes and describes becomes data when the researcher notes something as interesting and for that reason observes and describes it.

---

13 This idea of data-gathering is valid also for other means of method than fieldwork.

Because there is no standard definition of suitable fieldwork methods, both qualitative methods and quantitative methods are used. The most common methods are participant observation and qualitative interview, which together comprise the methodological basis for fieldwork. Various types of written narratives, for example diaries, are also sources of data. Likewise, video recordings, questionnaires and drawings are often applied in this field of research. The use of different techniques of data gathering to capture as many aspects as possible of the phenomena under investigation is often referred to as methodological triangulation.

Interviewing has already been described. Here we will note only that more informal interviews are often appropriate within fieldwork. Instead of formally scheduled interviews, a fieldworker may engage the people encountered in a particular location in spontaneous dialogue, without tape-recording the interaction. However, even informal interviews should be conducted with attention to openness and the necessary suspension of presuppositions.

Participant observation

van Manen (1990) describes participant observation as a procedure where lived experience can be examined. He refers to it as "close observation" (p. 68) in order to emphasize the difference between phenomenological observation and the more experimentally oriented observation of the social sciences, which are characterized by studying the phenomenon "from a distance". van Manen believes that, instead of distancing oneself with one-way mirrors or a secluded observation protocol, for example, researchers in the human sciences should enter into informants' domain in order to obtain information about their world. Seen this way, observation is a method that begins with a lifeworld approach that demands a researcher get close to the phenomenon as a field of knowledge.

Typically, fieldwork begins with observation so that researchers can get a sense of a particular group's culture or social life, the way that their lives transpire with respect to their work and their routines of daily living. Field observation is the better choice of method at this point because individual interviews or written narratives offer a limited view of a society. Cultures are created by the people within it. If the aim is to create a new culture and a new tradition the first step ought to be an illumination of the culture and tradition that is. Having been created by caregivers, patients, educators and students, the cultures of health care and education can be changed by them too. The way to a changed health care reality is through creating a new culture and new tradition, says Eriksson (1986). The same can obviously be said today about both the health care culture and the educational culture.

In order to improve and move on within a certain culture one must first understand that culture, in all of its complexity, with a method that acknowledges the intentionalities of individuals, their lived experience of the culture, and, as far as it is possible, the culture itself. Participant observation provides an interior perspective where one can see and come to understand phenomena in their natural setting. Interviewing teachers and students gives us a sense of the classroom milieu. But by observing the actual interaction, in the moment, between teachers and students we are privy to information that may never have been revealed in an interview.

The size of the field that one studies depends on the purpose of the research. It might be a country's entire health culture, or just a part of that culture, such as nurses' educational program (Pilhammar Andersson, 1992). It could also be something specific such as women's development as mothers as seen from a midwifery perspective (Bergum, 1992). Observation is a valuable alternative when for various reasons it may be difficult to conduct interviews or to obtain written narratives. According to van Manen (1990) study of small children is one such example:

> So to gain access to the experience of young children, it may be important to play with them, talk to them, puppeteer, paint, draw, follow them into their play spaces and into the things they do while you remain attentively aware of the way it is for the children. (p. 68)

Studies that include older children are also supported by observation.

Preparing for observation

Apprenticeship and supervision are important in all research training. In particular, the techniques associated with observation are best learned by doing. Just as no two interviews are exactly the same, the nature of fieldwork is unpredictable, serendipitous, and often ambiguous. There is no method that anticipates every imaginable instance of fieldwork. On the contrary, we have only a few concrete and practical bits of advice to pass along to those preparing for fieldwork. In doing so, we draw on the epistemology that is the foundation of this book.

Every researcher in the field approaches that field with some sort of pre-understanding. Either one has had personal and intimate experience of the field, or one's pre-understanding stems from the literature of the field. As in all research, it is to the researcher's advantage to be acquainted with published research reports and other types of literature regarding the field to be studied. As Gadamer (1995) has given us to understand, pre-understanding is a main ingredient in the development of knowledge. Despite the fact that the notion of pre-understanding is not a common part of anthropological or ethnographical research protocols, we call the reader's attention to the importance of adopting an attitude of self-scrutiny that supports a reflective approach and to restrain the pre-understanding, not only in the preparation phase, but throughout fieldwork.

Research in fields that are strictly regulated, such as healthcare or education, require meticulous planning. Gaining permission from an institutional research board (IRB) or another form of research ethical committee to conduct research can be a time-consuming process. Taking time to learn the particular regulations of the IRB from whom one seeks permission and then carefully preparing the proposal will make a timely response from the board more likely. As a written document, a good research proposal contains a thorough description of the anticipated procedures that will be carried out by the researcher. Typically, proposals give background and theoretical justification for the study, then a detailed account of the method that will be used to collect and analyze data. The members of an IRB are interested in the procedural details, but function primarily as protective agents for persons who will participate in

176

the study. Often ethical considerations are given inadequate attention in research proposals. A common shortfall is lack of descriptive detail about how participants will be identified and approached, as well as the nature of the relationship between researcher and participant. At the very least, there should be adequate description of the concrete measures, such as destruction of data that will be taken to protect the privacy of the persons who agree to participate. But equally important is evidence in the proposal of the researcher's obligation to the participants themselves as persons placing their trust in the researcher's commitment to treat them as sovereigns of their own lives.

Pilhammar Andersson (1996) emphasizes the importance of one whom she refers to as a "gate-keeper," that is, someone in the field who can facilitate the researcher's entry into the field and its social network. Hammersley and Atkinson (1987) understand gatekeepers as "actors with control over key resources and avenues of opportunity" (p. 38). Such gatekeepers "exercise control at and during key phases" and can, consequently, be valuable people for field working researchers. However, they can also hinder the research because of their own vested interest in seeing that the researcher gains as favorable an impression as possible of the field.

It is also of crucial importance to carefully consider one's role as researcher, when planning fieldwork (Pilhammar Andersson, 1996). One cannot assume the neutrality of this role. As a field researcher we become involved in various activities in the field of study, encountering persons who may want to draw us in or keep us out of these activities. In all cases it is important to be clear about one's role because fieldwork occupies the researcher in a more obvious way than any other type of research. Pilhammar Andersson relates in her preface that she had not understood how totally involved and engaged she would become the course of the years in a particular study. Neither had she considered how much energy and effort would be needed to conduct and complete the study. Similarly, Kullberg (1996) points out problems with the researcher role in fieldwork. In her viewpoint, fieldwork and participant observation are suited to a certain type of individual, one "who likes, wants and is capable of carrying through these contextual, reflexive, continuing, and extended (longitudinal) studies" (p. 67). These words by Pilhammar Andersson and Kullberg, both experienced in the fieldwork research, are important to consider for those who plan observational studies.

Likewise, Leininger (1985, 1991) shares her long and deep experience from this particular research, that is more complex and more complicated to learn than any other method. She and other researchers of like mind, emphasize the importance of maintaining the researcher/observer role. It can be temptingly easy for a teacher, for example, to revert to the teaching role while conducting education research, thus relinquishing researcher identity and its objective perspective. The caveat here, of course, is to be wary when conducting research in one's own territory, for example at one's place of employment.

Realization of fieldwork and observation

The beginning of fieldwork is dominated by observation. The researcher has to learn about a perhaps completely unknown field of activity. Here all the senses come into use and the researcher sees, listens, smells, touches and tastes, in short, uses every perceptual ability to get a picture of the research area. Subsequently, the researcher participates to an ever increasing degree in the activities of the field. This is when a more systematic approach to the study of the field becomes necessary, for example, one may begin to collect information about how people react to the researcher's presence. It is also appropriate to begin to identify persons who may be able to offer important information about the field. These individuals are typically referred to as key informants and may change as the course of the study proceeds.

Initially, everything is of interest when one first embarks upon fieldwork, but before long one's focus settles on specific areas, people or activities. So called "critical situations"[14], where events have made deep impressions on the informants in the situation, provide points of interest. When the field becomes familiar the scope of the research can be enlarged and other data gathering strategies such

14 By critical situation is meant here a decisive, cumulating, serious, exciting, curious, etc., situation that "stands out" from the everyday activity in the field of study.

as interviews and written narratives can be added to observation. The point is that all methods and techniques are potentially fruitful. Selecting the best method depends on the research problem, the goals of the study, and the nature of the field.

There are various strategies for taking field notes (see for example, Glaser & Strauss, 1980; Hammersley & Atkinson, 1983; Leininger, 1985; Kullberg, 1996; Pilhammar Andersson, 1996). Whether they are hand written or tape-recorded, notes are made as meticulously as the situation allows and always as concretely as possible. This means recording observed events as raw data, without interpretation. As in the observation and participation phases, a researcher must view the collected data as though from a distance, which often facilitates possibilities for new or complementing observations, and new strategies.

Even when every effort is made to avoid entanglement with what one is studying, involvement beyond the boundaries of good field protocol sometimes occurs. Researchers cannot help being emotionally affected with what they observe in the field, and it is all too easy to take a simplistic attitude toward the notion of maintaining a neutral researcher role. Most experienced researchers find it advantageous to postpone analysis until a certain distance from the activity has occurred. Ploug Hansen (1992) writes:

> Throughout my whole fieldwork it was clear that the observation situations in the oncological department could be described only to a very little extent while I was in the department. First in the evening, when I had gotten a little distance to the field, when the actual experiences had retreated into the background, was it possible to reflect about what had occurred. (p. 488)

It is a good advice to try to just stay as open as possible during the time of observation, and leave the more analytic reflections to situations when the researcher has some distance to the observations.

There is the temptation in field studies to "continue forever," to follow new leads and experiences that expand the focus of the field. It is, therefore, important to be able to conclude one's work. Often an advisor or colleague outside the research project can see more clearly a logical end point.

Ethical reflections on observing

The nature of this type of research is such that informants may, at worst, be coerced into divulging aspects of their lives that would ordinarily be private, or at least, may experience a sense of unease that they cannot express. The researcher's position of being immersed in and simultaneously removed from the field that they study is both a necessary, yet potentially disturbing state for both them and their informants. But there is no help for it. If the aim is to be open and sensitive to the phenomena of research it is simply not possible to avoid the often paradoxical complexities of the personal worlds into which we step as researchers. Because we do not rely on lock-step research protocols, we are obligated to be mindful of the ultimate sovereignty of those who let us into their worlds, making time to consider the entanglements of will and authority that inevitably arise in the course of lifeworld research. One such example is given below.

It is not uncommon that the proximity of participant/observation engenders an atmosphere of suspicion for participants: What is it that the researcher is *really* after? Leininger (1991), who has decades of experience of cross-cultural studies and observation, describes how this suspicion, often mixed with both wonder and uncertainty, can prevent the researcher from getting information that is important for the study. When a researcher is first truly accepted as participating in the culture or situation, "cultural secrets and private world information and experiences [are divulged]" (p. 83), she says. A common question arises whether researchers are willing to share their observations, especially field notes. This situation became apparent rather early in a study of physiotherapy (Dahlberg, 1995, 1997b). The problem was resolved in a general discussion at a ward meeting. The physiotherapists and other involved personnel were informed that in order for the researcher to do her job she needed to keep certain, possibly sensitive, material to herself for a while in order to reduce the risk that her observations would change the normal activity of the ward. She made it clear, that if the staff insisted on having access to her field notes she would avoid recording certain information, instead keeping private her observations until such time as she could put them in written form. The ward staff saw the problem, and since they were generally supportive of the research, they gave up the request to have access to notes and other information. An agreement was made that the researcher would regularly meet with the staff to inform them of the status of the research. These joint meetings served a dual purpose, providing staff with information, as well as additional opportunities for data collection at a time when the staff were together. For example, when the staff discussed various issues pertaining to their work, the researcher could observe these discussions first hand. The result of this agreement was reciprocal respect between researcher and informants, but it did not eliminate all suspicion. Curiosity about the field notes persisted despite an easing of the relationship with the agreed upon meetings.

A large part of the natural curiosity and suspicion that participant observation engenders can be avoided by continual dialogue with the informants of the field. It is important for researchers to balance the need for information with an unassuming and open manner to convey to informants that they seek to gain as objective and just picture of the field as possible. Nevertheless, participant observers learn to accept a certain level of suspicion about them and their work. That is part of the package.

5 Analyzing data and presenting results

In lifeworld research, analyzing data is a process that is directed towards finding meanings. In order that the meanings can be understood, critiqued and used by others, they must be presented in a comprehensible way. The results of a research study must be structured and summarized in scientific format, which affects the later process of the analysis. The analysis of data and the presentation of the findings, thus, belong together.   •

In chapter 3 on openness and its requirements and chapter 4 on data gathering, there were no actual distinctions outlined with reference to either phenomenology or hermeneutics, except a few words about the different approach to pre-understanding. This is a deliberate strategy to stress the common ground for phenomenology and hermeneutics, particularly as our aim is to outline some methodological principles for lifeworld research, rather than discuss issues philosophically. The struggle for scientific openness is basically the same whether one is doing phenomenological or hermeneutic research. The striving for openness is also central during the research phase, when data is analyzed. Whether the analytic process is descriptive or interpretive, there is an emphasis on openness and a sensitivity towards the phenomenon in focus. However, there is also an indisputable difference. While a phenomenological analysis is a descriptive work, the hermeneutic analysis is an interpretive one.

This chapter is divided into two main sections, the first presenting the phenomenological analysis (description), the second presenting the hermeneutic analysis (interpretation). Researchers intending to do hermeneutic analysis can benefit from reading about phenomenological analysis, and vice versa. Both sections include empirical examples which also serve as examples of how phenomenological and hermeneutic research findings can be presented. We then briefly describe phenomenographic analysis, a form of qualitative analysis that is common in educational research in Europe.

Phenomenological analysis – description

Our understanding of phenomenological analysis of qualitative data stems from the reading of Giorgi's phenomenological method (cf. 1985, 1989a, b, 1997). He emphasizes that in order to conduct phenomenological analysis, we first of all need the data to be analyzed which, in this case[1], is naïve descriptions from others. The researcher doing phenomenological analysis is also descriptive, that is, aims at describing a phenomenon and its meanings. Giorgi insists, that description involves avoiding interpretation, construction, or explanation. What is more important is that the researcher stays as close as possible to the original data.

The researcher's description is not a naïve one, as is the informant's. On the contrary, it is important that the phenomenological analysis is affected by reflection on the part of the researcher and informed by a certain awareness of one's involvement in the world in order to restrain one's pre-understanding. Our experience as researchers and supervisors suggests that beginners, but also more experienced researchers, easily fall into the trap of seeing what they "wish" to see, which is not necessarily a very conscious act. The pre-understanding, *wirkungsgeschichte*[1], that is, mainly tradition, affects not only the explicit course of understanding, but also the implicit understanding. Therefore, when involved in a scientific procedure of analyzing scientific data, researchers must restrain their pre-understanding and encounter data in an unspecified and open manner as possible. When the researcher remains true to the data and suspends pre-understanding, the result is a description of the phenomenon as it appears, as it shows itself to the researcher, with nothing taken for granted about its "real"

---

1 The concept was explained in chapter 2, p. 81, and in chapter 3, p. 134.

existence. A pure description of a phenomenon is, in this sense, a description of its meaning, based on the experience of "the thing".

Giorgi (1997) presents four basic principles of analysis, which underlie many qualitative methodologies. The basic approach to analysis in this book is in accordance with Giorgi's method however the general idea is understood in a slightly nuanced way. The first principle, *the reading of the data*, means the initial reading of data is done with the goal of retaining a sense of the whole. *The dividing of the data into parts* involves meaning discrimination where the data or text is divided into *meaning units*. These are separated by a mark where there is a transition of meaning. After these meaning units have been identified they are examined, probed, and re-described. Giorgi calls this *organization and expression of raw data into disciplinary language*. The content of the meaning units is transformed by the researcher, and is guided by her/his disciplinary perspective. *Expressing the structure of the phenomenon* is the final step of Giorgi's method. The aim is to have a single structure, a synthesis, combining meanings of data by the end of the analysis. Even if this final operation is at a somewhat abstract level, the general rule is to stay faithful to the data. One could say that the final and general structure is that which is allowed by data. The ultimate outcome, is to find structures as "essences and their relationships" which Giorgi identifies as "the structure in relation to the varied manifestations of an essential identity" of a phenomenon.

Giorgi's methodological principles were initially developed for the purpose of analyzing relatively short narratives, that is, each encounter with an informant would generate a couple of pages of text. Consequently, in such a study the entire data material would consist of 10–20 pages of textual data. Presently, in most qualitative studies, one single interview typically generates 20–30 pages of text, which means that a study that includes five interviews could potentially result in 100–150 pages of text to be analyzed! Complex phenomena often require extensive interviews. The method for analysis that Giorgi recommends is very detailed and means that the researcher "rewrites" every meaning unit a couple of times. This is manageable when the data consist of around 20 pages, but the strategy becomes awkward and cumbersome when data are 100 pages or more of text. Accordingly, our approach to phenomenological analysis is in line with Giorgi's but our way of implementing the methodological principles is somewhat different and aims at helping researchers to cope with an extensive amount of material.

Whole – parts – whole

Phenomenological analysis begins when data is scribed text, that is, the verbatim transcription of interviews, written or typed narratives, or journals kept by the informant. Also data composed of observations, that is, journals kept by the researcher, usually end up in some form of written text. In principle, they could be a part of lifeworld analysis, and especially this kind of data can be supportive of the phenomenological description of meanings. However, for a more autonomous analysis we advise that observational notes should be subject to interpretive analysis.

Analyzing data in texts that have never been anything else than texts is equally complicated as transcribed texts that were once in verbal form. There are challenges against the idea of seeing an interview as "text" but equal support in favor of transcription as valid text. Gadamer, the earlier described lifeworld oriented hermeneutisist, would concur. He does not make a big deal of the difference between, on the one hand, the explication of human experience in speaking, and on the other hand, the explication of human experience as text. Gadamer says (1995): "Recently Paul Ricoeur has come to the same conclusion: writtenness confirms the identity of sense and dissolves the psychological side of speaking" (s. 576). While he emphasizes the art of dialogue as a dialectic of question and answer, Gadamer also sees it as a valid source for understanding. The analysis guidelines we describe in this chapter are therefore independent of the form of the original data, and should include text as data.

All qualitative methods are governed by some general principles. The analysis of data has a tripartite structure and is described as a movement between whole – parts – whole. This movement is central to all understanding, within a natural attitude as well as in a scientific attitude. In the natural attitude the process of understanding is most often "naïve" and not reflected upon. In science we have to be aware of the process and raise this to an art of understanding. When analyzing a text for meaning, it is imperative that each part is understood in terms of the whole, but also that the whole is understood in terms of its parts. It is always a question of seeing the relationships in the text and carrying on a dialogue with it. Openness in terms of a sensitivity to the text thus means to be able to follow its movements, allowing the analysis to finish in a harmonic whole. Gadamer (1995) explains:

> Thus the movement of understanding is constantly from the whole to the part and back to the whole. Our task is to expand the unity of the understood meaning centrifugally. The harmony of all the details with the whole is the criterion of correct understanding. The failure to achieve this harmony means that the understanding has failed. (p. 291)

Gadamer calls this "the hermeneutical rule", but it can also be understood as a rule of understanding, valid for both phenomenological and hermeneutical research analysis. To understand the whole in terms of the detail and the detail in terms of the whole is a methodological principle that takes research into an art of understanding. The goal of research analysis is understanding the data on their own conditions. The requirement, "that a text must be understood in its own terms" (Gadamer, 1995, p. 291) is also a principle important in the art of understanding[2]. This means avoiding the temptation to explain speculatively, or (linear) causally, or in other ways go beyond the given meaning of the phenomenon. Instead, the emphasis is on being present to data as given (Giorgi, 1997). It might seem to be a "miracle of understanding", but it is not at all mysterious. It is not the matter of "communion of souls, but sharing in a common meaning", says Gadamer (1995, p. 292). The sharing is the researcher's encounter with the lifeworld. The challenge for lifeworld researchers is to be so sensitive to both whole and parts of the data and to the meanings of the phenomenon, and write so clearly and articulately, that the inherent ambiguity of the lifeworld and its meaning is captured. Such analysis provides poignant evidence of the ultimately unan-

---

2 Here we can see a reaction against the idea to reach into the other's inner world and that way, by putting oneself in her/his place, understanding the phenomenon.

swerable questions that characterize lifeworld experience and research. Ultimately, such descriptions will enable the human sciences and their praxis domains, such as caring and education, to clarify their realms and refine their stocks of knowledge.

Bengtsson (1991) points out in his description of a research process that the relationship between the whole and the parts is never static. He says that

> ... the actual knowledge of the whole generates questions about the parts and knowledge about the parts new questions about the whole. The answers to these questions have with them that new detail knowledge and whole knowledge comes into existence, which in turn generates new questions. (p. 19)

Even if this process of analysis and understanding a phenomenon seems to be endless, the researcher in each actual situation must decide when it is time to end the process.

At the beginning of data analysis is a familiarizing phase which means that the researcher reads the whole text, that is, the transcribed or written data material, a number of times to get a sense of it as a whole. The open-ended approach is significant in that the researcher does not intend to make anything of the data but just opens up her/his mind to the data and the meanings that are there. Similar to what has been said earlier about data gathering, the open approach while reading could be characterized by immediateness, which means that the researcher is close to and immersed in the text, and is curious enough to want to understand and to be surprised by the text. When this reading is completed the researcher should easily be able to briefly articulate the overall theme of a particular text, as well as the logistical information contained within it. When the researcher is able to describe that "the first interview (or narrative, or observation) is about a person of the age ... etc, who tells about this and that ... etc", then the first reading has probably been successful, and it is time to go on.

The importance of this initial reading should not be underestimated, especially if the data is extensive like in the case of interviews, it is important to have this sense of the whole material before starting the examination of the parts. Among other things, the sense of the whole helps the researcher to find her/his way through the data. It also helps in the struggle to put preconceptions aside; the more one becomes involved and acquainted with the actual data, the less one's pre-understanding gets in the way.

Phenomenological parts

When data becomes familiar as a whole, the character of the reading changes; the different parts begin to emerge. Based on the understanding of the whole, the concentration focusing on the parts of data, that is, the portions of the text, signals commencement of the actual analysis. Since one cannot analyze all of a text all at once and in order that one gain a deeper understanding of the data, the text must be divided up into smaller segments, preferably in relation to the meaning of the parts, that is, the meaning units (Giorgi, 1997). The next reading is focused on the meaning units, in order to understand the meaning of every unit or change of idea of the text. We advise researchers to set up the data text in such a way that a narrow segment of every page has the right hand side empty. This space is used for noting the emerging meanings.

It is not before this point in the research process that researchers begin to more fully understand their data, and to the extent it has value. Many researchers return from gathering data with interviews filled with superficial talk, which appears to give little information. The interviews seem to have been conducted within the best guidelines of the art, but are scattered and confusing. Sometimes, however, as the analysis progresses, interviews that at first glance looked completely worthless, are now demonstrating that they contain gold nuggets!

According to Gadamer (1995), articulating the meanings in a text, requires that the researcher "is prepared for it [the text] to tell him something" (p. 269). "The human scientist interrogates texts" (p. 240). The understanding of data is thus not a passive or distant act, but is characterized by an active and intensive dialogue with the text, that, so to speak, changes form. When we are trying to illuminate a phenomenon of interest, Gadamer says, "the questions a text puts to us can be understood only when the text, conversely, is understood as an answer to a question" (p. 576). We start to converse with the text, and then it moves from being an object for the researcher to becoming a subject that is ready for cross-examination. And the purpose is to understand the text, the text itself and nothing but the text. Let us repeat the important words

188

by Gadamer: "The important thing is to be aware of one's own bias, so that the text can present itself in all its otherness and thus asserts its own truth against one's own fore-meanings" (p. 269).

With the suspension of the potentially distorting pre-understanding in mind, the researcher carries on the analysis by way of questions being asked of the text; about what is said, how it is said, and what the content and, especially, the meaning is. A few examples: How does the interviewee describe the phenomenon? What does s/he really say here? Is a particular comment really an expression of an understanding of the focused phenomenon or is another object in focus? How do the different utterances fit with each other within the framework of a single person's narrative? Does the interviewee express more than one understanding? If so, do they agree with one another? Are there also opposing statements or observations? Is there something that is continually repeated? The questions posed to the text are at a general level related to the aim and goal of the study. That is, researchers are not posing just any questions to the data, but strive to come up with questions that are aimed at telling something about the particular phenomenon that is in focus. The questioning provides the researcher with answers from the various meaning units. Such an answer, "is revealing something about anger, or learning, or depression or whatever my phenomenon happens to be?" (Giorgi, 1989a, p. 50).

Since the goal of the analysis always is to understand data and the meaning of the phenomenon, the researcher should also attend to expressions of emotion or uncertainty, pauses and hesitations, and other expressive qualities which can give clues to the content of the conversation and its meaning. In a similar way, observational notes about what happens in the observed situation or surrounding a particular incident, influence how the event or the stories about it are understood.

Specific qualitative content including the special and unexpected descriptions of the phenomenon and its meaning can be separated and noted. Those parts of the text that refer to central aspects of the phenomenon are noted in another way than those parts that contain more marginal aspects. Sometimes a sentence or statement is noted because it seems especially interesting and important even if one does not know just then what makes it seem interesting.

During continued reading, similarities and differences in meaning are observed and in this way a pattern of understanding emerges. The process involves making the implicit explicit, that is, making the hidden and unspoken, spoken and clear. Giorgi notes the value of being sensitive to the expressions that describe the phenomenon, as well as never losing contact with the original data. The process of analysis is characterized by a balance between free discovery and attachment to certain scientific guidelines. Giorgi (1989a) clarifies:

> Overall, this method, without being structured, is a hesitant method. It's truly empirical since it allows for the discovery of meanings and it is not as bound up with a priori structures, although there are guidelines. This means that there's more spontaneity, a little more creativity, a little more making last-minute decisions and a bit more dwelling with things during the execution of the procedures. In some ways it's like not having to decide on anything until you really have to. It's as though one tries to be as patient as possible in order to dwell with the moments of the description as long as possible. One does not close off the phenomenon until one really has to. (pp. 50–51)

Here Giorgi illustrates, in a beautiful way, what we have said earlier about openness. Instead of imposing a meaning from the outside on the phenomenon, this methodical stance means to wait for the phenomenon to show its meaning to us. Therefore, we might have to be patient and wait, and we might have to stand the uncertainty and the "woolly" or awkward feelings that come when we do not know exactly what is going on and what the result will be.

An important piece of process in the analysis is described by Giorgi (cf 1997) as "transformation". The expressions by the informants from the natural attitude are transformed (re-gestalted, reconstructed, transfigured) into the general language of the discipline, with the focus on the phenomenon under examination. If, for instance, Giorgi is doing a study within the field of psychology, the understanding has a psychological perspective. In a study on learning, he makes the idea clear: "… the researcher assumes a psychological attitude toward the concrete description, and along with it, the set that the text is an example of the phenomenon of learning (in this case)" (Giorgi, 1985, p. 11). Up to this point the text has spoken with the original subject's voice, but after the transformation the content is expressed from a scientific perspective, and the focus is only on meanings. The tools in this process are reflection, and experiential respectively imaginative variation. This means that if the data gathering has been conducted in a productive way, it consists of variations, that is, a variety of naïve descriptions of experiences of the phenomenon, which is the basis for the search for an essence or a general structure of the data. The researcher can further use her/his own conscious ability to imagine or intuit further variations, in order to clearly see the essence or general structure.

Drawing from a developing awareness of the text as a whole, the researcher then begins organizing the parts in order to see and understand patterns, that is, clusters of meanings, that should be conveyed in a logical[3] way. Hereby the researcher moves back and forth in the material. This is especially important if data are based on interviews or observations spanning a long period, because in this case meanings could belong together no matter they are conveyed in the beginning or end, or somewhere else in the data. Here we can see the value of being patient during the initial reading. A researcher who knows her/his material well has the advantage at this point.

As one looks at all the data and reflects on all the emerging meanings, the similarities and differences related to meanings in the text become especially important. The emerging and transformed meanings are linked together; in other words, the meanings are grouped. This reflective and creative procedure has the potential of developing a meaningful pattern, like a beautiful and harmonic picture, as its goal.

Although lifeworld research is holistically oriented, the complexities of the lifeworld requires that researchers use analytical procedures and devise schematic representations that treat the whole as parts in order to understand meanings and create structure. All kinds of data analytical procedures should, however, be approached with an attitude of healthy skepticism and with an eye on the larger picture, because the whole is always more than the sum of its parts, as Gestalt psychology has understood so well (cf.

---

3 The word is here used in its everyday meaning.

Wertheimer, 1944). It could happen, for example, that the researcher has worked out a preliminary pattern of understanding, but then makes new discoveries when analyzing a rich material. The new discoveries must influence the previous description. Sometimes a preliminary result must be completely changed, a pattern completely destroyed, and sometimes it is sufficient to make some minor adjustments. The main thing is to keep one's mind open through the whole process and to be sensitive to nuances and changes in meaning. The meaning of minor pieces of the text sometimes change the whole of something that is developing, just as the whole of the text affects the meaning of the little piece.

A new whole

When the researcher believes that the text is "emptied" of all meanings, and these are neatly noted by the researcher, it is time to move on. The text is again treated in its entirety, as a whole, but now with a broader understanding than was initially present. The meanings are now being synthesized into a structure that binds them together. In so doing, there is a move away from concreteness toward a more abstract level of understanding.

A goal in phenomenological analysis is to arrive at some structure where "essences and their relationships" can be described (Giorgi, 1997, p. 248). The general structure of the phenomenon is reached by synthesizing the transformed and clustered meaning units in such a way that the phenomenon's inner structure, its essential core or essence, is illuminated. Husserl[4] (1973) describes how an essence can be understood. The basis lies in the fact that all phenomena, concretely experienced or imagined, can take different forms in consciousness. For example, the phenomenon horse can have various forms in consciousness. First one can think about the horses that one is familiar with, then one can imagine all possible horses, large and small, fat, skinny and lively, brown, gray, and black, with long or short tails, and bushy or tiny manes. Husserl (1973) explains that this operation

---

4 Husserl has a philosophical analysis in mind, but our understanding is based on an empirical transformation of the original meaning.

is based on the modification of an experienced or imagined objectivity, turning it into an arbitrary example which, at the same time, receives the character of a guiding "model", a point of departure for the production of an infinitely open multiplicity of variants. It is based, therefore, on a *variation*. (s. 340)

Even if the possible variations are endless there is an original "model" there which guides the variations and sets its boundaries. For example there is a "stop" when the horses in the example suddenly become donkeys, zebras or toy horses. Husserl explains:

> It then becomes evident that a unity runs through this multiplicity of successive figures, that in such free variations of an original image, e.g., of a thing, an *invariant* is necessarily retained as the *necessary general form*, without which an object such as this thing, as an example of this kind, would not be thinkable at all. (s. 341)

There is a general form or structure of the phenomenon, an essential meaning or essence to the phenomenon, which does not vary. In other words, this essence makes the object what the object is and thus we can speak of the object's, or thing's, essence or character. If that inner core changes, then it is another object. Horses, in the example, can also vary endlessly in one's consciousness; it is possible to imagine an endless number of varieties of horse, but there is something stable throughout that "conscious game", namely the essence, or the general structure, that makes a horse a horse and thus differentiates it from a donkey, a zebra or a toy horse.

It is, however, not always the case that a complete essence can be described. The researcher might not find a general structure in the data. But, according to Husserl (1973), an essence does not have to be exactly and completely described. At a certain time, in a particular study, a researcher can be satisfied with the description of a preliminary essence being outlined, and this may eventually be completed in a later study. If data are too superficial, if the dialogue has failed, if the questions have been asked in a self-affirming way, or if the interview has been characterized by too few follow-up questions, it might be a good idea to seek expert advice and possibly try once more. But if, at the very end, no complete general structure emerges, that may be the end. Then the researcher has to describe the structure, complete or incomplete, that is present.

A set of data always conveys *many* meanings. These can be "grouped" and described as themes of meaning, if the researcher fails to describe an essence. Differences and similarities in how people experience something within their lifeworlds can be described. Even if these descriptions cannot be synthesized and an essence thus created, it is still worthwhile to describe what has been found.

The art of reaching a new understanding is dependent on the researcher's ability to handle the paradox of sameness/uniqueness in the synthesis phase of the data analysis. The patterns that emerge in phenomenological analysis are in themselves paradoxical. Patterns of the lived world are at once consensual, portraying a commonly shared understanding that makes it possible for productive and meaningful coexistence with others, and simultaneously indicative of the uniqueness of the individuals to whom they refer. Researchers must make sense of the patterns that are seen in data in such a way that conveys the uniqueness of the persons who have contributed their experience to the study, while at the same time the sameness and the common structure is revealed. As the entire analysis process is a whole – parts – whole movement, there is a similar movement in relation to "the unique" and "the same". First, when gathering data, we search for the unique experience. Also when analyzing data, in the first part of it, we search for the meaning of the unique experience. At a certain point we move to searching the essentials, the structure of the phenomenon. In a way one could say that we are then searching that which is "the same" in the descriptions. We do not, however, leave the unique behind. As we shall see later on, when communicating the results of the analysis we show the basic structure as well as the variations of the phenomenon.

Dialogal research

Halling and Leifer (1991) have presented an approach to phenomenological research that takes seriously the demand to adopt an open stance towards the investigated phenomenon. This approach was developed in the context of studying the experience of moving towards forgiving a significant other (Rowe, Halling, Davies, Leifer, Powers & van Bronkhorst, 1989). The dialogal research they describe, a process-oriented response to the methodological principles that are described in this book, involves groups of researchers[5] who investigate a phenomenon together. In this research, "faithfulness to the data as well as depth of understanding are fostered primarily through open dialogue among the researchers in relationship to the phenomenon under investigation" (pp. 4–5). In addition to the general advantages that come from group work, such as sharing and distribution of tasks, Halling and Leifer found that, "research groups provide a means for readily recognizing bias and preconceptions through the presence of multiple perspectives" (p. 5). Such recognition also enables a richer understanding of data. Halling and Leifer emphasize the value of a genuine dialogue where each participant is confronted with her/his own limitations and is supported to move beyond them, while at the same time having the opportunity to expand, deepen, and enrich their relationship to the phenomenon and its meaning.

Halling and Leifer identified three levels of dialogue within the groups. First, a preliminary dialogue is an initial sharing of perspectives and, not least important, an identification of prejudgments. Second, in a transitional dialogue the participants share their own experiences of the phenomenon. They begin to explore the phenomenon and try to identify common themes of meaning. Third, in a fundamental dialogue "there is a discussion not only of personal accounts of the phenomenon, but of others' descriptions as well" (p. 6). There is a building on and interweaving of previous themes and, when successful, a collective understanding emerges. Halling and Leifer note that when the researchers can return to the data in an attitude of openness, a fundamental dialogue occurs and it is this open attitude, to the data and to the others' understanding, that is the core of the dialogal method.

---

5   The groups in the description of Halling and Leifer consisted of students and one or two faculty. However, dialogal research is not limited to certain group constellations. The described constitution proved to be an excellent way of providing training in research for students, but the approach is suitable also for research work in general.

An embodied moment of encountering violence and aggression in mental health nursing – an empirical example of phenomenology[6]

The following is an example of phenomenological research. We are using this study to give an illustration of a possible way to carry out descriptive phenomenological analysis, as well as how to present the results. First a few words about the context of the study.

The background of the study says that violence from patients/clients is a growing psycho-social problem in the health care working environment. The literature shows that nurses are physically assaulted, threatened and verbally abused more often than other professionals. In the first study of a series in this topic area[7], the phenomenon of a positive encounter with a violent client with good results was explored. The aim was to explicate "the good example". Five individuals, male and female, who were nurses or nurse assistants in psychiatric care were interviewed about their experience of encountering violent clients. Prior to the interviews they had contributed written narratives about one successful encounter with an aggressive client. The interviews began with a review of the caregiver's written narrative description, which served as creative form of "setting the scene," a step in drama interviewing (Drew, 1993; Carlsson, Dahlberg, Drew & Lützen, 2001). The interview continued with the directive, "tell me more about the described event." The data gathering and the phenomenological analysis of the data were guided by the phenomenological principles that are presented in this book.

Findings

The essential meaning of the phenomenon, caregivers' experiences with aggressive and violent clients that had a positive outcome, is understood as an embodied moment. An embodied moment is

---

6   The whole study has been published by Carlsson, Dahlberg & Drew, 2000, in *Issues in Mental Health Nursing, 21*(5), 533–545.

7   In the second study the same perspective, that is, the caregivers' experiences of aggressive encounters, was further explored. In the third and ongoing study the patient perspective is focused.

            © Studentlitteratur

characterized by pliability, which is the professional's ability to be close as well as distant at the same time, to be both actively and passively engaged, that is, the willingness to wait as well as to take action. In this embodied moment many crucial and spontaneous decisions are made. The caregivers acknowledge their own fears and instinctively choose the right manner of touch. Recognizing the shared mutuality, the human bond between themselves and their clients, they draw on their own capacity for steadfastness in response to the exigency of the moment. In this moment the care-givers decide how to set the boundaries for the situation and how to convey their understanding of the situation to the clients. Care-givers described themselves as moved by the events. They clearly remembered what had happened, often despite a long passage of time since the recalled event. And they also expressed a strong wish and hope that they had given something good to the clients.

This general structure can be further explicated by presenting and describing its seven constituents: Respecting one's fear and respecting the client, Touch, Dialogue, Situated knowledge, Stability, Mutual regard, and Pliability.

Respecting one's fear and respecting the client

Caregivers who encounter aggressive clients are likely to feel threatened and experience fear. This was true for the informants in the present study. A major finding, however, was that the care-givers did not try to avoid this experience, instead they acknow-ledged the threat to their safety and their own fear. During the interviews, when questioned about their feelings during such inci-dents, the informants answered for example, "*I was scared. Scared and hard pressed.*" The caregivers expressed feelings of anxiety and described themselves as initially "*terrified.*" However, once recog-nized, the feelings of fear decreased and lost their intensity, and were replaced by other, more positive reactions.

Instead of being paralyzed by their emotions, caregivers can re-spond to aggressive clients in a creative way that allow them to encounter the clients as unique individuals, with unique needs, and deserving of respect, this is evident in the following excerpt from an interview:

The client was brought in by violence, which means an insult to him as person. He was taken away from his home, he was handcuffed at the back, and brought away as a criminal. He felt extremely offended. He was brought to the emergency ward at the psychiatric clinic. It was obvious, that up till then, he had been met by nothing but aggression, violence, and degradation. Suddenly, he was encountering a quite different attitude, no violence, but a quiet, comforting and kind reception.

This client, as well as the others, appeared to feel redressed, relieved by the caregiver's calm and respectful demeanor. Because he was treated with dignity, he could cease behaving belligerently.

Touch
Encounters with aggressive clients that have positive outcomes are characterized by touch. The caregivers recalled moving close to and physically touching the clients, basing their action on the belief that bodily closeness and holding are calming, comforting, and help in releasing both physical and mental tensions within the clients. One caregiver described this approach:

> I think that a client could be extremely afraid, feel alone and abandoned. I think that everyone needs to have the experience that there is someone who can help, especially if they are in trouble, then you cannot stand at some distance and shout 'hey there, calm yourself,' you must instead come close, to be able to support him.

The bodily touch was also described as tending, for example in the form of dressing a wound. An attitude of "tending to" the client helps to create a calmer and more comfortable environment.

Dialogue
A third constituent describes the intersubjective communication within the encounter with an aggressive client as "bodily dialogue". The caregivers grasp the aggressive situation by reading and understanding the clients' signals. *"In a way one reads the client, one doesn't listen to the verbal language, but the non-verbal in some way, the body language, the facial expression, etc."*

In turn, caregivers also use their own bodies to communicate with their clients, either as complement, or as alternative, to the verbal message. They described silence as an important part of the dialogue and emphasized that the bodily message must correspond with the verbal one. One study informant stated, *"I know that I tried to say as little as possible; as much as possible, I nodded or with my eyes gave him the message that I heard him."* Congruent actions and speech facilitate and improve communication with the aggressive clients. Another informant said, *"I cannot talk in a soft way and at the same time seize hold of his arm, because the two actions don't agree and the client will then be confused."* The informants stressed that it is crucial that caregivers know how to listen in an active way because active listening is confirming for clients who are trying to be understood.

Situated Knowledge

The caregivers described finding themselves in a situation which they did not immediately know how to handle. They discovered what to do as they were doing it. When asked to explain this phenomenon, they described it as trusting in themselves, as well as in the client. The caregivers rely on an "inner knowledge," which they stated stems from their own experience, and especially their professional experience:

> It is an inner knowledge that one has, that is developed through life experience, even if I haven't had this particular experience so much, but experience from earlier situations like this one. I trust in myself, so to speak.

The internalized, lived, professional experience helps the caregivers to act and to manage the acute situation in a creative way. They also described placing themselves in the other's position in order to understand what is needed in the moment:

> Well, I think I try to meet with people in situations of crisis in a way that I myself would like to be met. (And what does that mean?) Well, I would like to be met by a calm, composed, and sensible person, I don't want to be met by someone who is, ah, who says a lot of things that do not make sense, or who is negative and discouraging to me.

When the caregivers talked about understanding aggressive situations from their clients' perspectives, their demeanor reflected a lack of self-importance or superiority in relation to the clients. At the same time the caregivers expressed confidence in themselves and their knowledge.

Stability

This theme refers to the caregivers' ability to be fully present in the situation, physically as well as mentally and emotionally. One of the study informants stated, *"I turned my eyes away and didn't stare at him, but I didn't back off either; I still sat there."* Another informant described remaining steadfast despite the risk of physical danger:

> I stayed there even though she threatened me and hit out at me, I didn't leave her, and that might be what made her trust me, I think that deep down within her she was scared. I had made up my mind that this was something that we had to do.

The caregivers remained in the same position where they were, they did not back away, and they did not leave the clients. By remaining calm and determined, and assuming responsibility for the situation, they created an atmosphere of security in which the client could let go of the threatening attitude.

Mutual Regard

The encounters between the aggressive clients and the caregivers were described as intense meetings in which something meaningful is shared by both. These encounters are characterized by mutual recognition between caregiver and client. The caregivers are absorbed by the situations and able to be fully present to the clients. A caregiver described approaching a client who was lying on a bed, in restraints, with a group of healthcare personnel standing around him: *"I saw only the two of us, it was like the others were taken away. (Was he given the injection then?) I am not sure, I am not sure what happened around us."* Here exists an openness and an emotional engagement, and the caregivers show an ability to be present in the encounters and to give from themselves. *"I gave him something. (What did you give?) I gave him a part of myself at this moment. (How did you do that?) Through being present, I was with him.* The informants' descriptions of these encounters depict an immediate and intense mutuality in which aggression is mitigated and a sense of peace emerges instead.

Pliability

Caregivers who seem to have an ability to encounter aggressive and violent situations in a positive way act with an intent to be calm and adaptable in the situations. They see themselves as pliable, present to the clients in such a way that they can subsequently understand the clients' unexpressed needs, desires. The caregivers described their sensitivity to the situations, their concern that the clients not feel threatened. When approaching the clients, they do so in a non-authoritarian, non-judgmental, and permissive manner, careful not to come too close, but to find just the right balance between nearness and distance: *"I waited and let him take the first steps."* Another informant stated:

> One cannot try to catch his eye, but at the same time one has to feel that there is a relationship, it is up to the client how much eye contact, and that one feels that we have a kind of relationship.

In a seeming contradiction, the caregivers are able to convey patience and watchfulness while at the same time taking action to resolve the situation.

Hermeneutic analysis – interpretation

As this book begins the task of outlining hermeneutical methodical principles, we want to make it clear that the approach is based on lifeworld hermeneutics, that is, we emphasize a phenomenological grounding for the understanding of hermeneutics. In this understanding of hermeneutics we do not abandon the scientific rigor proclaimed by Husserl. It is an approach that attempts to balance the complexity of the lifeworld with the objectivity claims of science.

Hermeneutisists ask the epistemological question, what kind of knowledge is needed in order for human phenomena to be interpreted and understood? According to Heidegger (1998) and Gadamer (1995), text interpretation involves finding the text's meaning and elucidating what the text says. When we read a text we cannot understand the text better than the author, but we can understand it in a different way by "seeing something new", as Gadamer describes it. It is important to recognize how we understand a text or a phenomenon different at various times or from other researchers or readers. Hermeneutic interpretation, as well as all forms of text analysis, means engaging in a thinking dialogue with the text's message. In Ödman's (1979) words, the act of understanding is a matter of "sense impressions, interpretations, understanding and language converging in a "lightning act" (p. 45). However, while the process of phenomenological analysis is often understood as a systematic work of analysis, most commonly, the act of hermeneutic understanding is understood without reference to distinguishable phases. And, of course, this is true in some sense. In neither phenomenological nor hermeneutical analysis researchers can follow locked steps. The overall principle of scientific openness makes clear that the main rule is to be open to the research data, that focused part or aspect of the world that is about to show itself, and every research question must give rise to new methodological considerations. But, at the same time, the principle of openness requires some kind of order, some kind of systematicality that differentiates the scientific and rigorous work from the unreflected approach that we have in the natural attitude. This balancing between the natural and the scientific attitude is captured by Diekelmann and Magnussen-Ironside (1998) who say: "The essence of hermeneutics lies not in some kind of mystic relativism but in an attitude of respect for the impossibility of bringing the understanding of 'Being' to some kind of final or ultimate closure."

However, articulating a hermeneutic method would still be counterproductive. Here we follow Gadamer who, as we wrote in chapter 2, argues against a general trust in a certain method. However, it is not the case that he is totally against the idea of methodological principles, in fact, our analysis of Gadamer's philosophy of science shows that it follows some principles that are relevant to developing some hermeneutical methodological ideas. Gadamer's first and overall methodological principle must be understood as openness. His main work, *Truth and Method* (1995), is an impressive discussion about the importance of a philosophical and scientific openness and how it is affected by tradition and its power over the human understanding. Second, an awareness of the power of tradition, understood as a personal history of effect, or *wirkungsgeschichte*, is an important principle of the hermeneutic approach. This awareness includes a healthy suspicion towards oneself as researcher. A third methodological principle we have found in the philosophy of Gadamer (1998) is a cautious use of theory to prevent pre-understanding from controlling the process of under-standing. The forth principle we want to put forward is the search for "the otherness", that is, the search for an understanding of a phenomenon that is not given by one's pre-understanding. We have transformed these principles of Gadamer into a scientific interpretational attitude.

A scientific interpretational attitude

Interpretation analysis within the framework of hermeneutic research cannot rely on the researchers' natural attitude to the world. The interpretations that are in focus when we talk about a scientific approach are *not* those that guide us within the natural attitude, that we earlier have described as ontological interpreta-tions. Those interpretations are basically the same as the inten-tional process when we understand something "as" something, without reflecting on it. Scientific interpretations are explicit and reflective methodological interpretations. Consequently, in distinc-tion to the understanding process that happens within the natural attitude, scientific methodological interpretations are to be described in terms of the following questions; what data are used in the interpretation and how were they gathered? What questions have been asked? How has openness been practiced? How has the relevance of the interpretations been verified? And, perhaps most important, what influence has the researcher's pre-understanding had on the interpretations?

When we try to understand the world around us we do so in rela-tion to the pre-understanding, the implicit knowledge that is there with us already. At a minimum, having a lifeworld is a pre-under-standing that we can never escape. It is also thanks to the pre-understanding that we can understand the world that we live in. In the natural attitude the pre-understanding comes to play in an uncritical and, most often, unreflected way. Not even in a profes-sional activity, where we are confronted by problems that demand a reflective stance from us, do we necessarily reflect on the pre-understanding that still governs the understanding. When it is mentioned it is instead named as maturity, life wisdom, profession-alism, etc. In hermeneutic analysis, as well as in phenomenological analysis, the researchers must be more aware of their pre-understanding. As was said before, we want to emphasize that even in hermeneutic analysis of data an optimal control of one's pre-understanding is of relevance. Some pre-understanding comes to play in interpretation: this is an important realization within hermeneutics. But the pre-understanding that runs the risk of being misleading should be "on hold", a term that signals a certain awareness and a temporally withholding and restraining of one's pre-understanding.

We have already dealt with notions on pre-understanding both in chapters 2 and 3. Here we will just add a few ideas that are important for the interpretive data analysis in particular. If one's pre-understanding was noted in the beginning of the study, if a "research diary" has been used, or if the researcher by other means has noted ideas and thoughts about the phenomenon and the proceeding research process, then these notes are important to consider during the analysis of data. All notes that help the researcher become reflective and aware of her/his pre-understanding are valuable. Only if the pre-understanding is illuminated can it avoid the pitfall of jeopardizing the process, or bringing it into question, which is what Gadamer (1995) expects of us.

A question that can be raised in relation to the notions of pre-understanding is how much of it and which parts should be written down in the research report. This question cannot be answered fully in a general way. Every researcher must make her/his own decisions as to what to mention of the reflected pre-understanding. The only answer we can give is that the pre-understanding that is reported should have a ready relationship to the research area and question. Even though, of course, one could make a connection between interpretations being made and one's childhood experiences, it would probably lead one too far astray to capture these kinds of biographical notes in a research context. But, for example, if the researcher has been working many years with patients with mental illness this is something important to note when a study in this area is reported. This and similar information helps the reader to judge the relevancy of the interpretations and questions of application and generalization.

Whole – parts – whole

The scientific attitude of interpretation is concretized in the circular process of understanding. In hermeneutical as well as in phenomenological research, grasping the meaning of data constitutes a spiraling movement from the whole to its parts and back to the whole again. The spiral starts from the object of research, that is, the phenomenon. Hence, even the hermeneutic analysis starts with reading the whole with the aim of gaining a preliminary understanding of the phenomenon and its context before "the parts" come into focus. Already in this initial phase of analyzing, the researcher starts to dialogue with the text of data. The reading is, at a minimum, a dialogue that gives some clues to what the whole thing is about.

In this initial phase, the researcher must practice openness. We noted this in the description of phenomenological analysis and the necessity of openness is no less critical here. On the contrary, due to the external input of interpretational help, the hermeneutic analysis is not bound to data to the same high degree as the phenomenological analysis and the interpreter must strive to remain open to data and its meaning. During the stages when the interpretation relies on external support, such as theories, the researcher must make sure that s/he still is close to the original experience. All through the research, and especially during the analysis, the searching light is on "otherness". As researchers, we want to see something new or in a new way rather than confirming what we already know. This means that already in the initial phase, the researcher is prepared for the data to tell her/him something (Gadamer, 1995).

The preliminary understanding, or the tentative interpretation, of the result of the first reading should be noted. For researchers practicing this approach for the first time, a good practice is to ask someone to read through the preliminary interpretation. A critical reading, either by oneself if one can establish enough critical distance, or by someone else, can help to judge if the pre-understanding has been too influential, and if openness has predominated during the first phase of the hermeneutic analysis.

Hermeneutical parts

When the researcher has arrived at a preliminary understanding of the data, a new dialogue with the text begins. Now the search is for the deeper, underlying, and sometimes hidden meanings. The task is to find the ideas and messages in the text that might not be evident at first. In Palmer's (1969) words: "The task of interpretation must be to make something that is unfamiliar, distant, and obscure in meaning into something real, near, and intelligible" (p. 14). Similar to phenomenological research, hermeneutics seeks to express meanings, and to transform them in a way that brings the unknown into something that can be understood by others than the researcher. However, interpretation includes an explanatory function that goes beyond the scope of phenomenological analysis that attempts description.

In the natural attitude much of the act of understanding has an explanatory function. Some examples: "When my friend told me that she had been disappointed with me since I had not invited her to come with me on the trip, I understood that unpleasant feeling I got when she called me the other day". "Opening the morning paper we found that they finally got married, and then we understood why they had been looking so mysterious the whole week." These are examples of everyday utterances that convey everyday explanations. In the natural and everyday attitude even causal and linear explanations are used: "Look, how dark the clouds are. I think it will rain". "I have to turn the burner up to make the water boil." In human sciences, we accept causal or linear explanations, not from the researcher, but from the informants, that is, we recognize that explanations are important parts of the stories they want to tell us. Interpretational explanations offered by the informants are to be understood as intentional. They belong to the realm of everyday human living and affect one's perceptions of the world, including the experience of understanding something *as* something[8]. Explanations clarify how something is perceived and understood. When descriptions from the informants include causal

---

8   If Husserl would express this he would say that the intentional explanation is noetic.

© Studentlitteratur

explanations and should be interpreted, we have to ask, What is the importance of this description for the understanding of the investigated phenomenon?

We want to emphasize that the explanations that are part of the understanding process are not truths per se. Everyday explanations are constructed for the purpose of making the world comprehensible and reasonable. As such, the interpretational explanations that we use are part of tradition and culture, and are referred to as "common sense"[9]. Interpretational explanations are contextual, providing a background of already accepted meanings. Thus, what we do in research is use the pre-understanding in general to understand something – and this is important – in a new way. In Palmer's (1969) words: "a fundamental problem in hermeneutics is that of how an individual's horizon can be accommodated to that of the work" (p. 25). In research, we do not, as we often do in the natural attitude, use common sense to confirm what we know beforehand in order to keep the experience of a stable world. On the contrary, the scientific attitude goes deeper and is more reflective than common sense, and with its open stance encourages us to be critical of the pre-understanding and treat it cautiously and explicitly in the process of understanding.

Interpretational explanations also stem from theory and prior research findings in the field. The use of theory in lifeworld research is not uncomplicated. We believe, that the important question is not *if* theory should be used, but *which* theories or *what* kind of research would best serve the inquiry. Consequently, we want to highlight the question of *how* to use theory in interpretive research. In lifeworld research, first, theory should not be used in a predictive[10] way, that is, we should not speculate what will happen. Secondly, "strong" theories could be used in such a way that the outcome of the analysis is more dependant on the theory than on data, which is not what we want. Thirdly, the input of theory too early in the interpretive process disturbs the interpretation more than it helps. In summary, the use of theory has one and only one purpose: to help us see data and its meaning better. And,

---

9   Gadamer (1995) talks about "sensus communis".
10 What we warn against here is prediction as it is used in quantitative research.

interestingly enough, this is a reason for Gadamer's (1998) some-what surprisingly positive attitude to theory. According to him, theory serves the purpose of controlling the pre-understanding. Even if theories also belong to tradition, in interpretive analysis they support the scientific attempt to see something else than what is offered by the natural attitude.

Sometimes researchers hang on to one theory throughout a study or an interpretation process. We claim, first of all, that a the-ory should not be chosen until the data has suggested the need for it, which means that a theory cannot be a fact already in the back-ground of a hermeneutic study. We also believe that it is worth-while to keep more than one theory in the interpretational process and let them compete, so to speak. It is important that the theory is chosen on behalf of the data, and that the opposite possibility be excluded when it no longer serves the interpretation.

A new whole

In order to arrive at a new whole, a "main interpretation" is laid out. The main interpretation is more than a narrative; it is a form of structure at a higher abstract level than the earlier interpreta-tions during the analysis process. We can compare this strategy with the phenomenological way of looking for essences. The essence cuts through all the meaning variations that are in the data. We argue that this should also happen in the hermeneutic analysis; the main interpretation should cut through all the tenta-tive interpretations. Consequently, one could say that the main interpretation concludes the earlier interpretations. The main interpretation makes up "an umbrella" that guides the reader through the former interpretations and contributes in a primary way to the reader's aha!-experience. Besides following the herme-neutic rule and letting the interpretations bring light and make intelligible that which is strange and obscure, this form of interpre-tation also makes possible an understanding that goes a bit further than the context that is given in the study, that is, such a result opens up the possibilities of generalization.

We propose, that a hermeneutic research study should not end with the phenomenon (or experience) being illuminated from dif-ferent perspectives. Diekelmann and Magnussen Ironside (1998) conclude that "there is a danger in closing down on scholarly inquiry too early" (p. 1354)[11]. We believe this is true. Researchers should continue their analysis one step further than just expressing diverse experiences, and strive to find an interpretation that connects the different perspectives that have emerged in the analysis.

The ideas about a new whole that ties together all the interpretations leads us to some notions on how the interpretations can be verified, which is an important part of the hermeneutic research if it is to pass as scientific work.

Trying out the interpretations

If one's daily life is characterized by openness, one is willing to reinterpret old ideas in favor of new ones and, in that way, able to learn something new. We call this personal development. In a scientific attitude we reconsider and challenge our interpretations and their strength in a more systematically reflective, open and explicit way. As soon as an interpretation is presented it should be tried out. Trankell (1972) found that criteria for estimation of reliability in evidences used in the process of law are also useful in hermeneutic studies. One of his followers, Ödman (1994), has further developed the idea of trying out interpretations in hermeneutic research. On the basis of the ideas of Trankell and Ödman, we propose the following criteria for the "trying out" of interpretations:

- An interpretation should illuminate the actual piece of data. An interpretation that leaves a considerable amount of data unexplained is viewed as weak.
- With regard to the time dimension, one pays attention to the history of a phenomenon as well as its future and its possibilities. By reconstructing a phenomenon's temporal context the understanding of it expands.

---

11 Even if they have a somewhat different topic in mind, discussing doctoral education, their idea is in favor of in-depth exploration in scholarly work.

These criteria work well when the interpretations refer to an external world. However, interpretations that refer to the internal world, like existential interpretations, need further criteria. Ödman (1994) explicates a dimension in the understanding of existential meaning that can complete the criteria for testing interpretations:

- The focus dimension emphasizes the connection between the external and internal world. A basic idea is that an explication of phenomena in the external world clarifies even the internal world (see the example that begins on next page).

The level of abstraction is connected with the principle of parts and whole. There must be a consistency in the system of interpretations in the sense that interpretations with a higher degree of abstraction, for example the main interpretation, frame the interpretations at more concrete levels, such as the interpretation of parts. The consistency of the interpretations can thus be affirmed when the researcher makes sure that no important parts fall out of the interpreted whole. The dimensions of time and focus can be challenged as the researcher makes sure that nothing in the background or in the external world contradicts the interpretations of the lifeworld. Consequently, a good interpretation is one that is not only enough but is in itself necessary to illuminate all the data. Then other possibilities of interpretation can be excluded. In particular, this criterion is necessary when evaluating the validity of the main interpretation:

- The main interpretation should by itself be able to illuminate all the data.

An interpretation that is congruent with well-known facts and accepted theories is probably a "fair" interpretation. However, at the same time this approach to interpretation may prevent the emergence of a new understanding through the interpretive process. People in general are inclined to move towards consensus, because in the natural attitude we do not favor an understanding that goes against what is commonly believed. Working within a scientific attitude demands from the researchers that, on the one hand, they create interpretations that are consistent with a common understanding, but also, on the other hand, they have an open mind and are clear that understandings that go against a previously accepted "truth" might well be discovered.

Historians are well acquainted with the problem of how two interpretations can seem to be equally good even while they are mutually exclusive (Ödman, 1992). Because of this, historians must often accept as valid portrayals of the reality in question, only interpretations that give a complete and reasonable explanation of the information available. In practice, Ödman argues, this means that researchers must go forward in two directions. Researchers must hunt for new information, and at the same time they must try to create an interpretation which gives a complete and reasonable explanation of the data. For historians it may be difficult to find new information because the sources of material are often scanty. If this is the case, the researcher must go through the material over and over again, and try to discover new possibilities.

Finally, we want to emphasize that the trying out of interpretations could be done in more ways than we have noted. What is important, however, is that the above principles are considered in one way or another. And what is most important is that the trying out of interpretations constantly involves a serious awareness and an open scrutiny of the researcher's own pre-understanding, including the personal "history of effect" and one's hopes, wishes and feelings in relation to the topic under investigation.

The enigma of severe mental illness – an empirical example of hermeneutic analysis[12]

In order to make explicit the practice of hermeneutics we include a summary of a Swedish research project within the area of psychiatric care. We want to give an example of the interpretive procedures previously described. The aim is also to show how interpretive research findings can be presented. First a few words about the

12 This study is a part of a published dissertation, Nyström, M. (1999). *Allvarligt psykiskt störda människors vardagliga tillvaro* (The everyday life of people with severe mental illness). Acta Universitatis Gothoburgensis, Göteborg Studies in Educational Sciences, no 145. A paper will also appear in Scandinavian Journal of Caring Sciences 2001.

study's background and method so that the interpretive procedure can be followed.

What does it mean to live with severe mental illness? This question was the starting point of a research project focusing on the daily life of former patients in institutional psychiatric care with diagnoses of psychotic disorders. A point of departure for the study was the critique that, for the most part, the nature of the support provided for these individuals is determined by ideologies and political considerations, and not by the essential needs of the people themselves. Their interpretations of the world are private and sometimes impossible for other people to understand. In order to treat and care for these persons in an appropriate way, we have to deepen the understanding of the enigma of severe mental illness. The aim of the study was to understand the existential meaning of the daily life of persons with severe mental illness. The main questions were: How do persons with severe mental illness experience their daily life? What characterizes their experiences of the internal world and the world around them?

The study was hermeneutic and guided by lifeworld theory. The research was carried out in a an averaged sized Swedish community with a population of 100 000 citizens. In the first phase of the study twenty-four individuals with severe mental illness living in the geographical area were interviewed. The strategy was to find as many variations as possible that would provide information to the research questions. The interview protocol was not established. The purpose of the interview was to get in-depth information about the daily life of persons with severe mental illness. Consequently, the participants chose what to talk about in relation to the research question. The interviews were tape-recorded and transcribed to text.

The analysis began with reading the interviews several times to get a sense of the whole and compare the informants' statements. Five main common themes emerged; living conditions, the content of ordinary days, conceptions about self and others, psychiatric nursing, social care and experiences of psychiatric symptoms. A tentative interpretation was then conducted to find some preliminary meanings within the themes. The focus of the interpretation was the internal world of the informants.

In the second phase of the study, two years later, seven of the twenty-four informants were contacted again. This sample consisted of informants who could describe their daily life experiences in a way that made their lifeworld visible in all its variation making communication a criterion for participation. Consequently, acute psychotic persons were excluded from this part of the study. After the second interview the tentative interpretations concerning those informants were reexamined.

The next step of the analysis was to compare the interpretations and, finally, to formulate a main interpretation including all the interviews. The criteria of quality in interpretative methods, such as striving for openness and reflecting on the pre-understanding, were used in all steps of the process.

The reading of the interviews, taking them at face value, was matched by a critical reading in order to make, what Ricoeur (1976) calls, intentional explanations. The explanations were supported by well-known theories of severe mental illness, particularly psychodynamic theories and especially object-relation theory (Klein, 1989). Gradually interpretations influenced by existential philosophy (for example Sartre, 1998; Heidegger, 1998; Gadamer, 1995) shed more light upon the existential meaning of living with severe mental illness.

Below is an example of the process of interpretation concerning one informant that is reported in a more thorough way than the others. The other six cases are reported on in the form of a brief summary of data and the existential interpretations. In the next section, the existential interpretations are compared. The analysis is completed with a main interpretation that draws upon all the data.

Findings

Margaret, forty-five years of age, lives in her own apartment in a community care unit for severely mentally ill citizens. She said that her childhood was unhappy, and that she suffered from psychiatric problems as early as five years of age. In her mind this was due to her parents' separation. She describes her mother as being very cruel at that time of her life. Margaret lost contact with her beloved father because her mother did not want her to see him. He died a long time ago, but she still longs for him. Margaret had a younger sister, Helen, and she believes that her mother only had sufficient love for Helen. Helen also began to treat Margaret badly when their mother died, Margaret claimed. Today Margaret's mother and her sister are both deceased, and she says she does not miss either of them.

Margaret became involved with a man when she was seventeen years old. They had a daughter, Anne, but Margaret never married Anne's father. She did love him, however, and they lived together for quite a while he passed away and Margaret states that she misses him a lot. When Anne left home, Margaret had a terrible time because she longed so deeply for her daughter. Currently, Anne lives abroad.

As is often the case with patients who later on become diagnosed with psychotic disorder, Margaret became a psychiatric patient due to panic attacks. At the psychiatric hospital the personnel often annoyed her. There were too many of them, she thought, and they did not understand her needs. However, she did really like one nurse, but they lost contact when Margaret had to leave the nursing home.

Because of psychiatric de-institutionalization, Margaret had to move back to her community against her will, to live in a community-based living arrangement. A social welfare worker, Charlotte, was her "contact person". Margaret was angry because Charlotte did not understand her need for help and support. Charlotte just talked to Margaret, and Margaret had to manage by herself concerning cooking and cleaning. Margaret also believed that other people in her apartment building were stealing her food and siphoning gas through the mail slot. Sometimes, however, she thinks this is a fantasy.

Tentative interpretation. The transcribed interview was preliminary interpreted with help from the theory of primitive psychical defense mechanisms (Kernberg, 1983; Klein, 1946; 1998/1934) since it could explain Margaret's feelings of intrusion. Margaret's own interpretations about her interpersonal relations seem to be influenced by her experiences of unsatisfying and frustrating relations during early childhood. She seems to understand other people as either bad (her mother, sister and personnel) or good (her father, her fiancée, her daughter and one nurse in the mental hospital). This can be explained by a process called splitting, which serves the purpose to save good interpersonal relations by denying everything not good in them. However, she seems to have lost all good relations, while more recently relations symbolize everything bad in Margaret's daily life.

Currently, Margaret is free of her "wicked mother and sister", but she still experiences threats from unknown people. She is not sure whether the intrusions are true or not, but the experience is frightening. Tentatively this experience can be explained in terms of the defense-mechanism projection. Margaret seems to see other people as aggressive, but perhaps some of this aggression is her own feelings transferred to other people.

The next interview with Margaret took place two years later. She then talked more about her mother and sister. Margaret thought that her mother was mentally ill. She hated Margaret and maltreated her. Perhaps this was because of her own early psychiatric problems, Margaret reasoned. She described herself as a "difficult" child. Later Margaret's sister Helen had to take care of Margaret's daughter Anne, and Margaret felt that her daughter was stolen from her. Today Anne again lives in the same community as Margaret, and they have some contact. However, Margaret is disappointed because Anne does not understand her hate for her mother and sister. Margaret also believes that her mother and Helen persuaded Anne's father not to marry her because of her psychiatric problems.

Since the last interview Margaret has been diagnosed with diabetes, and she spoke a lot about this condition. She now has two doctors and likes to confide in them. She still does not trust the mental health personnel in the community setting, but she likes her "contact person" Charlotte much better than she did two years ago. Charlotte was present during a part of the interview and it was apparent that these two women had a warm and positive relationship.

Evaluation of the validity of the tentative interpretations. During the second conversation with Margaret she talked a lot about lacking basic love and care during her childhood. This can explain why it was so hard for her to trust other people. It is also understandable that Anne does not agree with her mother that the aunt was wrong in taking over the responsibility for her. At the same time, we can understand Margaret's disappointment in feeling that Anne is not loyal to her. The preliminary interpretation that Anne was experienced by Margaret as entirely good did not seem to be relevant any longer. Rather, Margaret seems to have ambiguous feelings towards her daughter.

The relationship with the social care worker, Charlotte, has, however, developed for the better. Charlotte appears to have been able to establish a constant and trusting relationship with Margaret in spite of the latter's negative attitude two years ago. Now, Margaret's psychical illness symbolizes the "bad". Perhaps this shift has reduced some of her interpersonal problems. She did not talk about intrusion from her neighbors any more.

Existential interpretation. Margaret's need for safety and love has never been satisfied, and she became suspicious of the world around her. Later on this suspiciousness sometimes brought about feelings of threat and persecution, i.e. paranoia. However, this is not the most important consequence of her mistrust. More strikingly, mistrust seems to be the source of many problems in her interpersonal relations today. Hence, Margaret lacks experiences of long and lasting trusting relationships. A constant and accepting milieu in the community care unit has made Margaret feel more secure. Today Margaret appreciates the available support, even if she is sad when thinking about the missed opportunities in her life.

The second participant in the study, twenty-five year-old **James**, lives in a community care unit because of a psychotic disorder. As a teenager, James got into trouble with the police and he lost both self-esteem and support from his parents. Because of his psychosis, James was an in-patient several times during his teens. At the time of the first interview James was involved in work-training, and he talked about soon being "normal" and not needing so much psychiatric support any more. But two years later he quit the training because of panic attacks. He reported that he could not handle frustrations when being criticized. Psychiatric consultations have increased because of his feelings of being despised by others. At the same time, James still talks a lot about soon being strong enough to live an ordinary life as an employed person with friends.

Existential interpretation. James seems to be caught in a static pattern. Sartre's (1992/1943) concepts "facticity and project" illustrate two dimensions of humans' dreams about the future. "Facticity" symbolizes the past, the well known. "Project" represents what we are planning and dreaming about. The past being well known is experienced as security. The future plans are hazardous. Most people strike a balance between the safe and well known on one hand, and the unknown and challenging on the other hand. The well-known in James' life is the role of being a psychiatric patient, but he wants something else. James repeats his plans of not needing support and being able to work, that is, to live an ordinary life. His unconscious project, to eliminate all emotional risks and stressful factors, is, however, overwhelming the project of living an "ordinary life".

Tom is a middle-aged man living in his own apartment. During a trip abroad twenty years ago he experienced a psychotic episode for the first time. Since then he has been a psychiatric in-patient several times, "but I could have been a managing director if I wanted". In fact, Tom continued, "if I want to say something I write to the Parliament." When he was asked if he received any social welfare services, he became angry and left the interview.

Two years later Tom seems to be more willing to talk about his need for support. He recognizes his need for other people, especially his primary care giver, a nurse. Tom also receives psychotherapy, but he complains about the therapist being "too distanced". This makes him feel distressed and frustrated but he wants the health care professionals to be strong and persistent in case he tries to do "bad things". He believes it is better being cared for by a nurse because she can take care of "the whole of me", medication as well as social support.

Existential interpretation. Tom does not experience himself as an adult. Sometimes he responds to feelings of being small and powerless by trying to make other people feel as small as he perceives himself to be. This process was noticed several times. Feelings of being a small boy was humiliating for Tom at a time when he was talking about being a managing director and writing to Parliament. He became angry and left the room, abruptly leaving the interview. During the next interview two years later, he talked about his needs and his difficulties concerning daily life. He appreciates personnel who stay close to him even when he becomes angry or contemptuous. If Tom, in spite of his varying attitudes and childlike behavior, is confirmed as a person who is "good enough", he seems to accept his needs for interpersonal relations.

Fifty-year-old **John** lives with his mother at their family farm. He never left home and he has never had a girlfriend. As a child and teenager he mostly engaged with his brother and his friends, due to having no friends of his own. About fifteen years ago he began hearing voices inside his head. Beyond this behavior, he reports, there are no problems in his life, even with a diagnosis of schizophrenia.

In the second interview John still complains about hearing voices all the time. He says now that the auditory hallucinations started fifteen year ago, the same week that his father suddenly died in a car accident. John, who was the eldest son was expected to take over his father's responsibility, but he failed to do so. He did not know how to run the farm by himself. Consequently the activity at the farm decreased substantially after the death of his father. Currently John works at the farm as much as he is able to, but he also takes part in activities for severely mentally ill community members.

Existential interpretation. John remained in the role of his parents' son while others of his own age left home and established their own families. He seemed to avoid emotional challenges as long as he was able. The death of his father frightened him and he did not know how to handle either his own life or the farm when he lost the leadership and guidance of his father. Today John, as well as his family, seems to be aware of his need to take part in activities where he can socialize with others as well as his difficulties in maturing emotionally.

Tommy, a man in his late forties, is living in a rural community care unit. He was a psychiatric patient as a child but he is unable to recall why. He does remember being about seven years of age and having a father who wanted control him. When his parents were divorced, Tommy reports to have felt abandoned and was free to do as he liked. In his teens he began to illicit psychotic symptoms. During the first interview he reported that it was very frustrating to live at a community setting.

During the time of the second interview Tommy was discharged from the community care unit. He claimed that the personnel humiliated him and controlled everything he did because of his inclination to abuse drugs and alcohol. He had no plans concerning his new life in his own apartment, but he did look forward to being able to take a drink if he wanted. On the other hand, he added, he was a little bit worried and fearful of being psychotic again. He did not want any interpersonal relations and an ordinary life is a boring option, according to Tommy.

Existential interpretation. Tommy believes an "ordinary life" is no longer a possibility and he feels like a failure. His problematic attitude was reported as the cause for the personnel to treat him as a child. The controlling personnel made Tommy feel distressed and frustrated, and as a consequence he did not wish to pursue interpersonal relationships. If Tommy can receive respect from the personnel, even if he is childlike and seeks pleasure in a naive way, he might perhaps, participate in an ordinary life, even if he sometimes would find it boring.

Thirty-eight-year old **Hannah** lives in her own apartment with support from social welfare service. She is diagnosed with schizophrenia and has been an in-patient many times. Hannah feels lonely other people. On the other hand she finds it difficult to socialize with others. She also hopes to meet a kind and loving man, and to get married. On the other hand, she does not wish to have close relations with men at all. In fact, she feels very lonely, but can only socialize with the personnel by "being their job". Two years later in the interview, Hannah still hopes for a husband. She says that her mother always favored her sister. Hannah's mother has been dead for several years but she still longs for a *real* mother, as she puts it.

Existential interpretation. When Hannah is thinking about her childhood she recalls the lack of love from her mother and feelings of being envious of her younger sister. She did not learn how to cope with her own family and she is still not able to establish close relations with others. Because of this, as well as her dislike of men, it is surprising that Hannah dreams about getting married. Perhaps her longing for a good, kind and loving husband symbolizes her fantasy about a "real" mother. Hannah still seems to be a little girl competing with her sister for their mother's love and attention. Even today she does not want to compete with other patients with severe mental illness for the attention of personnel. Rather, she wants the personnel to consider her wants and needs as "their job". This is the only way of being guaranteed that the professionals would not loose interest in her, as her mother did.

Fifty years old **Michael** lives in his own apartment. He visits a day care center in the community. When he was younger he was working, but he always felt odd and alienated from others. He was a lonely child without friends, and he lived with his parents until he was middle-aged. When his parents died and he lost his job he felt alone and fell into despair. He became verbally aggressive and destroyed his apartment. The neighbors called the police, and Michael was hospitalized. He appeared very embarrassed when talking about this.

Existential interpretation. Michael tried to do everything he thought a young man "should" do. He worked, left his parents' home, and socialized for as long as possible. He seems embarrassed when talking about losing control and the psychotic episode. Now, as a middle-aged man, he finally accepts his disability. When he succeeds in living without working, and adjusts to daily life within his emotional capability, he feels better than during the time when he tried to follow "conventions" as to what he "ought" to be doing.

Comparative analysis of the existential interpretations

The stories of the participants encompass seven individuals' actual situations and their perceptions of their lives. Through lifeworld based interpretations, we have gained a glimpse into how they experience themselves and their everyday world. They all search for feelings of security and self-esteem. All the participants in this study have problems with interpersonal relations, and they would be isolated, most of them completely isolated, without contact with health-care professionals.

The participants seem to be unable to develop genuine interests but do not appear preoccupied with this absence from their lives. They seem to attempt to avoid feelings with the tendency to project their negative feelings upon others. As a consequence of projecting aggressive feelings onto other people, they often experience *them* as "bad" and frightening. Some participants experienced intrusion in the form of burglary (e.g. Margaret) or "voices" (e.g. John). Others had feelings of being despised by others (e.g. James).

220

By viewing other people as bad, or as competitors concerning nursing care, it is also possible to deny the need for others (e.g. Tommy and Hannah).

Problems in interpersonal relations, inability in putting up with feelings of frustration and disappointment, as well as lack of engagement and interests seem to be predominant themes in their lives. These problems make it difficult for them to live a meaningful life with other people.

On a personal level, the participants appear preoccupied with numerous memories of frustrating events. They were all "outsiders" in some way during their childhood. They were either too close to their parents (e.g. John and Michael) or experienced lack of love and support (e.g. Margaret and Hannah). They got into deep trouble and did not want further control by their parents (James and Tommy). The participants experienced their growing up without sufficient emotional support, and, as a consequence, they are unable to handle frustrations and disappointments, and have lost their ability to develop a secure base within themselves.

It is fair to assume that all humans need internal security to be able to call old fantasies into question and to thereby benefit from new experiences. Accordingly, it appears that these people do not develop emotionally over time in relation to their contemporaries. After the second interview, it was easier to recognize "time standing still". The participants were all firmly oriented to "objective" time, but when talking about their former experiences, time seemed to stand still. They did not work through the past and they do not try to reinterpret earlier suffering or old insults.

The main interpretation – an interpreted whole

"It is the tyranny of hidden prejudices that makes us deaf to what speaks to us in tradition", Gadamer says (1997, p. 270). Pre-understanding is not a priori mobile. Gadamer, who we primarily consulted methodologically, appeared to be a valuable source even when aiming at a main interpretation of the lifeworld of people living with severe mental illness. He differentiates a dynamic pre-understanding from a pre-understanding that limits our thinking and further understanding. Through this distinction Gadamer's philosophy sheds light on fundamental problems in a severely mentally ill persons' understanding of self and others. An individual who has a dynamic pre-understanding is open and curious about new experiences, while a person who has a narrow or static pre-understanding tries to avoid every semblance of internal changes in the perspective used to understand the world.

Existential loneliness is an obvious theme in the stories of the participants. Their only "friends" are the mental health personnel. People with severe mental health illness seem to experience themselves as outsiders, alienated from others, even when they are together with other people. The foundation of this alienation can be described in terms of a static pre-understanding. The participants seem to live with an unconscious internal fantasy, that it is necessary to live through intersubjective encounters without letting oneself be affected by them. This makes it difficult to share experiences with other people, and consequently it is also difficult to benefit from new experiences in a productive way.

Phenomenography[13]

Phenomenography is a qualitative research approach that was developed in Sweden at the University of Gothenburg, Department of Education and Educational Research. It was presented by Marton (1981) as a research program with the aim to find and systematize forms of thought in order for people to interpret aspects of reality. Phenomenography builds on the assumption that things or events in the human environment can be experienced in qualitatively different ways by various people (Marton, 1976). This research approach ideally strives to take a lifeworld perspective, most commonly in its approach to interviews. Marton emphasizes the aim of making "deep dives" under the level of every-day opinions, with respect to humans' understanding and experience in different forms. If this "deep diving" is carried out correctly, he believes we can discover that seldom is anything understood in the same way.

---

13 It could be argued, that phenomenography does not belong to the lifeworld approach, and consequently falls outside the focus of this book. However right this may be, phenomenography could still be applied phenomenology.

Even if the concept of understanding is central in phenomenography, other concepts have come to be used to describe the relationship of the human consciousness to the world. In English descriptions of phenomenographic studies the terms "conceptualize" and "experience" are used. In one study of learning, the researchers make clear that they use "experience" and "conceptualize" interchangeably (Marton, Watkins & Tang, 1997). In other words, in some descriptions of phenomenography, "understand" is made equivalent to "experience".

What are the reasons for describing different conceptions of a phenomenon? In answer to that question Säljö (1988) writes:

> The answer is related to the particular knowledge interest that is prominent in educational contexts. Teaching and learning are communicative activities and they involve attempts to change people's conceptions of reality in order to adopt the particular forms of thought characteristic of specialized linguistic and cognitive communicative communities such as the ones represented by physicists, geographers, historians, etc. The use of insights from phenomenographical research provides intellectual tools that can be used when planning teaching. (p. 44)

The phenomenographic epistemology is the description of humans' qualitatively different ways of conceptualizing phenomena of interest (Marton, 1988b). This is of special interest since learning, within phenomenography, is described as a change in understanding (Marton & Säljö, 1976; Marton, Dahlgren, Svensson & Säljö[14], 1983). This implies, according to Kroksmark (1987), that there is a pedagogical potential in phenomenography. Learning can be defined as a qualitative change of a conception. With this shared view of knowledge, comes an interest in showing what conditions are necessary if a conception is to go through a qualitative change. Kroksmark believes that qualitative differences in understanding, identified through phenomenographical research, are a basis for didactic choices in the educational setting. If that which is understood in different ways is of importance and understandings

---

14 F. Marton, L-O. Dahlgren, L. Svensson, and R. Säljö, together with C-G. Wenestam, are often described as the original group of phenomenographic researchers. Later on, T. Kroksmark and S. Larsson also joined that group.

differ in important ways, then it is worthwhile to describe these different understandings in order to achieve an improvement which takes the form of a deeper understanding (Marton, 1976).

The relationship of phenomenography to phenomenology is ambiguous. Marton (1986) explains that in terms of its origin phenomenography did not consciously draw upon phenomenological philosophy. Instead, he says, phenomenography developed from empirical research that was focused on learning and teaching. Eventually, there grew a need for a deeper theoretical and epistemological understanding of phenomenography. Marton writes: "We thought that phenomenology – based on the Husserlian imperative to return to "the things themselves" – offered a philosophical explanation for what we were doing" (1986, p. 40). Some years later the tendency to join phenomenography to the phenomenological philosophy was strengthened by Marton (1992). In one interview, he clearly expressed the goal of developing the theoretical aspects of phenomenography with the help of phenomenology. In Marton's understanding then phenomenography is "an empirical phenomenology" (p. 48). He names two important aspects in the phenomenological foundation that is important in the development of phenomenography. They are phenomenology's focusing on the experience of the world and phenomenology as a philosophical school, useful in the development of phenomenography. A year later Marton, Dall'Alba, and Beaty (1993) described the result of a longitudinal phenomenographical study where conceptions of learning were the focus. The analysis of the transcribed interviews was described as interpretive, guided by what they call "the hermeneutics of phenomenography" (p. 282).

Another attempt to join the phenomenographic approach to phenomenology and hermeneutics and, thereby, reconstruct a phenomenographic ontology was done by Kroksmark (1987)[15]. He discusses the relational aspect of phenomenography, that is, its point of departure in the lifeworld, its intentionality, and its emphasis on intersubjectivity.

Phenomenography has moved in several directions in the past decade and may no longer be understood as a unitary tradition.

---

15 Kroksmark is the researcher within phenomenography who first explained "phenomenon" as "that which shows itself ".

The most important notion is that the tie to phenomenology was cut when Marton and Booth (1997) declared that phenomenography and phenomenology are related no more than cousins by marriage. They are implying that there is no real relationship at all. Further, Wenestam (2000) notes that phenomenography is "a way of approaching research on human thinking and understanding" (p. 98). He makes clear that the theory background of phenomenography is not phenomenology. Instead, Wenestam says, the basic assumptions of phenomenography are linked to the theories of cognitive psychology, Piagetian developmental psychology, and Gestalt psychology. Phenomenography, Wenestam says, is concerned with "the study of human cognition, that is, functions like thinking, understanding or remembering. This is one of the most important characteristics of phenomenography" (p. 98). Since cognition seems to be the focus within recent phenomenography, phenomenography is best applied in research concerning clearly defined phenomena, such as, how a student solves a mathematical problem (Friberg et al., 2000).

Categories of understanding

The traditional picture of phenomenography is that a number of different understandings[16] exist, are categorized and described. The categorized descriptions of understanding are seen as the main result of phenomenography (Marton, 1981) and there is no search for an essence, a main interpretation, or any such summarizing step of the analysis. On the contrary, the qualitative different understandings or conceptualizations are the point of phenomenography.

The analysis of data that leads to the categories of understanding have been described with the help of relatively simple characteristics (see e.g. Larsson, 1984; Wenestam, 2000). After the transcribed interviews have been read in their entirety a number of times, attention is directed towards the qualitative similarities and differ-

---

16 The categories, as the outcome of the analysis, are built on what in Swedish is called "uppfattningar", a concept that covers understandings, conceptualizations, and experiences.

ences that appear in the data material. "It is by comparing the differences that an understanding achieves a gestalt – through the contrast with other understandings one sees the characteristics of an understanding" (Larsson, 1984, p. 31). By working with these similarities and differences a pattern appears, the qualitative different categories of how people understand and conceptualize something appear.

The categories of understanding are basically made up of individuals' ways of reasoning about a phenomenon. Understandings, to the extent that they show qualitative similarities, are placed together in categories that thus describe the observed qualitative variations on a super ordinate level. Individual understandings are defined as intersubjective understandings of the actual object. It is important that it is the understandings that are categorized, and not the individuals. This means that one person's understandings can be part of different categories. Each category represents a qualitative way to understand a phenomenon.

The qualitatively different ways to understand and conceptualize a phenomenon, that are shown as categories are limited in number, according to Theman (1985) and Marton (1986). Marton maintains that in phenomenographic research, it has been often found that "each phenomenon, concept, or principle can be understood in a limited number of ways" (p. 31). This implies, according to Kroksmark (1987), that a categorized description of qualitative different understandings defines the total possible knowledge at a specified time. The descriptive categories together form an "outcome space" (Wenestam, 2000), that is composed of all the possibilities of statements and categories of understanding.

In summary, phenomenography in recent literature, is an empirical research approach without an explicit epistemological basis. It is, however, our belief, that phenomenography could be based upon phenomenological and hermeneutic epistemology, and, especially, upon lifeworld theory. Such an epistemological framework would stabilize the empirical work of phenomenography[17].

---

17 We believe that the phenomenographic problem is a common methodological problem within the qualitative research approach. All qualitative methods would benefit from an explicit epistemological foundation.

6 Generalization and validity in lifeworld research

Is it possible to generalize results and build theories from qualitative studies? This question has been debated and often the claim is put forward that generalization and theory creation do not belong to phenomenological research, and especially not to hermeneutical research. The impossibility of doing so is explained first of all with reference to the lack of randomization in qualitative studies. Also, qualitative research in general is understood as too context dependant to be generalized, and thus, no theory can be created from the results either. Our view is that these arguments are marks of a mixed discourse. Results from qualitative studies *can* be generalized and theories *can* be created out of qualitative research. However, the idea that generalization and theory creation from results from phenomenological and hermeneutical research cannot be concretized in general, that is, since lifeworld research is much more complex than mathematically based research, outlining the conditions of generalization and theory creation that must be, require an empirical context. What we will do here is explicate the main ideas as far as possible and then briefly discuss them in relation to the empirical examples we used earlier in this chapter.

The main assumption behind the idea of generalization and theory development is that the data analysis can be expressed in the form of a general structure, which in phenomenology would be an essence and in hermeneutics a main interpretation. This does not mean that the result is completely de-contextualized. On the contrary, phenomenological and hermeneutical research results are always contextual. Phenomenological and hermeneutical research results are thus never to be understood as universal. The general structure means that the result is lifted above the concrete level, but that it is still within a certain context, such as American health care or European education[1].

The possibility of generalizing the research result and creating a theory is dependent on the quality of the result. We have argued, that it is an art to reach a new understanding in research. In order to outline some ideas of generalization and theory creation, we want to emphasize the act of reaching a result that is a new understanding. For that purpose high quality data are of crucial importance, as is the ability to restrain or hold one's pre-understanding in abeyance so that the phenomenon can present itself to an open, sensitive and curious mind.

The earlier described principle of whole-parts-whole moving in the analysis is central also to generalization and theory creation. The principle of understanding each part in terms of the whole, and the whole in terms of its parts, guides the act of generalization as much as the creation of theory. Consequently, it is still a question of seeing the relationships in the data and carrying on a dialogue with the data, in order to be able to complete the project with a conclusion that is a harmonic whole.

Application of the results to new contexts

Informants in scientific studies are chosen because of their ability to give meaningful and varying data. This was done, for example, in the study of Carlsson, et al. (2000) and Nyström (1999). Their findings are applicable in the same context, that is, psychiatric care in western societies. This does not mean that the results have no meaning in other contexts. For example, the result showing the essence of an encounter with aggressive patients that had a positive outcome for both participants could be applied and tried in another context. Caregivers in home care, where violence from caretakers is an increasing problem, could read the research report and apply the result to their specific context moving from the institution to the community or home setting.

---

1   In the same fashion, even natural science empirical results have defined parameters in which results can be generalized.

The idea of application could be understood as an endless process of understanding, which also is depicted in the metaphor of the hermeneutic spiral. According to Gadamer (1995) this idea of application is a natural part of understanding. He says:

> ... that understanding always involves something like applying the text to be understood to the interpreter's present situation. ... The current state of the hermeneutical discussion is what occasions my emphasizing the fundamental importance of this point. We can appeal first to the forgotten history of hermeneutics. Formerly it was considered obvious that the task of hermeneutics was to adopt the text's meaning to the concrete situation to which the text is speaking. The interpreter of the divine will who can interpret the oracle's language is the original model for this. But even today it is still the case that an interpreter's task is not simply to repeat what one of the partners says in the discussion he is translating, but to express what is said in the way that seems most appropriate to him, considering the real situation of the dialogue, which only he knows, since he alone knows both languages being used in the discussion. (p. 308)

The quote shows that Gadamer considers application as integral a part of the hermeneutic work as understanding and interpretation. Application also makes the hermeneutic analysis a unified process that bridges temporal as well as other contextual distances.

Application of the results to new contexts involves theory creation. A basic idea of theory creation is to internally compare and relate the different meanings of empirical data in order to reach a higher descriptive level. Glaser and Strauss (1980) are researchers in the field of sociology who speak of theory creation building in qualitative research. They advocate a method that is a theory development with its basis in each study of theirs. Their individual studies become parts of a whole, that is, a theory about "the thing being studied".

Accordingly, the main idea of theory creation is based on a research design where projects are composed of several studies of a common phenomenon. In this process empirical data can also be compared with theoretical data. By way of a new analysis, often referred to as a meta analysis, the results of the different studies can be understood in a new way. Through this work, where the principles of data analysis we explained earlier in this chapter are processed, a more sophisticated understanding, a theory, may be created.

Validity and objectivity

In this book, we have chosen to use the terms validity and objectivity to describe the scientific value of a lifeworld research study. Our understanding and use of these terms supercedes the division of scientific traditions and is, therefore, applicable in human science and lifeworld research. Polkinghorne (1986) says:

> The traditional notions of validity and reliability in research design imply a system of concepts that is stable, context-free, and clearly delineated from one another, yet human existence points toward a conceptual system that changes, is context-dependent, and is organized around prototypical instances. (s. 129)

According to Polkinghorne, human science demands that scientists discuss the theoretical or metatheoretical points of departure and the contextual factors, which influence the form of research and its results. We believe that general scientific rules, based in an assumption of a measurable world, are insufficient when the questions of objectivity in lifeworld research are discussed. A problem here is that the early movement of qualitative research took over the positivistic definitions of validity. Kvale (1989) argues that researchers within qualitative research approaches have long been expending energy trying to validate themselves externally in the scientific community in an attempt to show that qualitative research is as scientific and as trustworthy as mainstream science and research. The result has been that the internal discussion has not developed to a similar degree. "The field has been characterized by an unfortunate polarity of a positivist reification and a humanistic neglect of validity in social research", as Kvale (1989) has purported since the early 1980's.

Researchers, claiming to produce scientific results worthwhile for a broader audience beyond the researchers themselves, cannot ignore involvement in the discussion of objectivity and validity. The alternative is relativism and/or subjectivism, and scientific malpractice. The issues of objectivity in human science research must proceed from the context of the epistemological assumptions within human science research. The whole idea with objectivity and validity "has to be rethought from a phenomenological perspective because its assumptions are different than those of logical-empiricism" (Giorgi (1986c, p. 15). Giorgi begins the discourse regarding the starting points for such discussions within human science research and, in particular, phenomenological research.

A human science research understanding of the problem of objectivity and validity is discussed by Lindström (1990), a Swedish hermeneutisist. As Kvale and Giorgi, Lindström argues that basic epistemological questions must be mirrored in the debate about objectivity. Lindström (1990) shows how objectivity (as opposed to ontological objectivism) belongs to a human science research approach. Objectivity is a condition for knowledge and it brings certain ethical consequences for research, claims Lindström. He names the following characteristics of objectivity: "Intellectual honesty; thoroughness in reasoning and in view of conditions and consequences; prohibition of favoring one's own person, skewed sampling, omission of negative evidence, one sided maneuvers and wishful thinking – everything = subjectivism" (p. 62). These demands for objectivity are as fundamentally necessary in human science as in all science.

The thoroughness in reasoning, mentioned by Lindström, is often labeled as a "coherence criterion" of validity (Kvale (1987a). The coherence criterion involves a research result that presents an inner logic, that is, it should be possible to follow the researcher's reasoning all through the study. There should be a "red thread" and it should be visible the whole way through the description of the study. The presentation of a research study may not contain internal contradictions if it is to be judged as valid. This is not less important in hermeneutic studies, with their input on external meanings in the form of theories that support or illuminate the interpretations.

However, the basic line of lifeworld research, founded in the philosophies of phenomenology and hermeneutics, is to go to the things themselves. Objectivity and validity in this context, above all other criteria, means being open, susceptible, and sensitive to these things, that is, the phenomena in focus. Palmer, who understands hermeneutics as a tradition with strong roots in phenomenology says, that openness in research "is the objectivity of allowing the thing that appears to be as it really is to us" (Palmer, 1969, p. 179). Openness thus supports objectivity in research and the objectivity claims of human science research therefore relates to openness.

Actually, quite a bit has already been dealt with concerning objectivity in this book, albeit, it has not been labeled as such. For example, the scientific openness is central in such a discussion and the limitations to openness that have been described apply even to objectivity and validity. The aim in this separate chapter is to further reflect about the issue of objectivity in human science lifeworld research, and thereby, draw upon our own experiences from empirical research.

The researching subject

Sometimes it is asserted, that while objectivity is emphasized in natural science research, it is subjectivity that is important within qualitative and human science research, thereby having subjectivism and relativism in mind. The argument indicates a general confusion around the mixing of objectivism with objectivity. As we have noted before, objectivism implies the possibility of carrying out research and gathering knowledge and truth from a position that lies outside of the actual research sphere and resultantly, is without any sort of "bias". Such traditionless, pre-understanding-free, history-free or in other way context-free research does not exist, by any standards. Every researcher has a lifeworld and that is still active and present during the research process. This is obvious not only within human science research. Within modern physics objectivism is problematized. There are physicists such as Bohm (1980) and Capra (1991) who epistemologically explicate the dilemma of objectivism. The circle is closed – both in human sciences and natural sciences, researchers acknowledge the researching subject. Within both fields of research a great amount of effort is put into the work of understanding the researching subject and eliminating the negative influences on it, while at the same time, trying to keep the positive and, for lifeworld research, necessary aspects of subjectivity.

The main reason for this objectivity debate is the irrefutable fact that researchers are subjects. Researchers are living contextualized people. Researchers have lifeworlds. Accordingly, researchers have consciousnesses and are intentional, that is, when we approach the world, it has meaning. The researcher's intentional consciousness is integrally involved in the account of any phenomenon. If such intentionality is neglected in phenomenological research, then the labors of what we call phenomenological research are nothing more than the sorting, classifying, and describing what scientists have done since Aristotle. We want to do more. As human science researchers working on illuminating the human being, we want to reveal the meaning that is the core of the lifeworld. We cannot, then, stand outside, but instead have to vividly encounter being. Using the full potential of ourselves as subjects we must, as researchers, satisfy the objectivity claims by being open enough for a new perspective and new knowledge of the world and the phenomenon that we investigate.

The methodology of empirical research in general entails the sorting, categorizing, understanding, and conceptualizing of objective data. However, empirical research in general does not require the scientific awareness of what we, as researchers, have to contribute to an investigation. If we simply describe a phenomenon, however succinct and exquisite the description, we have not given a phenomenological account of it. It is not enough to write about our informants' experiencing; our contribution in the process of data gathering and data analysis belongs to the data as well. To quote Giorgi (1998), "Phenomenology is empirical and it is more."

Consequently, we cannot avoid reflecting on ourselves as researching subjects. Zaner (1970), speaking of the phenomenologist, says that

> ... since his aim is to develop his discipline as rigorously as possible, and since that signifies that he must obtain the best possible evidence for the things to be studied, then clearly, the phenomenologist must turn to his own mental life. (p. 122)

Husserl repeatedly gave us the understanding that scientists look at their own conscious processes as well as the phenomena they describe. He saw science as naïve about methods, unaware of the destructiveness of its objectivism, which is that detachment from, and dismissal of the subjectivity, the self-interest, that launches all scientific projects (Husserl, 1970b). He believed that in phenomenology he had developed a first philosophy of science, and conveyed a caveat to all scientists and researchers for the necessity of self-awareness.

Self-awareness is the ability of every human being to affect one's pre-understanding of something in the world upon which we focus. We discussed this matter extensively in chapter 3. Here we will just briefly recapitulate some meanings of this discussion in relation to the problem of objectivity and validity.

For Benktsson (1985), the importance of self-understanding is clear: " Of course, self-understanding is needed, if one wishes to understand others, since a twisted understanding of oneself can only lead to a caricatured view of others" (p. 49). Without self-awareness there is no basis for the understanding of others or others' lifeworlds. This understanding of self-awareness leads us to notions of self-awareness within psychology and psychotherapy. Perls (1977) talks of a "filter knowledge", which implies that only that which one can see in oneself, one can deal with in relation to other people. The basis for knowing others lies in knowing oneself. In more everyday language one could say "through oneself you know others". Self-knowledge is therefore an indisputable claim in psychotherapeutic practice. This does not mean that every researcher must go through psychotherapy. One can come a long way with common sense and it belongs, or should belong, to the everyday practice of professional human existence, to examine oneself, one's assumptions and values, along with one's actions and non-actions. We must, however, accept that we fall short in some aspects here. No matter how much psychotherapy and self-examination we do, the human subject can never be completely "self conscious". That belongs to the lifeworld ambiguity that we must live with. Objectivity and validity as self-awareness does not just mean the strife for knowing one's self better. It also means to be conscious about the limits of self-awareness.

In some studies, the researcher chooses not to tell the interviewees about the basic profession (nurse, teacher, therapist). This means that the interviewees have been extremely detailed when they describe their experiences of health care and the medicine they have had, or the educational or learning experience. Such descriptions might otherwise be omitted, since it is such disciplinary knowledge that the professional should have prior to the interview. At the same time, the researcher has professional knowledge that supports the understanding of the descriptions, and also makes it possible to generate good following-up questions. However, in studies of persons' lifeworlds, when the interviews treat existential and other difficult questions and the interviewees can be incited in such a way that their thoughts about life and death come to light, we advice researchers not to leave their researcher role. Instead, the professional (i.e. caring) knowledge can provide for a secure feeling between the researcher and interviewee and support the research event to go on, even in the face of tension. With the disclosure of discipline, after the interview is over, the researcher's role can be discarded and the informants with all their feelings that the research awakens can be met in a supportive, caring, professional way.

The researcher is sometimes viewed as an expert, which can create problems in research. If the research is within one's own area of expertise there is a particular risk that the researcher lets go of the research role and acts or talks like a nurse, or a teacher, etcetera. The opposite can also happen. The study can be influenced by suspiciousness that a researcher can encounter. The researcher comes from "outside" and is judged to never understand what it "really" is all about. The researcher can also be seen as a spy, who is out to reveal the truth and use it actively. This can be a serious problem, especially if the investigation is to be used as a basis for economic or political, administrative or organizational decisions.

The above described expectations and experiences of the research role appear in all types of field studies, but also in interviews and less comprehensive studies. When one is carrying out an observational or an interview study, the effects can be mitigated when the researcher's time "in the field" is long enough. What is "long enough" can, of course, vary. The effects can also be modified by an optimal contact between the researcher and the research area, where dialogue and information are important factors. When conducting interviews, it is crucially important not to end the interview too early, or, which is even more important, not to end a question area too early. We have too often faced the fact that interviewers stay at a conversational level and accept responses as "it was good", or "he was the best one of all my teachers". It might be of interest to get this information, but of more interest are statements that would follow if the researcher asks "how": *how* is it good? *How* or *in what way* is he the best teacher? And so on. It could also be important to listen to descriptions of contextual factors that could improve the researcher's understanding of the phenomenon. Even if these activities could be conducted in a short time, a researcher has to be prepared in the event that it could also take a longer time. Due to objectivity and validity reasons, the researcher must plan for enough time for the data gathering. Poor data gathering means poor validity.

Validity of the data analysis

Typically, when we conduct phenomenological research we transcribe interview dialogue and then undertake repeated reviews of the transcripts. We transform our interviewees' accounts of their experience into conceptual form and select language with which to describe the phenomenon under investigation. In the process of examining a transcript and recalling the interview, some passages of the dialogue will stand out to us as important; in other words, the phenomenon shows itself to us.

It is this "standing out" that phenomenological researchers consider, for it signifies the intentionality that Husserl emphasized as central to phenomenology. Natanson (1973), discussing Husserl's insight, makes the point that when we look at an object or event in phenomenological research, we must do more than simply consider what is going on and then describe it. The researcher must also look at her/his own process of seeing, which is the researcher's perception of the phenomenon. "Intentionality carries with it a reflexive dimension which distinguishes it from what otherwise might be thought of as simple, straightforward inspection of data ... done by some naturalists" (Natanson, 1973, p.13). The phenomenon of standing out is the initial part of the decision-making process through which a matrix of ideas emerges, and ultimately, lifeworld description and interpretation are created. The researcher's account of this process is a crucial component for the objectivity and credibility of a study. When a passage in an interview transcript stands out, it does so because it signifies inherent meaningfulness to us; it stands out to us because we have already been involved with it (Heidegger, 1989, 1967; Gendlin, 1967). Such meaningfulness invites explication; it holds the key to our experience of the study and therefore the potential for our objectivity about it. "Phenomena, unlike gods, are not self-generating; they point back to where they have come from and to how they have traversed their constitutive path" (Natanson, 1973, p. 98). We hold, that when we see our personal connection to the phenomena we investigate, we have begun the process that separates phenomenology and hermeneutics from other empirical research.

When we look at our relationship with the thing that we are studying, we take a step back from our mundane researcher persona who works in a reflective manner. We want to know how well we are explicating the way that the phenomenon is constituted in the lifeworld. In so doing, we temporarily abandon our everyday mode of the natural attitude and of uncritical acceptance. And yet, we never entirely cut ourselves loose from the natural attitude. All of our "thematic cognitions in the end refer back to [the natural attitude] as the continual situation of the one phenomenologizing" (Fink, 1995, p. 136). As long as we remain in the natural attitude we take for granted that the world is an absolute, existent unity that is quite independent of us, and outside of which, there is nothing. But the scientific work with and awareness of our pre-understanding teaches us that what we have held as absolute is partly a product of our constituting subjectivity (Fink, 1995) and therefore subject to our particular history, our particular lived experience. We slacken the threads of intentionality, as Merleau-Ponty (1995) so elegantly describes the reflective activity. This reflective pause is taken in order to objectify our method so that we can talk about it, plan our approach to it and critique our work. We want to know if the work that we are doing, our phenomenologizing, as Fink (1995) expresses it, is going to produce a valid description, one that elucidates the essential structures of the phenomenon that we are studying.

Because we are scientists, we are concerned with objectivity and with the validity of the clarifications of human experience that we create. The stance, from which we begin, from which we step aside, and to which we return countless times throughout our work as researchers, is also an object for phenomenology. When we pause to consider the phenomenon that is being studied and identify the way that it is lived uncritically in the lifeworld, we have the opportunity to meet ourselves and discover what is meaningful to us, to discover the role that such meaningfulness takes in our experience of the phenomenon. Again, looking at a transcribed text, we reflect on why a particular passage of dialogue stands out as important, pondering the experience that the interviewee has shared, and equally as important, wondering about our own choice of that particular passage. Mulling this over, we begin to identify preconceptions about the phenomenon or commonly held assumptions that society may have. These common, social assumptions are generally not so difficult to identify and can be discovered within the usual dialogue with one's research colleagues. Less obvious, however, is one's own history with the phenomenon and the assumptions contained therein. One's own reasons for seeing a passage as signifying something important about the phenomenon are likely to be hidden. But hiddenness is just that characteristic of the lifeworld that makes it what it is. Standing in the midst of our own experience, we can look at it only from within, which means that some part of it always remains obscure. This is what Heidegger (1962) means when he says that that to which we are closest is precisely what is most hidden from us.

A phenomenological or hermeneutic analysis aims normally at describing respectively and interpreting the deeper underlying meaning of data. We have to show the readers of our results how we have come to the conclusions we hold as objective assumptions of a phenomenon. For validity reasons, but also for clarity in general, it is advisable to illustrate the analysis with excerpts from the interviews or other excerpts from the data. Giorgi always describes his analysis carefully (cf. 1985, 1989a; see also von Knorring-Giorgi, 1998). Step by step the reader can follow his work with the text and its meaning, all the way to a description of the essence or general structure. He summarizes the phenomenological validity with the statement: "If the essential description truly captures the intuitive essence one has validity in a phenomenological sense. This means that one adequately describes the general essence that is given to the consciousness of the researcher" (Giorgi 1988, p. 173). It is easier to grasp the value of this description if one allows the reader to see the development of the analysis.

Giorgi's way of giving full access to data is problematic if the data is made up of hundreds of pages of transcribed interviews. Even with ethical considerations in mind it is difficult to give out all the data. The goal that Giorgi has in mind can be achieved, however, by relating the process of analysis as carefully as possible. An evaluative reading is easier if the description of the method clarifies how the text has been worked with, how it has been divided, how abstractions have been made, transformed, and synthesized, and how the description of the general structure of the phenomenon took form.

Concluding reflections

Husserl gave us the epistemological elements of phenomenology: the notions of intentional consciousness, transcendentality, intersubjectivity, and lifeworld. These ideas are addressed philosophically, leaving to the ingenuity of the researcher the manner in which to address the human capacity for reflecting on our pre-theoretical and uncritical involvement with the subject matter of a study. In order to conduct truly phenomenological or hermeneutic research, we need to develop concrete ways to gather and analyze data, as well as to examine how researchers, as residents of the lifeworld, influence or constitute their research results.

In the work of his later years, Husserl thoroughly thematized the lifeworld and attested to our experiencing of it as the primordial nature of consciousness, that is, a non-critical involvement with the things that we meet in our experience. Experience equates with the lifeworld; experience can only be considered within the lifeworld, for that is where we live and conduct our ordinary, day-to-day tasks and projects, the walking, eating, musing, that make up the lifeworld. It is only in the lifeworld that we find the truth about being, our ontology, for the lifeworld is the home of both our subjective experiencing and our scientific role as logically objective observers. In Husserl's acknowledgment of everyday reality and the lifeworld, he saw that it is not enough to explicate consciousness as a process or to explicate the stages of the interaction between perception and its objects. More important is understanding that the way that we live out our perceptions in the everyday world is the concern and realm of phenomenology. It would be a mistake, however, for us to dismiss Husserl's preoccupation with conscious processes and overlook the significance that his thinking about consciousness has for phenomenology. The goal of understanding lived experience depends on thoughtful consideration of the reciprocity between consciousness, perception, and the lifeworld and how consciousness and perception contribute to lived experience. This goal also implicates the knowledge of how to make scientific the understanding of lived experience.

Consequently, working with lifeworld research with the aim to illuminate the human being, must in one way or another make explicit the researchers' involvement with lifeworld, which is, at the same time, a very simple and rather complicated task. An easy way to understand lifeworld based research is to focus the way we, as worldly citizens, relate to the world and our existence, how we perceive the world, and how consciousness and intentionality work. To do research, then, is simply to slow down this process. As researchers we scrutinize the encounter with the world. That which makes this endeavor somewhat complicated is the natural attitude that we have to the ongoing encounter with the world. Even if we try our very best to explicitly examine what is happening, it is inevitable that when we perceive an object we oversee something that we take for granted.

The nature of the lifeworld makes this research a challenge. The lifeworld is constituted by the never-ending experiencing of the daily lives of its members, thus, the subject matter of phenomenological research is limitless. For meanings that can be understood from the lifeworld are always incomplete. The lifeworld concept reminds us of what we know instinctively, that the immediate, the concrete – that particular experience of a flower, or that particular moment of understanding between nurse and ill patient – has a primacy and significance that outweighs any theorizing. A challenge in lifeworld research is to capture this primacy and significance.

Another challenge for researchers in the new century is to meet, be open to and sensitive of the named richness of the lifeworld, while, at the same time, remaining scientific. We claim that qualitative studies have to be more "pure" than we see today. Human science researchers have to be suspicious of and careful with the increasingly glamorous research designs presented as qualitative research. Too little attention is paid to the coherence among the epistemological assumptions, research questions, methods, and results of investigations and their values. Weak philosophical and epistemological insights easily end up in a mishmash of methods.

Phenomenology and the reflective lifeworld approach offer a consistent epistemology that form a solid basis for research, a firm foundation that prevents the researcher from scientific malpractice.

Bibliography

American Psychiatric Association (1987). *Diagnostic and Statistical Manual of Mental Disorders, DSM IV R* (4th ed.). Washington, DC: Author.

Anderson, N. (1981). Exclusion: A study of depersonalization in health care. *Journal of Humanistic Psychology, 21*(3), 67–78.

Ashworth, P. (1996). Presuppose nothing! The suspension of assumptions in phenomenological psychological methodology. *Journal of Phenomenological Psychology, 27*(1), 1–25.

Ashworth, P. (1997). The variety of qualitative research. Part one: introduction to the problem. Part two: non-positivist approaches. *Nurse Education Today,*17, 215–224.

Ashworth, P. (2000). The representation of openness of consciousness in some current theories of human nature. Presented at the International Human Science Research Conference, Long Island University, Southampton, US.

Bandura, A. (1977). Self-efficacy: Toward a unifying theory of behavioral change. *Psychological Review, 84,* 191–215.

Bateson, G., Jackson, D., Haley, J. & Weakland, J. (1956). Toward a theory of schizophrenia. *Behavioral Science*, 1, 251–64.

Beck, A.T. (1963). Thinking and depression. *Archives of General Psychiatry, 9*, 324–333.

Bengtsson, J. (1987a). *Edmund Husserls filosofi. En introducerande översikt över hans fenomenologi och dess inflytande* (The philosophy of Edmund Husserl, an introduction). Göteborgs universitet, sociologiska institutionen, forskningsrapport nr 90.

Bengtsson, J. (1987b). *Maurice Merleau-Pontys filosofi. Några grunddrag* (The philosophy of Merleau-Ponty). Göteborgs universitet, sociologiska institutionen, forskningsrapport nr 91.

Bengtsson, J. (1991). *Den fenomenologiska rörelsen i Sverige. Mottagande och inflytande 1900–1968* (The phenomenological movement in Sweden 1900–1968). Göteborg: Daidalos.

Bengtsson, J. (1993a). *Sammanflätningar* (Intertwinings). Göteborg: Daidalos.

Bengtsson, J. (1993b). Theory and practice: two fundamental categories in the philosophy of teacher education. *Educational Review,* 3(45), 205–211.

Bengtsson, J. (1994). *Reflektion i läraryrket. Ett bidrag till bestämningen av självreflektionens möjligheter och gränser* (Reflection in teaching). Göteborgs universitet, institutionen för metodik.

Bengtsson, J. (1995). What is reflection? On reflection in the teaching profession and teacher education. *Teachers and Teaching: Theory and Practice,* 1(1), 23–32.

Bengtsson, J. (1998). *Fenomenologiska utflykter* (Phenomenological excursions). Gothenburg: Daidalos.

Bengtsson, J. (1999) (ed.). *Med livsvärlden som grund* (The lifeworld approach). Lund: Studentlitteratur.

Benktsson, B-E. (1985). *Varat och tiden. Introduktion till Martin Heideggers tänkande* (Being and time. An introduction to the philosophy of Martin Heidegger). Stockholm: Liber.

Benner, P. (1984). *From novice to expert.* Menlo Park, CA: Addison-Wesley.

van den Berg, (1955). *The phenomenological approach to psychiatry.* Springfield, IL: Chalser Thomas.

Bergson, H. (1992/1889). *Tiden och den fria viljan* (Time and the free will). Övre Dalkarlshyttan: Nya Doxa.

Bergum, V. (1992). The dialectic approach to clinical judgement in nursing. Paper presented at Third International Invitational Pedagogy Conference. Victoria, Canada.

Binswanger, L. (1963). *Being-in-the-world* (J. Needleman, Trans.). New York: Basic Books.

Blumer, H. (1969). *Symbolic interactionism.* Englewood Cliffs, NJ: Prentice-Hall.

Bohm, D. (1980). *Wholeness and the implicate order.* Norfolk: Lowe & Brydone.

Brante, T. (1981). *Vetenskapens struktur och förändring* (The structure and development of science). Karlshamn: Doxa.

Bredo, E. & Feinberg, W. (1982). *Knowledge and values in social and education research.* Philadelphia: Temple University Press.

Bärmark, J. (1984). Vetenskapens subjektiva sida. (The subjective side of science) In J. Bärmark (ed.): *Forskning om forskning eller konsten att beskriva en elefant* (Meta science – the art of describing an elephant) (pp. 63–104). Lund: Natur och Kultur.

Buber, M. (1970). *I and thou* (W. Kaufman, Trans.). New York: Scribner.

Capra, F. (1991). *The Tao of physics* (3rd ed.). Boston: Shambala.

Carlsson, C., Dahlberg, K. & Drew, N. (2000). Encountering violence and aggression in mental health nursing. A phenomenological study of tacit caring knowledge. *Issues in Mental Health Nursing, 21*(5), 533–545.

Carlsson, C., Dahlberg, K. Drew, N. & Lützen, K. (2001). Reenactment interviewing as a way to reveal tacit caring knowledge. An epistemological and methodological analysis. Submitted.

Charon, H. (1989). *Symbolic interactionism.* Englewood Cliffs: Prentence Hall.

Coenen, H. (1986). Improvised contexts: Movement, perception and expression in deaf children's interaction. *Journal of Phenomenological Psychology, 17* (1), 1–31.

Comer, J. P. (1995). *School power: implications of an intervention.* New York: Free Press.

Comte, A. (1979). Om positivisen (On positivism). Gothenburg: Korpen.

Cooper, D. (1970). *Psykiatri och antipsykiatri* (Psychiatry and antipsychiatry). Stockholm: Aldus/Bonniers.

Crouter R. (1996). Introduction. In F. Schleiermacher: *On religion. Speeches to its cultured despisers.* Glasgow (UK): Cambridge University Press.

Dahlberg, K. (1992). *Helhetssyn i vården. En uppgift för sjuksköterskeutbildningen* (Holistic care – an issue in nursing education). Acta Universitatis Gothoburgensis, Göteborg Studies in Educational Sciences, no. 90.

Dahlberg, K. (1993). *Kvalitativa metoder för vårdvetare* (Qualitative methods for the health sciences). Lund: Studentlitteratur.

Dahlberg, K. (1995). Qualitative methodology as caring science methodology. *Scandinavian Journal of Caring Sciences 9*(3), 187–190.

Dahlberg, K. (1997a). *Kvalitativa metoder för vårdvetare* (Qualitative methods for the health sciences) (2nd ed.). Lund: Studentlitteratur.

Dahlberg, K. (1997b). Kroppen – vår tillgång till världen (The body as the access to the world). *Nordisk Fysioterapi*, 1, 10–14

Dahlberg, K. & Drew, N. (1997). A lifeworld paradigm for nursing research. *Journal of Holistic Nursing*, *15*(3), 303–317.

Dahlberg, K. & Halling, S. (2000). Human science research as the embodiment of openness: swimming upstream in a technological culture. Paper presented at the International Human Science Research Conference, Long Island, US.

Dahlberg, K., McClelland, J. & Plihal, J. (1999). University students' bodily learning experiences. Paper presented at the International Human Science Research Conference Sheffield, England.

Davidson, L., Hoge, M.A., Merill, M.E., Rakfeldt, J. & Griffith, E.E.H. (1995). The experiences of long-stay inpatients returning to the community. *Psychiatry*, 58, 122–132.

Diekelmann, N. & Magnussen-Ironside, P. (1998a). Hermeneutics. In J. Fitzpatrick: *Encyclopedia of nursing research* (pp. 243–245). New York: Springer Publ.

Diekelmann, N. & Magnussen-Ironside, P. (1998b). Preserving writing in doctoral education: exploring the concernful practices of schooling learning teaching. *Journal of Advanced Nursing*, *28*(6), 1347–1355.

Diesing, P. (1991*). How does social science work? Reflections on practice*. Pittsburgh, PA: University of Pittsburgh Press.

Dilthey, W. (1989/1883). *Introduction to the human sciences. Selected works*. Oxford, GB: Princeton University Press.

Drew, N. (1986). Exclusion and confirmation: A phenomenology of patients' experiences with caregivers. *Image*, *18*(2), 39–43.

Drew, N. (1989). The interviewer's experience as data in lifeworld research. *Western Journal of Caring Research*, *11*(4), 431–439.

Drew, N. (1993). Reenactment interviewing: A methodology for lifeworld research. *Image,25*(4), 345–351.

Drew, N. & Dahlberg, K. (1995). Challenging a reductionistic paradigm as a foundation for caring. *Journal of Holistic Caring,13*(4), 332–346.

Eisner, E. W. (1992). Are all causal claims positivistic? A reply to Francis Schrag. *Educational Researcher*, *21*(5), 8–11.

Elliston, F. (1977). Husserl's phenomenology of empathy. In F. Elliston & P. McCormick (eds): *Husserl. Expositions and appraisals* (pp. 213–231). London: University of Notre Dame press.

English, H.B. & English, A.C. (1958). *A comprehensive dictionary of psychological and psychoanalytical terms: A guide to usage.* New York: Longmans Green.

Eriksson, K. (1986). *Introduktion till vårdvetenskap* (Introduction to caring science). Stockholm: Almquist & Wiksell.

Eriksson, K. (1999). *Den trojanska hästen* (The Trojan horse). Institutionen för vårdvetenskap, Åbo Akademi, rapport 1.

Farber, L. (1964). Will and anxiety. *Review of Existential Psychology and Psychiatry, 4*(3), 195–212.

Fink, E. (1995). *Sixth Cartesian meditation. The idea of a transcendental theory of method.* (with textual notations by Edmund Husserl) (R. Bruzina, Trans.). Indianapolis: Indiana University Press.

Frid, I., Öhlén, J. & Bergbom, I. (2000). On the use of narratives in nursing research. *Journal of Advanced Nursing, 32*(3), 695–703.

Freud, S. (1968/1900). *Drömtydning* (The interpretation of dreams, Die Traumdeutung). Stockholm: Alb. Bonniers tryckeri.

Freud, A. (1969/1946). The writings of Anna Freud, vol. II, *The ego and the mechanisms of defense.* New York: International Hallmark Press.

Friberg, F., Dahlberg, K., Nyström Pettersson, M. & Öhlén, J. (2000). Context and methodological decontextualization in nursing research with examples from phenomenography. *Scandinavian Journal of Caring Sciences, 14*, 37–43.

Gadamer, H-G. (1976). *Philosophical hermeneutics* (D. Linge, Trans.). Berkely: University of California Press.

Gadamer, H-G. (1994). Truth in the human sciences. In B. R. Wachterhauser (ed.). *Hermeneutics and truth* (pp. 25–32). Evanston, IL. Northwestern University Press.

Gadamer, H-G. (1995/1960). *Truth and method.* Second revised edition (J. Weinsheimer & D Marshall, Trans.). New York: The Continuum Publishing Company.

Gadamer, H-G. (1996/1993). *The enigma of health* (J. Gaiger & N. Walker, Trans.). Stanford, CA: Stanford University Press.

Gadamer, H-G. (1998/1983). *Praise of theory. Speeches & essays* (C. Dawson, Trans). New Haven: Yale University press.

Gendlin, E. (1962). *Experiencing and the creation of meaning.* Glencoe, IL: The Free Press of Glencoe.

Gendlin, E. (1967). *An analysis of Martin Heidegger's What's a thing?.* Chicago: Regnery.

Gendlin, E. (1978). *Focusing*. New York: Everest House.

Giorgi, A. (1985). Sketch of a psychological phenomenological method. In A. Giorgi (ed.): *Phenomenology and psychological research* (pp. 8–22). Pittsburg, PA: Duquesne University Press.

Giorgi, A. (1988). Validity and reliability from a phenomenological perspective. In W. Baker, L. Moz, H. Rappard, H. Stam (eds): *Recent trends in theoretical psychology* (pp. 167–176). NL: Springer Verlag.

Giorgi, A. (1989a): One type of analysis of descriptive data: Procedures involved in following a scientific phenomenological method. *Methods, 1*(2) 39–61.

Giorgi, A. (1989b). Some theoretical and practical issues regarding the psychological phenomenological method. *Saybrook Review, 7,* 71–85.

Giorgi, A. (1989c). The status of qualitative research from a phenomenological perspective. Paper presented at the Eight International Human Science Research Conference, Aarhus, DK.

Giorgi, A. (1992). Description versus interpretation: Competing alternative strategies for qualitative research. *Journal of Phenomenological Psychology, 23*(2), 119–135.

Giorgi, A. (1997). The theory, practice, and evaluation of the phenomenological method as a qualitative research procedure. *Journal of Phenomenological Psychology, 28*(2), 235–260.

Giorgi, A. (1998). Paper presented at the Conference on Phenomenology and Hermeneutics. Revealing meaning for nursing and health. Minneapolis, MN, USA.

Glaser, B. & Strauss, A. (1980). *The discovery of grounded theory: Strategies for qualitative research*. New York: Aldine publishing co.

Halling, S. & Leifer, M. (1991). The theory and practice of dialogal research. *Journal of Phenomenological Psychology, 22*(1), 1–15.

Hammersley, M. & Atkinson, P. (1987). *Ethnography, principles in practice*. London: Tavistock Publ.

Heidegger, M. (1967). *What is a thing?* (W.B. Barton & V. Deutch, Trans.). South Bend, IN: Regnery/Gateway.

Heidegger, M. (1998/1927). *Being and Time* (J. Macquarrie & E. Robinson, Trans.). Oxford: Blackwells.

Helenius, R. (1990). *Förstå och bättre veta* (Understanding and knowing better). Malmö: Carlssons.

Husserl, E. (1907). *Die Idee der Phänomenologie*. Husserliana.

Husserl, E. (1977/1929). *Cartesian meditations* (D. Cairns, Trans.). The Hague: Martinus Nijhoff.

Husserl, E. (1964/1928). *The phenomenology of internal time consciousness* (J.S. Churchill, Trans.). London: Indiana University Press

Husserl, E. (1970/1900 a). Logical investigations: Vol. 1. Prolegomena to pure logic. (J. Findlay, Trans.). London: Routledge & Kegan Paul.

Husserl, E. (1970/1936 b). *The crisis of European sciences and transcendental phenomenology* (D. Carr, Trans.). Evanston, IL: North Western University Press.

Husserl, E. (1973). *Experience and judgement* (J.S. Churchill & K Ameriks, Trans.). Evanston, IL: North Western University Press.

Husserl, E. (1992/1929). *Cartesianska meditationer En inledning till fenomenologin* (Cartesian meditations, D. Birbaum & S-O. Wallenstein, Trans.). Göteborg: Daidalos.

Husserl, E. (1998/1913). *Ideas pertaining to a pure phenomenology and to a phenomenological philosophy* (F. Kersten, Trans.). Dordrecht: Kluwer Academic Publ.

Isaac, J.R. & Armat, V.C. (1991). *Madness in the streets*. New York: Free Press.

Keeves, J. P., & Lakomski, G. (eds). (1999). *Issues in education research*. New York: Pergamon.

Kernberg, O. (1966). Structural derivations of object relations. *International Journal of Psychoanalysis* 47, 236–253.

Klein, M. (1998/1934). *Love, guilt and reparation*. London: Vintage.

von Knorring – Giorgi, B. (1998). *A phenomenological analysis of the experience of pivotal moments in therapy as defined by clients*. PhD-thesis, Universite du Quebec a Montreal.

Kroksmark, T. (1987). *Fenomenografisk didaktik* (Phenomenographic didactics). Acta Universitatis Gothoburgensis, Göteborg studies in educational sciences, no 63.

Kuhn, T. (1970/1962). *The structure of scientific revolutions* (2nd ed.). Chicago: Chicago University Press.

Kullberg, B. (1996). *Etnografi i klassrummet* (Ethnography in the classroom). Lund: Studentlitteratur.

Kvale, S. (ed.) (1989). *Issues of validity in qualitative research*. Lund: Studentlitteratur.

Kvale, S. (1996). *Interviews*. Thousand Oaks, CA: Sage.

Lagemann, E.C. & Shulman, L.S. (1999). *Issues in educational research: Problems and possibilities.* San Francisco: Jossey-Bass publishers.

Laing, R.D. (1964). *Det kluvna jaget* (The divided self). Stockholm: Bonniers bokförlag.

Lakoff, G. & Johnson, M. (1999). *Philosophy in the flesh: The embodied mind and its challenge to western thought.* New: York: Basic Books.

Larsson, S. (1984). *Kvalitativ analys. Exemplet fenomenografi* (Qualitative analysis, phenomenography as an example). Göteborgs universitet, institutionen för pedagogik, didakta nr 1.

Lawner, P. (1981). Reflections on the "unknown" in psychotherapy. *Psychotherapy: Theory, Research and Practice, 18*(3), 306–312.

Lear, M.W. (1980). *Heartsounds.* New York: Simon & Schuster.

Leininger, M. (1985). *Qualitative research methods in nursing.* Orlando: Grune and Stratton.

Leininger, M. (1991). *Culture care, diversity and universality. A theory of nursing.* New York: National League for Nursing Press.

Leininger, M. (1995). *Transcultural nursing. Concept, theories, research & practices.* New York: MC Graw-Hill inc.

Lepp, M. (1998). *Pedagogiskt drama med fokus på personlig utveckling och yrkesmässig växt. En studie inom sjuksköterske- och vårdlärarutbildningen* (Educational drama in nursing and teacher education). Stockholm: Almqvist & Wiksell International.

Levin, H.M. (1988). *Accelerated schools for at-risk students.* New Brunswick, NJ: Center for Policy Research in Education.

Lindholm, S. (1981). *Vetenskap, verklighet och paradigm* (Science, reality, and paradigm). Stockholm: Awe/Gebers.

Lindholm, S. (1985). *Kunskap. Från fragment till helhetssyn* (Knowledge. From fragments to a holistic view). Stockholm: Liber.

Lindroth, S. (1975). *Svensk lärdomshistoria* (History of Swedish philosophy). Stockholm: Norstedts

Lindström, I. (1993). Arbetsterapi igår, idag, imorgon (Occupational therapy yesterday, today, and tomorrow). *Socialmedicinsk tidskrift, 7/8,* 339–340.

Lindström, J. (1978). *Hermeneutisk vetenskapsteori för samhällsvetenskap och humaniora* (Hermeneutics for social sciences and humanities). Göteborgs universitet, institutionen för vetenskapsteori, rapport nr 106.

Lindström, J. (1988). Ett förslag till en hermeneutisk vetenskapsteori (An introduction to a hermeneutic theory of science). Göteborgs universitet, institutionen för vetenskapsteori, nr 157, supplement nr 2.

Lindström, J. (1990). *Tillämpad hermeneutik.* (Applied hermeneutics). Göteborgs universitet, institutionen för vetenskapsteori, rapport nr 157.

Lübcke, P. (1995). *Vår tids filosofi* (The philosophy of our time). Stockholm:Forum.

Makkreel, R.A. & Rodi, F. (1989). Preface to all volumes. In W. Dilthey: *Introduction to the Human Sciences. Selected Works.* Oxford, UK: Princeton University Press.

Malm, U., Lundin, L. & Rutz, W. (1990). *Att bistå vid schizofreni* (To be of assistance in schizophrenia). The psychiatric clinics in Gothenburg, Jonkoping and Visby

van Manen, M. (1990). *Researching lived experience.* New York: SUNY Press.

Margulies, A. (1984). Toward empathy: The uses of wonder. *American Journal of Psychiatry, 141*(9), 1025–1033.

Marton, F. (1976). *Omvärldsuppfattning hos vuxna – projektbeskrivning* (How people conceptualize the world around them – a project design). Göteborgs universitet, institutionen för pedagogik, rapport nr 143.

Marton, F. (1981). Phenomenography – describing conceptions of the world around us. *Instructional Science,* 10, 177–200.

Marton, F. (1986). Phenomenography – a research approach to investigating different understandings of reality. In R.R. Sherman & R.B. Webb. (eds): Qualitative research. *Journal of Thought, 21*(3), 28–49.

Marton, F. (1988). Phenomenography: Exploring different conceptions of reality. In D.M. Fetterman (ed.): *Qualitative approaches to evaluation in education. The silent scientific revolution* (pp. 176–204). New York: Praeger.

Marton, F. (1992). Profilen: Ference Marton (An interview with F. Marton). In S. Selander (red.): *Forskning om utbildning,* 1, 47–52.

Marton, F., Dahlgren, L-O., Svensson, L. & Säljö, R. (1983). *Inlärning och omvärldsuppfattning* (Learning and understanding the world around us). Stockholm: Almqvist & Wiksell.

Marton, F., Dall'Alba, G. & Beaty, E. (1993). Conceptions of learning. *International Journal of Educational Research*, 19, 277–300.

Marton, F. & Säljö, R. (1976). Utveckling är inlärning är utveckling (Development is learning is development). *Forskning om utbildning*, 3, 6–14.

Marton, F., Watkins, D. & Tang, C. (1997). Discontinuities and continuities in the experience of learning: an interview study of high-school students in Hong Kong. *Learning and Instruction*, 7(1), 21–48.

Marton, F. & Booth, S. (1997). *Learning and awareness*. Mahwah, New Jersey: Lawrence Erlbaum Associates publ.

Maso, I. (1995). Trifurcate openness. In I. Maso, P.A. Atkinson, S. Delamont & J.C. Verhoeven (eds). *Openness in research: The tension between self and others* (pp. 7–19). Assen, The Netherlands: Van Gorcum.

Mead, G-H. (1934). *Mind, self and society. From the standpoint of a social-behaviorist*. The University of Chicago, IL, USA.

Merleau-Ponty, M. (1964). *The primacy of perception* (J. Edie, Trans.). Evanston, IL: North Western University Press.

Merleau-Ponty, M. (1968/1948). *The visible and the invisible* (A. Lingis, Trans). Evanston, IL: Northwestern University Press.

Merleau-Ponty, M. (1987/1960). *Signs* (R. McCleary, Trans.). Evanston, IL: North Western University Press.

Merleau-Ponty, M. (1991a/1964). *Consciousness and the acquisition of language* (H. Silverman, Trans.). Evanston, IL: Northwestern University Press.

Merleau-Ponty, M. (1991b/1969). *The prose of the world* (J. O'Neill, Trans.). Evanston, IL: North Western University Press.

Merleau-Ponty, M. (1995/1945). *Phenomenology of perception* (C. Smith, Trans.). London: Routledge.

Milne, A.A. (1990/1928). *The house at Pooh corner*. London: Mammoth.

Moran, D. (2000). Heidegger's critique of Husserl's and Brentano's accounts of intentionality. *Inquiry*, 43, 39–66.

Natanson, M. (1973). *Edmund Husserl. Philosopher of infinite tasks*. Evanston, IL: North Western University Press.

Nationalencyklopedin (1989). (The national encyclopedia). Höganäs: Bra Böcker.

Newton, N. (1996). *Foundations of understanding.* Amsterdam: John Benjamins Publ. Comp.

O'Driscoll, C. (1993). The TAPS Project 7: Mental hospital closure – a literature review. *British Journal of Psychiatry, 162*(19), 7–17.

Ogden, T. (1982). *Projektiv identifikation och psykoterapeutisk teknik* (Projective identification and psychotherapeutic technique). Stockholm: Natur och Kultur.

O'Toole, J. (1992). *The process of drama. Negotiating art and meaning.* London: Routledge & Kegan Paul.

Ottosson, J-O. (1995). *Psykiatri* (Psychiatry.) Gothenburg: Almquist & Wiksell.

Palmer, R.E. (1969). *Hermeneutics. Interpretation theory in Schleiermacher, Dilthey, Heidegger and Gadamer.* Evanston, IL: North Western University Press.

Peplau, H. (1991). *Interpersonal relations in nursing.* London: Mac Millan Education Ltd.

Perls, F. (1969). *Gestalt therapy verbatim.* Moab, UT: Real People Press.

Piaget, J. (1980). *Adaptation and intelligence. Organic selection and phenocopy.* Chicago: University of Chicago.

Pilhammar Andersson, E. (1992). *Det är vi som är dom. Sjuksköterskestuderandes föreställningar och perspektiv under utbildningstiden* (About nursing students' ideas of their education). Acta Universitatis Gothoburgensis, Göteborg studies in educational sciences, nr 83.

Pilhammar Andersson, E. (1996). *Etnografi i det vårdpedagogiska fältet – en jakt efter ledtrådar* (Ethnography in health care didactics). Lund: Studentlitteratur.

Ploug Hansen, H. (1992). På feltarbeide – om antropologiske forskningsstrategier i et projekt om onkologisk sygepleje (Field research – anthropological research in oncological care). *Socialmedicinsk tidskrift,* 9/10, 486–493.

Polanyi, M. (1966). *The tacit dimension.* London: Routledge and Kegan Paul.

Polanyi, M. (1978). Personal knowledge. London: Routledge and Kegan Paul.

Polkinghorne, D.E. (1986). Conceptual validity in a nontheoretical human science. *Journal of Phenomenological Psychology, 17*(2).

Popkewitz, T.S. (1992). Cartesian anxiety, linguistic communism, and reading texts. *Educational Researcher, 21*(5), 11–15.

Popper, K. (1988). *En intellektuell självbiografi* (An intellectual autobiography). Göteborg: Doxa.

Ricoeur, P. (1976). *Interpretation theory. Discourse and the surplus of meaning.* Forth Worth: Texas Christian University Press.

Robinson, F.A. (1998). Dissociative women's experience of self-cutting. In R. S. Valle (ed.). *Phenomenological inquiry in psychology: existential and transpersonal dimensions* (pp. 209–225). New York: Plenum.

Rolf, B. (1991). *Profession, tradition och tyst kunskap. En studie i Michael Polanyis teori om den professionella kunskapens tysta dimension* (Profession, tradition and tacit knowledge, a study of Michael Polanyi's theory of professional knowledge and its tacit dimension). Övre Dalkarlshyttan: Nya Doxa.

Rowe, J., Halling, S., Davies, E., Leifer, M., Powers, D. & van Bronkhorst, J. (1989). The psychology of forgiving another: A dialogal research approach. In R.S. Valle and S. Halling (eds), *Existential-phenomenological perspectives in psychology* (pp. 233–244). New York: Plenum.

Sachs, L. (1992a). *Vårdens etnografi* (Health care ethnography). Stockholm: Almqvist & Wiksell.

Sachs, L. (1992b). *Medicinsk antropologi* (Anthropology in medicine). Stockholm: Almqvist & Wiksell.

Sartre, J-P. (1998/1943). *Being and nothingness* (H. Barnes, Trans.). New York: Pocket Books, Simon & Schuster.

Schachtel, E.G. (1959). The development of focal attention and the emergence of reality. In *Metamorphosis: On the development of affect, perception, attention, and memory* (pp. 251–278). New York: Basic Books.

Schleiermacher, F. (1996/1799). *On religion. Speeches to its cultured despisers.* Glasgow, UK: Cambridge University Press.

Schrag, F. (1992). In defense of positivist research paradigms. *Educational Researcher, 21*(5), 5–8.

Slavin, R.E. & Madden, N.A. (1987). *Effective classroom programs for students at risk.* Baltimore, MD: Center for Research on Elementary and Middle Schools, Johns Hopkins University.

Smaling, A. (1995). Open-mindedness, open-heartedness and dialogical openness: The dialetics of openings and closures. In I.

254

Maso, P.A. Atkinson, S. Delamont & J.C. Verhoeven (eds). *Openness in research: The tension between self and others* (pp. 20–32). Assen, The Netherlands: Van Gorcum.

Smith, S. (1992). Physically remembering childhood. *Phenomenology + Pedagogy. A Human Science Journal*, 10, 85–106.

SOU 1992: 73. *Välfärd och valfrihet* (Welfare and freedom of choice). Stockholm: The ministry of health and social affairs.

Stolt, C-M. & Dahlberg, K. (1998). Relationen mellan kropp och själ. Ett medicinhistoriskt och fenomenologiskt perspektiv (The relationship between body and soul. A medicine historical and phenomenological perspective). *Svensk Medicinhistorisk Tidskrift*, 2(1), 165–188.

Sullivan, H.S. (1953). *Interpersonal relations in psychiatry*. New York: W.W. Norton & Company inc.

Sundström, B. (1996). *Studenters upplevelse av bekräftelse under handledning i yrkesmässig växt. En fenomenologisk studie av grupphandledning i sjuksköterskeutbildningen* (Students' experience of confirmation in group supervision during nursing education). Vårdhögskolan i Göteborg.

Theman, J. (1979). *The interview as a research instrument*. Reports from the Department of Education, University of Göteborg, nr 86.

Theman, J. (1985). *Likhet genom olikhet. Ett fall av kontextuell analys* (The same and the unique, a contextual analysis). Göteborgs universitet, institutionen för pedagogik, rapport nr 15.

Toombs, K. (1993). *The meaning of illness – a phenomenological account of the different perspectives of physician and patient*. Philosophy and Medicine, nr 42. Boston: Kluwer Academic Publishers.

Trankell, A. (1972). *Vittnespsykologiska arbetsmetoder* (Reliability of evidence). Stockholm: Beckmans.

Törnebohm, H. (1982). *Att forska över paradigm* (To investigate paradigms). Göteborgs universitet, institutionen för vetenskapsteori, rapport nr 136.

Törnebohm, H. (1985). *Vad betyder vetenskapsteori* (What is philosophy of science?). Göteborgs universitet, institutionen för vetenskapsteori, rapport nr 145.

Warncke, G. (1987). *Gadamer. Hermeneutics, tradition and reason*. Cambridge, UK: Polity Press.

Wenestam, C-G. (2000). The phenomenographic method in health research. In B. Friedlund & C. Hildingh (eds). *Qualitative research methods in the service of health* (pp. 97–115). Lund: Studentlitteratur.

Wenestam, C-G. & Dahlberg, K. (1990). Interaction between people and society as seeing and not-seeing. Paper presented at International Human Science Research Conference, Quebec, Canada.

Wertheimer, M. (1944). Gestalt theory. *Social Research, 11*(1), 78–99.

Wertheimer, M. (1961). *Productive thinking.* London: Tavistock publications.

Winnicot, D. (1967). Mirror-role of mother and family in child development. *Playing and Reality,* 197, 111–118.

Wolcott, H.F. (1983). Adequate schools and inadequate education: The life history of a sneaky kid. *Anthropology and Education Quarterly, 14*(1), 3–32.

Zaner, R. (1970). *The way of phenomenology.* Indianapolis, IN: Bobbs-Merrill.

Zetzel, E. (1961). Melanie Klein 1882–1960. *The Psychoanalytic Quarterly,* 3. 420–425.

Ödman, P-J. (1979). *Tolkning förståelse vetande* (Interpretation, understanding, knowing). Stockholm: Almqvist & Wiksell.

Ödman, P-J. (1992). Interpreting the past. *Qualitative Studies in Education,* 5(2), 167–184.

Index

accessories for dramatization 165
anthropology 169
apperception 57
application 229
appresentation 57
art works 164

bracketing 60

categories of understanding 226
close observation 174
clusters of meanings 191
cognitive psychology 129
coherence criterion (of
    validity) 231
conceptualize 223
critical situations 178
curiosity 98

description 182
dialogal research 194
dialogical openness 100
dramatized interviews 161
drawing 164

educational drama 162
embodied knowing 54
epistemology 42
essence 192
ethical reflection 167, 180
ethnography 169
exegesis 71

experiential variation 191
explanations 206

field notes 179
fieldwork 169, 172
filter knowledge 234
focal attention 102

gate-keeper 177
general structure 192
generalization 227
gestalt therapy 162

health 53
hearkening 100
hermeneutic analysis 201
hermeneutical rule 186
hermeneutics 70
hidden meaning 206
history of effect 81
horizon 57, 84

illness 53
imaginative variation 191
immediacy 99, 161
institutional research board
    176
intentionality 45, 55
interpretation 182, 201
intersubjective openness 112
intersubjectivity 63, 112
interviewer memorandum 164

language 88
leading questions 159
lifeworld 46, 91
lived experience 75

main interpretation 208
meaning 113
meaning units 188
meta analysis 229
method 110
methodological
    interpretations 203
music 164

naïve description 183
natural attitude 45
non-verbal 166

objectivism 44, 232
objectivity 44, 98, 230
observation 169
ontological interpretations
    203
ontology 77
open-heartedness 100
opening question 158
open-mindedness 100
openness 81
otherness 205
outcome space 226

paradigm 25
participant observation 174
phenomenography 222
phenomenological "turning
    point" 78
phenomenological parts 188
phenomenon 45
philology 71
poetry 164
practical research 171
prejudices 83

preliminary interpretation 205
pre-structure 119
presuppositions 120
pre-understanding 94, 117
protention 59
psychodrama 162

questioning 126

reduction 60
re-enactment 162, 163
relativism 232
research dialogue 157
research diary 204
retention 58

scientific interpretations 203
self-awareness 62, 94, 234
self-knowledge 234
self-understanding 234
sequence of the interview 158
setting the scene 196
standing out 236
strong theories 207
subjective body 49
subjectivism 232
synthesis 192
system of interpretations 210

tape recorder 165
tentative interpretation 205
themes of meaning 194
theory creation 227, 229
theory of interpretation 71
time-consciousness 58
tradition 25
transcendentality 59
transcription 166
transformation 190
trying out interpretations 209

uniqueness 116

validity   230
variations   193
view of science   31

world view   28